FAMILY TRUSTS

by *Frank J. Croke,*

with William F. Croke
Attorney-At Law

Capital Management Press
A division of Carolina Capital Management, Inc.
Wilmington, North Carolina 28403

Cover design: Mary Croke
Text Design: Mary Croke
Illustrations: Mary Croke

Library of Congress Cataloging-in-Publication Data

Croke, Frank J., 1928-
    Family trusts, good or bad : financial errors in trusts. how to
avoid and correct them / by Frank J. Coke with William F. Croke
        p.   cm.
    ISBN 1-892879-12-3 (pbk.)
    1. Living trusts--United States--Popular works.   2. Estate
planning--United States--Popular works.   I. Croke, William F.,
 1963- . II Title
KF724.Z9C76   1998
346.7905 '2--dc21

                                                                98-45094
                                                                    CIP

This book may be ordered by mail from the publisher.
Please include $3.00 for postage and handling.
But try your bookstore first!
This publication is available for bulk purchase.
Capital Management Press Publishers
A division of Carolina Capital Management, Inc.
Post Office Box 5905
Wilmington, North Carolina

This publication is designed to provide accurate and authoritative information in regard to the subject matter covered. It is sold with the understanding that the publisher is not, by virtue of distributing this publication, engaged in rendering legal, accounting or other professional service. If legal advice or other expert assistance is required, the services of a competent professional person should be sought. *Adapted from a Declaration of Principles jointly adopted by a Committee of the American Bar Association and a Committee of Publishers and Associations.*

INTRODUCTION
William F. Croke, JD, LLM

The purpose of this book is to help the reader prepare a financial plan for their estate. It has been prepared for the laymen who wants to establish a Trust to provide for family and reduce estate taxes.

The book presents many financial options that a person should consider based on the needs of their family. Understanding the reasons for these financial options requires each person to carefully consider them and then determine what options would be of benefit to their family.

By taking the time and using this book to develop a solid financial plan you can save hours of legal time that you would otherwise have to spend with your attorney. Without a good financial plan, however, an attorney cannot provide you with all of your true options and cannot prepare the best estate documents for your situation. This book will allow you to spend the time you need to identify and present your financial needs to your attorney who can then give you the best advice in preparing your estate documents.

This is not a book that can be used to create an estate without the help of a qualified attorney. If you are determined to avoid legal fees then you may try to use one of the pre-packaged legal kits, or you may try to shop around for a lawyer who will prepare your estate documents for the lowest set fee. However, not one of the financial options that are presented in this book will be available to you from basic legal forms. A number of the options in this book can save a very substantial portion of your estate if they are properly tied to your financial plan. Good legal advice to assist you with this will be a tremendous benefit to your family and is always worth paying for.

When your financial picture is clear, your legal choices become much easier to identify and put into effect. This is where you avoid unnecessary legal fees. Getting the best lawyer you can find to help you complete your estate documents will be the best way to insure that you can take full advantage of your options. To get the best legal advice at the least expense you need to have a proper financial analysis of your estate and estate assets, including the needs of your family. This book will help you save costs by investing your own time to develop a financial plan that you can then share with your attorney.

INTRODUCTION

Proper estate planning involves a number of important decisions about an individual's investments, their assets and their family's financial needs. The decisions involved require the individual to understand the full value of their property and the value that property will have five, ten and even twenty-five years in the future. This book will help the individual lay out these values and show how to develop an actual financial plan for their estate. It will even show how to review their plan and their estate every few years to see if any important changes are required to their estate documents.

All of this is laid out step by step with examples that the reader can follow and may even want to discuss with the attorney who prepares their estate documents. The key to estate planning is to take proper advantage of the legal options you have. The key to identifying which options will be the most beneficial for your estate is to take the time to lay out a solid financial plan for your assets. This book will help you do just that.

This book is not intended as a legal work on Trusts although lawyers may also find it useful. Providing individuals with financial information on their estate options is the real purpose of this book. In many cases references to the law have been given but this has only been done to alert the individual to the legal basis of their options along with certain restrictions that may exist. Once the objectives of the Trust are determined, the individual should obtain legal counsel to prepare the necessary documents.

In guiding you through the many options that are so often overlooked, this book focuses on a number of basic concepts. The reader will learn about these concepts in detail as they work through this book but it will be helpful to briefly introduce some of these basic principles here.

One of the most critical concepts is the existence of State "Default Rules" which can greatly affect how your Trust or estate will be managed. These Default Rules rarely appear in an actual estate document and few lay persons even know that they exist. Yet they often govern important aspects of an estate including how Trust funds or estate assets should be held or invested.

Default Rules are not mandatory. They simply apply where an individual has failed to give specific instructions or directives in their estate documents. The

INTRODUCTION

existence of these Default Rules fills in the gaps for many Trusts and estate documents that would otherwise fail. It is the Default Rules that make the simple legal forms that are available in pre-packaged kits legally complete. The Default Rules make the basic forms effective by giving instructions for all of the issues that the standard forms never address. When you use the standard legal forms to save money, the Default Rules end up making most of your investment decisions for you. This causes you to bypass choices that can enhance the value of your estate. Most people don't even know that these choices exist or what options are available to them in making such choices. This book presents a number of important options and allows the reader to make their own decisions about the investments and treatment of their estate property that would otherwise be governed by "Default Rules."

Default Rules generally require more conservative types of investments than many individuals routinely choose to make in their normal lives. This is laudable when we are safeguarding the property of a third party but the "security" of such investments is now challenged by the tremendous impact that inflation has. Inflation can do as much to decrease the value of money as other potential risks of investment. Understandably, investors are now as concerned about growth as they are about the security of their investment.

Large, diversified stock portfolios have become common place with small investors participating in these portfolios through large mutual funds. These investment vehicles and techniques greatly offset the danger of loss from a single stock and allow the overall growth of the market to provide a more secure and steady return. None of these investment options are presented on the standard legal forms which are available in estate "kits" and they are rarely discussed when an individual contracts with an attorney to have standard estate documents prepared for the lowest "set fee." You need an attorney who will work closely with you and the real options you have to effectuate the financial plan that you are able to prepare with the help of this book. Fortunately, before you ever speak to an attorney, this book will already have given you a good idea of how valuable their work will be to you and what financial benefits they will be able to help you attain. Then you will have the true comfort of knowing that your legal fees are being well spent.

The second major concept that is dealt with in this book is the distinction between "income" and "principal." These have always been relative terms but in former generations the average individual could generally rely on a simple application of their meanings. When farming land was at issue, the land itself was, clearly enough, the "principal" and the crops it produced were the "income." Under the Default Rules, a significant portion of estate funds are generally held in CDs or treasuries which pay a certain amount of "income" for the "principal" invested.

Under these concepts, its was easy to define what part of an inheritance was intended for the "Income Beneficiaries" (often the surviving wife or husband who needed such funds for ongoing support). The "principal" was generally held, and protected, for second heir, or "Remainderman" (those who would receive the estate after the Income Beneficiary died or the Trust terminated) Under the old Restatement of Law an inherent conflict of interest was recognized between these two parties.[1] The more money that was paid out as income, the less money was left to grow as part of the principal. It was believed that helping one party would invariably harm the other and no possible exception to this conflict could be conceived.

Today, however, the concept of a "Total Performance Trust" has emerged. Income Beneficiaries and Remaindermen (those who receive funds during the Trust and those who receive the remainder) are no longer seen as rivals. They are both seen as partners who benefit mutually when Trust or estate funds grow strongly from investment.

More and more individuals who invest in their everyday lives seek to invest in growth stocks. More and more Trusts and estates are starting to take advantage of these same investments. When investing in growth stocks it is the expected increase in their actual value which is more critical than any dividends or "interest" those stocks actually pay. The growth in the value of the stocks themselves represents the true gain on the investment. When any portion of those stocks are sold off, it is the actual return on this investment that is measured against the original "principal" invested.

(1)   Restatement (Third) of Trusts note 5, Section 227 cmts, e-h.

INTRODUCTION

What portion of this gain will be paid out to heirs or what portion will remain invested is no longer a simple matter of choosing "income" versus "principal." Again the standard legal forms that are often prepared for a "set-fee" do not address these investment options or the allocation of investment "growth" between the Income Beneficiaries and Remaindermen. Legislation is responding to these changes slowly.[2] However, such laws cannot account for every situation and still require special legal drafting to take proper advantage of. In short, the individual needs to decide for themselves what decisions they want to make for their estate and need to have these choices clearly laid out in their estate documents by a competent attorney.

Finally, it is important for the reader to understand the critical limitations that can exist in the preparation of their estate or Trusts that only an attorney can help guard against. Individuals are free to dispose of their own property during their normal lives and they are given broad powers to do so in their wills and Trusts as well. Included in this power is the ability to delegate many decisions and choices to their heirs and beneficiaries. At some point, however, these delegated powers can become so broad that they amount to general control of the property itself. In such a case the taxing authorities may treat this property as if it had been given to these individuals outright. This can result in exactly the type of direct tax on the estate and the beneficiaries that the Trust was intended to avoid.

While the general powers to leave an inheritance remains, many of the specific Trusts that are available today are statutorily defined, with very specific limitations on what kind of powers may be granted and who may be granted such rights. Combinations of powers that are acceptable under certain statutory Trusts may be invalid when combined in another. These statutory Trusts involve a number of legal prerequisites that must be met and the need to consult a competent attorney in these areas is more critical than ever. In addition, problems involving heirs' rights to an elective share, invalid perpetuities and other legal pitfalls can prevent you from receiving the benefit of your estate plan and require the assistance of an attorney.

(2)   see The Uniform Principal and Income Act, Section 104 (Commissioners Draft of May 19, 1997).

INTRODUCTION

Simply put, the estate planning that you will be shown in this book does not replace good legal counsel. It enhances it. It will help to make the time you need to spend with your attorney more efficient. It will allow you to use options that require specific legal assistance to make effective. Given the financial benefits that some of these options can provide, the cost of qualified legal help should prove more than worthwhile. It is the time you personally invest in planning your estate that will give you your best value for legal costs and your greatest financial benefit.

ACKNOWLEDGMENTS

This book, like Trusts, was a family affair. Without the support and assistance of my wife and six children this book would not have been written.

My wife, Frances, is the editor. My son, William, an attorney, reviewed the material for legal content and made numerous suggestions. My daughter, Mary, designed the art work. Another son, Frank, Jr., designed and implemented the internet site and made numerous editorial recommendations. My other children, Frances, Matthew and Diana assisted with suggestions, advice and encouragement.

Gerard B. McCabe, a friend, librarian and author of many books was of great assistance.

Mr. W. Y. Alex Webb, a Trust attorney and CPA, and his associate Rick E. Graves, an attorney with a Masters in Tax, practicing in Aberdeen and Wilmington, North Carolina were of great help. Their estate planning work represents the best interests of the client.

And I must thank the hundreds of Trust attorneys from North Carolina, South Carolina, Georgia, Kentucky and Virginia who have attended my six-hour Continuing Legal Education Course over the past five years and freely discussed the public's misconception regarding limited options in their trusts.

And, to the many friends who encouraged me in this work, I sincerely thank each and every one.

Frank J. Croke

It's a letter from Santa to you. It says

Dear Bob,
    I understand you still haven't fixed Your Trust.
You have until December 24th or you are off my list.

                    Your friend,
                    Santa

Contents

Contents

Contents

Part One

UNDERSTANDING WHY MOST TRUSTS DO NOT PROVIDE THE BENEFITS YOU DESIRE FOR YOUR FAMILY.

Surely you must see that I have to go back to revise my Trust.
My family is not properly provided for and besides
I have frequent-flyer miles left.

CHAPTER 1

Discovering the Common Problems of Most Trusts

People establish a Trust for many reasons such as providing support for others who may not be able to handle investments or are too young to be given large sums of money. Another reason people establish Trusts is to take advantage of the federal estate-tax laws. These laws allow a person to leave up to $625,000 tax free to their children and others in 1998. This amount increases each year to eventually reach $1 million in the year 2006.

By establishing such a Trust, the income from it can be used to support the surviving spouse; then, upon the death of that spouse, the funds in the Trust go to the children, tax free.

The amounts of the federal estate-tax savings double when a husband and wife each establish a "Credit Shelter Trust." These tax savings are substantial. In 1998 as much as $1.25 million can be left by parents to children and other heirs, free of federal estate taxes. This amount increases to $2.0 million in 2006.

But most people at the time they establish a Trust, do not realize that they have many financial and management options. They do not plan what they want their Trust to accomplish prior to visiting their attorney. As a result, most Trusts are governed by the Default Rules of the state in which the Grantor resides. It is these state adopted rules that will control the financial results of a Trust if you fail to make those decisions yourself.

Just a few examples will indicate why any person establishing a Trust would want to avoid the state's Default Rules.

At today's dividend and interest rates, you or your wife as the surviving spouse will only receive about $19,000 a year (before state and federal income taxes) from a typical $625,000 Trust. A very low return.

This amount gradually increases, as the amounts you are allowed to leave free of federal estate taxes increase to $1 million. In the year 2006, when you can leave $1 million, your surviving spouse will only receive about $30,000 a year. That is 3%, a very poor return.

To achieve this poor return, assets had to be removed from your family holdings to fund the Trust. The annual income on such an investment commitment should and could be much higher. A Trust funded in 1998 with $625,000 could have produced $50,000 per year. A Trust funded in 2006 with $1,000,000 could have produced $80,000. You, the Grantor, informed of your rights, must exercise and state those rights in your Trust.

The value of the Trust for children could have been much higher if the Grantor was aware of his rights and options.

The end-value of a Credit Shelter Trust that starts at $625,000 in 1998 could be worth a million dollars or more for the children if the Grantor used options missing from most Trusts. This increase in the end-value for children could be much greater for a $1 million Trust in 2006. Options that can help obtain this for children and other heirs are presented in Chapter 7.

If you used a family member or friend as your trustee, chances are you neglected to provide for the security and safety of the Trust's assets and a continuing strong family relationship. See Chapter 18.

If you do not clearly indicate what you want to have happen to the funds you place in your Trust, state law will determine how these funds are to be invested. They will control the financial options in your Trust, if you fail to state them. The resulting income your surviving spouse will receive, and many other important financial decisions associated with your Trust will be governed by these Default Rules.

The Dictionary's definition of a "default" is a failure to act - neglect.

In Law, a "default" is defined as "an omission."

Every Trust we have reviewed has had omissions. Important options were left out. And, the major reasons the Grantor left out options was because he did not plan the financial objectives he wanted his Trust to accomplish.

We all know that if we die without a valid Will, the state will determine who is to receive our possessions. But what most people do not understand is, that if they do not direct what they want to have happen with the assets they place in their Trust, the state under the Default Rules will make that determination also.

4

The Default Rules governing how funds are to be invested will cause your surviving spouse to receive a low annual income from your Trust. Most people are unaware of this. In addition, the end-value of your Trust, for your children can be substantially lower than what they could have had.

State Default Rules, once understood, are not what most people would want. But they can be overridden, and options to accomplish this are available to everyone. But these options must be known, their inherent value appreciated, and they must be used in the Trust.

Yet why is it that most people do not try to learn about their rights and options when their Trusts are being prepared?

Years ago I was giving a talk to senior citizens. An elderly lady stated that her stockbroker had advised her to do the opposite of what I was recommending.

I answered her by first asking those in the audience if they had a family doctor. Most raised their hands. I then asked what they would do if their family doctor said they needed an operation ? All said, "get a second opinion."

"Fine" I said, "now that you have the second opinion and if it also indicates that you need the operation, will your family doctor perform the operation?" The answer was, "No, a specialist would do it."

You know that your family doctor spent many years of study and was an intern before he started his work. Yet, you want a second opinion and a specialist, if needed.

We know so much about handling doctors yet we know so little about others we deal with such as a stockbroker, a CPA, an attorney, or a financial planner. Keen discernment is called for in all these instances, too.

What is your knowledge of other important professions in your life? A CPA studies accounting and tax laws and is licensed by the state after field experience and passing examinations. An attorney generally studied liberal arts in college and then studies the law for three years in graduate school. A stockbroker passed a multiple-choice examination for his license, but that exam contained not one question on how he would invest a person's funds. And unfortunately the title "Financial Planner" is not based on any state or national standards. Anyone can call themselves that.

Knowing some of these limitations, how many people obtain a second opinion when dealing with a CPA, an attorney, a stockbroker or a financial planner? Very few.

We have been asked to review many Trusts for their financial implications. Most Grantors once they understood their options, (options missing from their original Trusts) wanted them included. They did this through a Trust revision.

Hopefully for most people, this book will allow you to form your own second opinion on your Trust.

In many of the chapters, I will use as an example a "Credit Shelter Trust." It is the most common type of Trust utilized to take advantage of the federal estate-tax exemption. " A Credit Shelter Trust has many other names such as a "Bypass Trust," an "A and B Trust." A Credit Shelter Trust can be in a Will or in a "Living Trust" (to avoid probate).

We will offer information on the financial aspects of other types of Trusts. One of them, a Charitable Remainder Unitrust can greatly reduce estate taxes while providing a high annual lifetime income for the Grantor. At the Grantor's demise, another person, such as a child can also be provided with this income for their lifetime.

For those whose assets are limited but who still have a need for a Trust to provide for their spouse or others, this book can provide them with important financial options they have and should consider.

CHAPTER 2

Basic Facts about Trusts

Our purpose in this book is to show that you must first make a plan indicating what you want to have happen with your assets.

Anything you leave to your surviving spouse will usually pass to that person free of federal estate taxes.[1] This is called the Marital Deduction. There is no limit on the amount of assets you can pass to your surviving spouse free of federal estate taxes.

In addition to the Marital Deduction, you may also leave up to $625,000 in 1998 to others (typically children and grandchildren) through your individual federal estate-tax exemption. This exemption is annually increasing in increments until it reaches $1 million by the year 2006.[2]

If your surviving spouse needs the income from your individual exemption of $625,000 or more, and in addition may need some of the principal, you can establish a Credit Shelter Trust. This type of Trust is the most common type used by married couples. When both the husband and wife together establish such a Trust, they can leave $1,250,000 tax free to their children in 1998 and $2 million tax free starting in the year 2006 and thereafter.

Assets placed in a Trust over the amount of your individual federal estate-tax exemption are taxed at the time of your death.[3] The remaining amount, after payment of your estate taxes, will go into the Trust.

An exception is a Marital Trust that you establish for the benefit of your surviving spouse. There are no federal estate taxes when this type of Trust is established. Everything you place in it passes free of federal taxes to the Marital Trust at the time of the Grantor's death.

(1)   Exception: A surviving spouse who is not a U. S. citizen - See an attorney for alternative suggestions.

(2)   The individual federal estate-tax exemption amounts for the years 1998 to 2006 is in Appendix "B" for this chapter.

(3)   Although not commonly done, this is "pre-paying" a tax that normally can be postponed until the surviving spouse's subsequent death. Consult your attorney on this.

However at the death of your surviving spouse, the value of the assets remaining from the Marital Trust will be added to any other assets your surviving spouse owns at that time. Estate taxes will be paid on this combined amount over the limit of the individual's federal estate-tax exemption. In summary, the unlimited transfer between spouses is eventually funneled into the single exemption of the surviving spouse.

Here we re-emphasize that when you place assets in a Trust you must consider your financial and management options and then make decisions on what you want your Trust to accomplish. You have the right to state in your Trust(s) what decisions you have made concerning your assets. If you do not do this, the Default Rules will control your Trust and produce results that you may not want and that you could have changed.

The Basic Form of a Trust

Person:
a) Established a
      Trust.
b) Funds the Trust
   With Assets.

Note: Many Trusts are established in a person's Will or in their Living Trust [3]

Assets

Assets are placed in the Trust. These can be cash, securities, real property or anything else of value. Assets may continue to be placed in the Trust after it is established.

Beneficiaries of

the Trust

Generally there are two types of Beneficiaries of a Trust: 1) The person(s) [4] who are to receive income from the Trust during their lifetime or for a stated period. And 2) the persons [5] and organizations who receive the principal when the Trust is terminated.

(3)   A Living Trust is established to avoid probate for those items that are placed in this type of Trust. See Chapter 21.

(4)   These people are called the Income Beneficiaries.

(5)   These people and organizations are usually the Remaindermen.

The Purpose of a Trust

In the above diagram, a person established a Trust. Let's use the example of a man who wanted to provide after his death for the care of his wife. After his wife's death, he wanted to have the assets in the Trust given equally to his four children. Key questions that need to be asked, and an example of what the answers might be follow.

What is the purpose of the Trust?
To provide a lifetime income for my wife's needs after my death.

After the purpose of the Trust is satisfied, who is to receive any assets left in the Trust?
They are to be divided equally among my four children. And, I may name other people and charities to receive a part of my Trust.

Who is to be the trustee of the Trust?
A Trust department of a bank or one of my children or a friend. [6]

There are a few additional questions such as the age the children are to be when they receive their share of the Trust. But in most instances only the above three questions are presented. They, along with the answers given, are expected to supply a body of information from which can be prepared a financially effective Trust.

But unfortunately, the answer to the first question is often forgotten when the Trust is prepared. Problems can and do result in the document itself and for the family it is supposed to protect and benefit. More information must be requested and supplied.

Some key questions never asked are:

1. *What will be the specific income needs of your wife after your death?*

2. *What portion of her income needs must come from the Trust?*

Most people never ask or plan for the answers to these last two questions. The question of the wife's income needs from the Trust was never discussed with the preparer of the Trust.

[6] Your surviving spouse could be a co-trustee. A spouse could also be the sole trustee. Important safeguards and restrictions on her access to the principal of the Trust would be required.

The explanation given by most people is that they thought the income their surviving spouse would receive was controlled by Trust law and the tax code. They did not know that they had an option in determining exactly what that amount would be.

Most people who invest their money want to know about return, safety and growth in value.

However, when it came to investing $625,000 of family assets in a Trust, they never directed a single question to these important factors. In short they chose to disregard their usual fiscal discipline of return, safety and growth. They did so at the time they were making an important investment decision. As a result, the Trust prepared for them was "silent."[7] It was silent on how the funds in the Trust would be invested; silent on the annual income their surviving spouse (the Income Beneficiary) would receive; and silent on an estimated end-value of the Trust for their children (the Remaindermen).

Most people are shocked to learn that if they placed $625,000 in a Trust for the support of their wife, she would only receive about $19,000 a year from that Trust, further reduced by state and federal income taxes. But this is what can happen.

The reason is the Trust investments are determined by the Default Rules. Today's low interest and dividend rates give the surviving spouse an annual income of about 3.0% of the value of the Trust. Such a meager income can result if the options available are not used when preparing a Trust.

As mentioned in the first part of this chapter, under the current federal estate-tax rates, each person can leave up to $625,000 free of federal estate taxes in 1998. This amount increases to $ 1 million in 2006.

Many people establish a Credit Shelter Trust because they want to take maximum advantage of their lifetime federal estate-tax credit.

When a husband and wife each establish a Credit Shelter Trust they can shelter $1.25 million of their assets by combining their individual $625,000 exemptions in 1998. For a couple who does this, their combined federal estate-tax exemption increases to $ 2 million in 2006.

(7)   "Silent" is a legal term meaning that the document neglected to state what the Grantor wanted.

How a Husband and Wife Establish Credit Shelter Trusts

The husband has a Will prepared and the wife has a Will prepared. In each Will a Trust is established with the maximum amount of an individual's federal estate-tax exemption. Each Will states that at their death their maximum exemption from federal estates taxes is to be placed in a Trust for their children (or others) and the income paid to their surviving spouse. This is shown below.

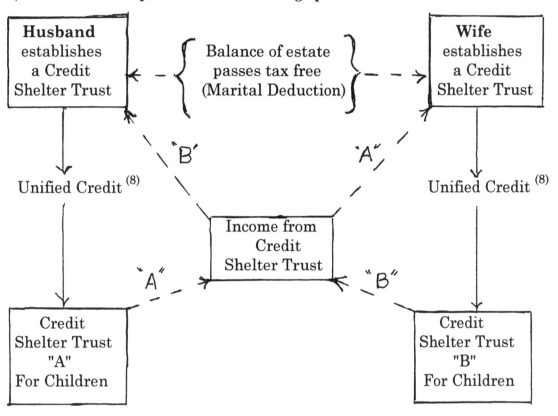

Notes: 1. In the event the husband dies first, his Credit Shelter Trust "A" is established and the income from his Trust is paid to his wife. In this case, the wife's Credit Shelter Trust "B" is no longer required[9] since her husband has died.

2. If the wife had died first, her Bypass Trust "B" is established and the income from her Trust is paid to her husband. In this case, the husband's Credit Shelter Trust "A" is no longer required[9] since his wife has died.

(8)   The Unified Credit is the term the federal government uses in the estate-tax code. It is this tax credit that allows each individual to leave $ 625,000 free of federal estate taxes in 1998. This amount increases in the following years to $ 1 million in 2006.

(9)   Exceptions such as restrictions that defer distribution to children and grandchildren until certain ages are obtained.

When the above Credit Shelter Trusts are written both the husband and the wife are alive and able to execute legal documents. Each document generally states that if that person dies first, the maximum amount of their assets allowed under the Unified Credit are to be placed in their Credit Shelter Trust. It is to be held there for the benefit of their children and the income is to be paid to the surviving spouse.

After the death of the surviving spouse, the funds in the Trust are given to their children or any other persons or organizations, such as a charity, according to the terms of their Credit Shelter Trust.

In most cases, the first to die is the husband. At that time, his Credit Shelter Trust is activated. All or part of the other assets the husband has can pass tax free directly to his wife. Or, he could have placed all or some of the assets in a Marital Trust. These assets would also pass tax free at the time of his death. But the assets that remain in the Marital Trust may be taxed at the time of the wife's death if, combined with her other assets, they exceed her Unified Credit.

When she dies, up to $625,000 of her estate in 1998 (allowed by the Unified Credit) goes tax free to the children. In 2006 and after, this amount is $ 1 million.

Combining the husband's federal estate-tax credit with the wife's tax credit results in providing $ 1.25 million in 1998 that they can leave free of federal estate taxes. In 2006 this increases to $ 2 million that they can leave to their children tax free.

By doing this, the couple save at least $235,000 in federal estate taxes. There can also be an additional tax-saving based on the estate-tax rates of most states.

Trusts to be funded after the death of a person are generally documented in that person's Last Will and Testament. There is the option of establishing a Living Trust"[10] while you are alive that can also establish a Credit Shelter Trust and other Trusts after your death. Living Trusts are generally established to avoid probate and can have other advantages over a Trust established in your Will.

You can also establish an Irrevocable Trust and many other kinds of Trusts during your lifetime. Trust attorneys are well versed in all of the different types of Trusts available to you.

.[10]   Living Trusts are discussed in Chapter 21.

The important issue in planning a Trust is determining what you want to accomplish with your estate. This requires decisions that can only be made by you. The financial and management options available to you and placed in your Trust will then make it an effective document.

Laws Governing Trusts

The laws governing Trusts are of two types:

1. Laws of the first type deal with tax issues such as how much of your estate you can leave tax free; limitations on the powers of the Income Beneficiary, etc. These laws are mainly federal government laws. States also have estate-tax laws. You cannot change these laws. Your Trust must conform to them. Your Trust attorney should be well trained in this area. When he prepares your Trust he will make continual reference to the various tax code sections. [11]

2. Laws of the second type deal with issues Grantors neglected to address in their Trust. These are state Default Rules that control what will happen to the funds in your Trust and hence the resulting income to your spouse, the expected end-value of the Trust for your children and many other important issues. You have the authority to override these Default Rules. When you do not use your options to do so, your Trust is said to be "silent" on an option. Therefore, the state will now determine how these most important issues will be handled. It's like dying without a Will.

It is in this second area of Trust law that you control and use your options. Your Trust attorney knows the Default Rules of your state. He also knows how your Trust will be handled under them. If a Grantor does not take the time to plan what their Trust is to provide, the attorney can only prepare a Trust that will be controlled by these Rules.

(11) There are numerous regulations that Trust attorneys continually study for guidance in Trust work. These include: the Internal Revenue Code; Private Letter Rulings issued by the IRS; Official Rulings of the IRS; Treasury Regulations; and statutes and court rulings of their state.

You have a right to override the Default Rules of your state. This right is found in the new "Uniform Prudent Investor Act" (UPIA) [12] currently the law in twenty-three states and being considered for adoption by many others.

SECTION 1. The "Uniform Prudent Investor Act" states:

> **(a)   Except as otherwise provided in subsection (b), a trustee who invests and manages assets owes a duty to the beneficiaries of the trust to comply with the prudent investor rule set forth in this [Act].**
>
> **(b)   The prudent investor rule, <u>a default rule,</u> may be expanded, restricted, eliminated or otherwise altered by the provisions of a trust. A trustee is not liable to a beneficiary to the extent that the trustee acted in reasonable reliance on the provisions of the trust.**

Carefully read what section 1 (b), above, says. The new law itself is a Default Rule that you have the right to change [as stated in section 1 (b)]. You have the right to put into your Trust what you want to have happen with the funds in your Trust - how they will be invested and managed. You can better determine such things as the income your surviving spouse will need and the potential end-value of the Trust for your children and other heirs.

You have the right to expand upon, restrict, eliminate or otherwise alter this law to accommodate your wishes. Your trustee is to act upon these Directives and is not accountable to a beneficiary of your Trust for following your clearly stated instructions.

In some cases, even where a Default Rule is favorable, you should consider stating these instructions openly to avoid problems that arise from changes in law.

We will give an example of how a $625,000 Credit Shelter Trust can provide $35,000 a year in 1998, instead of $19,000. In the year 2006 the same example can provide $70,000 instead of $30,000. You will also learn about other important financial and management options you have.

(12)   See Appendix E for a listing of states that have adopted this UPIA, a copy of it, and comments on key sections of the Act.

A second look at your rights under the law can be found in Federal Regulations of National Banks. National banks are supervised by the Comptroller of the Currency, a federal office.

Under Federal Law:

> "The Fiduciary (your trustee) must manage investments in accordance with the terms of the governing instrument, which is the primary determinant of a fiduciary's powers and duties. . . .
>
> If the instrument is silent as to authorized investments, the trustee is guided by provisions of local law."
>
> From: Page 49, "Comptroller's Handbook for Fiduciary Activities," Comptroller of the Currency, Administrator of National Banks. Code of Federal Regulations regarding trusts.

The statement above is another example of your rights to override the Default Rules of your state government.

We will show you examples of how powerful your rights are under the law. You can state in your Trust how you want your assets invested. So powerful are your rights that if you stated that 100% of your assets must be held in cash, the courts in all likelihood would not change your Directive.. They may agree to a petition to at least hold the cash in insured savings accounts in order to obtain a small amount of interest.

The courts are very reluctant to issue a ruling to change Directives stated in a Trust.

> **Except where impossible, illegal, or where a change of circumstances occurs which would impair the purposes of the Trust, the nature and extent of the duties and powers of a trustee are determined by the Trust instrument."[13]**

In Chapter 6 we will present differences in income needs between a husband and a wife. In most Trusts, they both will receive the same low annual income no matter who the surviving spouse is. Why?

---

(13)   Allen v. Pacific National Bank 99 Wash.2d 394, 633 P.2nd 104

With the exception of the differences in their names, the Trusts of most husbands and the Trusts of their wives read the same. Why?

If you and your spouse already have Credit Shelter Trusts, compare one to the other. Place them side by side and on a separate page write the name of each article in the Trusts. Note any difference in the sections between the husband's Trust and the wife's Trust.

You will find, as have many, that the provisions of a husband's Trust and wife's Trust are basically the same and do not address the different economic needs. This usually is a failing. Economic needs are rarely the same.

In addition, the Trusts that were reviewed contained no instructions to override the Default Rules. This strongly suggests that the Grantor was not aware that these Rules would govern the Trust. No power to override weakens a Trust and seriously impacts financial benefits to the heirs.

In the next sections, we will explain each of your major financial options and the economic benefits of using them. Part Four, summarizes the financial issues of each option presented that should be considered in every Trust.

CHAPTER 3

The Attorney / Accountant Dilemma

Introduction

A person requiring estate planning documents needs to be aware of the information presented in this chapter.

Background

Most of the revisions in the various state Default Rules came about through changes in the types of securities (approved by state regulatory authorities) in which Trustees may invest. Prior to World War II, state laws required bonds of high quality to be the investments held by trustees. After World War II, a small portion of your stocks were approved for Trusts. The holding of stocks, as approved trustee investments, has steadily increased since then. Now it is considered reasonable to have 50% in stocks and 50% in bonds to achieve a "Balanced Trust."

These stock and bond percentages were selected in order to provide fairly for the Lifetime Income Beneficiary, usually the surviving spouse, as well as for the Remaindermen, generally the children and other heirs. The concept is that the bonds will provide a higher income, but are not expected to increase in value. The stocks, with their lower income, will increase in value to preserve the purchasing power of the Trust when it is distributed to the heirs.

Unfortunately during this same period of regulatory change, the taxation of estates has increased. New types of Trusts are now approved by the federal government that could reduce a person's taxable estate.[1] There are some exceptions especially in the total credits allowed by the various states.[2]

---

(1)   These new types of Trusts are covered in the following chapters and in Chapter 19.

(2)   As an example: When the federal tax exemption on a person's estate was $600,000, some states adopted a lower state exemption of $500,000. And, recent changes in federal tax regulations have not yet been adopted by some states due to legislative delays in adopting the new changes.

These changes in the tax laws and their complexity have created a legal speciality in Trusts. And, it can be a frustrating professional speciality due to the administrative delays of the taxing authorities in releasing tax rulings.

These new and complex changes place on Trust attorneys the continuing burden of understanding constantly changing laws and regulations. The Trust attorney must determine what combinations of the numerous regulations allow which of the many types of estate planning techniques in order to produce the greatest estate tax savings for the client.

The Rights of the Grantor

Throughout the above process of change, however, the Grantor always had many financial and management options that could override the Default Rules of the various states. When the state Default Rules, prior to World War II, required a trustee to only invest in high quality bonds, a Grantor could state that 100% of the investments were to be in stocks. If this was stated in the Trust then the trustee had to follow these instructions.

A Grantor can override the Default Rules. This requires a Grantor to plan what they want to accomplish either prior to visiting their legal Trust specialist or with the assistance of their legal advisor.

The authority of the Grantor, however, carries with it a requirement: either the Grantor understands the benefits of their numerous financial options available to their family or the Grantor can engage a person who does.

The Issue

Must this person who advises a Grantor on their financial and legal options in estate planning be an attorney? Are the skills required to do this work different from those taught in law schools?

Many different professions advertise to the public that they are specialists in estate planning. But if their work includes the financial and management options to be placed in a client's estate planning documents, are they engaged in the unauthorized practice of law?

This is a critical issue for a CPA who must also hold a state license to practice. Some CPAs, working in this field, might be asked, are they engaging in the unauthorized practice of law? This is very doubtful if they were not drafting the legal wording to accomplish a Grantor's objective The issue can apply to others who may not be attorneys licensed to practice in a particular state.

I particularly call this matter to the attention of CPAs since they, by their financial training, are clearly able to assist a client in the estate planning process.

The Potential Resolution of the Issue

I believe that this issue can be resolved by answers to the few questions that follow:

1. Is it the unauthorized practice of law for a person who is not an attorney to read a legal contract or a draft and inform their client of the financial implications of the contract?

2. Is it the unauthorized practice of law for a person who is not an attorney to recommend financial options that would be to the client's benefit if included in the contract?

And lastly, just to bring this third item into the discussion:

3. Is it the unauthorized practice of law for a person who is not an attorney to recommend that the client consult another attorney, other than the one they are using, for a second opinion?

Does the professional responsibilities of a CPA to their clients, in the area of estate planning, require that the CPA:

A. Explain the financial options and the expected results when these options are used in Trusts.

B. Periodically review for clients, their existing Trusts for significant changes in the client's objectives and financial resources.

These same professional responsibilities of CPAs to clients would apply to others who engage in estate planning.

The problem of advising properly is recognized by the legal profession and they recognize the need for professions other than attorneys to assist clients. The "Model Rules of Professional Conduct"[3] of the American Bar Association state:

"RULE 2.1 ADVISOR

In representing a client, a lawyer shall exercise independent professional judgment and render candid advice. In rendering advice, a lawyer may refer not only to law but to other considerations such as moral, economic, social and political factors, that may be relevant to the client's situation."

The model rules go on to state:

"[4]   Matters that go beyond strictly legal questions may also be in the domain of another profession. . . . Where consultation with a professional in another field is itself something a competent lawyer would recommend, the lawyer should make such a recommendation."

(3)   Pages 54 and 55, 1994 Edition, "Model Rules of Professional Conduct" published by the American Bar Association, 750 North Lake Shore Drive, Chicago, Illinois 60611

Chapter 4

How This Affects You

Most Trusts do not accomplish what you want. The reason is simple: a plan was not prepared prior to visiting a Trust attorney. A person establishing a Trust has numerous financial and management options. Being aware of them and using them properly are what make a Trust truly beneficial to a family. This book explains your key financial and management options and provides examples of each option that you can discuss with your attorney.

If a person does not consider the key options they have and fails to present them to the attorney, that attorney can only prepare a general Trust document that will be governed by the "Default Rules" of the state.

The Default Rules of the state you reside in may not be the best way to control your Trust. They may not provide a sufficient income for the surviving spouse and they can result in reduced benefits and protection for your family and other heirs.

Think back on your past experiences with an attorney. Think about the work you did and the work your attorney did.

For most people buying their first home was the initial experience with a lawyer. You told the attorney the location of the house, the price you would pay for it, mortgage requirements, the maximum interest and any extra items to be part of the purchase price (appliances, lawn mowers, etc.).

The attorney made notes on all of this information. He probably advised you that a mortgage lender would require a title guarantee policy and that you would pay that expense. A survey of the property and a certificate of occupancy may have been required. Termite and other inspections should be made of the property. The attorney prepared a contract based on the information you gave him.

This is the work an attorney does. He represents you and what you want.

Unless your attorney was a family member or close friend, he did not advise you on what type of home you should have, where it should be or in what school district. He did not advise you on any of the other details associated with the home you selected and decided to buy. This is not what an attorney does. It is what you do.

It is not very different if you ever bought or started a business; or invested large sums of money in a company. You selected what you would invest in, based upon your plans, your forecast of the growth, and the financial returns from your investment.

Your attorney does not select the business you should buy or start. Nor does he select the investments you should make; it is not his job to calculate the risk or the return on your investments. A study of the many financial and management issues associated with your investments and businesses is not what your attorney does. This is the work that you do.

And when you establish a Trust, the procedure is the same. You should plan what you want to accomplish before obtaining the assistance of a Trust attorney.

Properly preparing the objectives of your Trust before visiting your attorney has three important results.

1. You will have clear written intentions about what you want.

2. Your attorney will be better able to legally accomplish exactly what you have planned.

3. Your attorney's fees in the long run, will be less. You know exactly what you want. Your attorney does not have to spend time on general Trust discussions.

This is true in buying a home or starting a business, and, it is certainly true when you decide to establish a Trust.

Before you visit an attorney, you must determine many things you want your Trust to accomplish. Attorneys can only start with the federal laws and regulations for a particular type Trust. You cannot use preprinted Trust forms. The items covered in this book are not included in these forms.

Very important items such as the income needs of a surviving spouse are not adequately provided for in most Trusts. You may well ask "Why?" since this is one of the most important aspects of the Trust. The answer is one of the oddities in Trust work.

If an attorney told the client that they must first make a financial plan, most clients would not do this. They would go to another attorney.

The general public does not understand why a financial plan or any plan is required prior to the preparation of their legal Trust document. The main reason for this is that the pubic believes that they have few if any options for their Trust. They are uninformed and believe that their Trusts are controlled by state and federal laws with no financial options. So why should a person take the time or spend the money to have a financial plan prepared?

Because of this misconception, the public "shops around" for an attorney who will prepare their estate planning documents for the lowest fixed fee. They receive what they pay for, a poorly planned Trust that deprives their family of the financial benefits they could receive.

The public does not understand that there are Default Rules that will control their Trusts for each area where they neglect to give specific instructions in the Trust document. The legal profession needs to try to correct this widely accepted misconception that Grantors have no financial options.

These Default Rules do not take into account the specific needs of the client or the family. The Default Rules provide only a fraction of the income the surviving spouse often thinks they are going to receive from the Trust.

The Default Rules do not maximize the potential end-value of the Trust for the children and other heirs.

The Default Rules can result in Trust management that is unproductive and finances that are deficient.

It is possible to avoid all of this in a properly prepared Trust. But to do this requires serious consideration given to the specific needs of the family. I have been asked many times: What does a good estate plan cost?

Time is the major expenditure in the planning period. Only you can give the time required.

What you must do

If you want to properly provide for your family, you need to select the financial and management options you want for your Trust. These financial options are not difficult to understand. Most of them are just plain common sense such as:

1. How much money will the surviving spouse require from the Trust? Use the form: "Income needs of Each Spouse" as the starting point. (The need for this is explained in Chapter 6.) You are then able to place this amount, in current year's dollars, in the Trust. You increase this for inflation and an additional percentage (to cover higher inflation costs for seniors not provided for in government data).

2. If a Grantor wants a high end-value of the Trust for his children, use Directives[1] to increase the percentage invested in good quality common stocks to 75% or higher. (This is discussed in Chapter 8.)

3. Consider using a custodian for the funds if a family member is trustee and require the custodian to send copies of the Trust statements to all heirs. (This option is presented in Chapter 18.)

4. If you wish to help provide for a spouse of a second marriage but still provide for your own children. (see Chapter 12.)

5. Providing other benefits and options after your death that will help make your Trust more responsive to changing family needs.

This workbook explains the above financial options and many other important options. Information on each option is presented so that you can determine if you want that option in your Trust. These are options that you have a right to place in your Trust. With your instructions, your attorney will be able to put each option in proper legal form to comply with existing Trust regulations and case law. Your trustee will be required to follow your clearly written Directives.

In many states attorneys are not permitted to give investment advice and in respecting that caveat, many of them avoid asking even basic financial questions. So, you as the Grantor of a Trust must tell the attorney exactly what you want. It is the same as when you bought your home or started a business - you tell the attorney what your decision is.

[1] A Directive is an instruction given as to what is to be done such as "I direct my trustee to pay my surviving spouse $35,000 a year starting on the date this Trust was executed and increased 3% a year from that date."

If an attorney were to spend the time reviewing with you all of your options presented in this workbook, your legal costs would increase. However, the benefits to your family would far outweigh that expense.

Good planning and the use of your most important options are the key to a successful Trust. Both subjects, planning and options, are addressed in the following chapters.

This book, a financial manual on Trusts, follows the format of a workbook. It will enable you to develop a financial plan for your family. If you already have a Trust, these "work pages" will allow you to review your document and determine if it excludes financial and management options you would want included.

Use this material seated at a desk or other writing surface. Make notes on the key items presented. Use a yellow high-lighter to mark things important to you. Use a paper clip for key pages that you want to use to plan your Trust. Make copies of summaries of key financial and management Directives that you want to address in your Trust and bring them with you to your Trust attorney.

If you take the time to use the ideas presented in this book, your attorney will have a very clear understanding of what you intend to financially accomplish through your Trust.

Many of the important options you have are financial ones. These are missing from many Trusts. Your attorney may want to review with you why it is so important that these options be included in your Trust. You can use this workbook to present the intended financial benefit of each option you have selected.

Chapters 23 to Chapter 27 summarize the options presented in this workbook. Mark those options that you want in your Trust and give them to your attorney. Your attorney will prepare the proper wording based on the federal regulations and the laws of your state and to conform to prior court rulings. [1]

---

(1)   There are numerous regulations and court rulings that Trust attorneys continually study for guidance in Trust work. These include: the Internal Revenue Code; Official Rulings of the IRS; Private Letter Rulings issued by the IRS; Treasury Regulations; and statutes and court rulings of their states.

Prior to making a commitment for the services of a Trust attorney, it is recommend that you interview attorneys. Often there is no charge for an interview to discuss your needs, the attorney's services and fees. If the attorney, during this initial interview, has trouble understanding financial options that are important to you or presents objections on why you would want them, you may wish to consider another attorney.

Before we address these important financial and management options, a review should be made of what you want to accomplish. This is discussed in the next chapter.

CHAPTER 5

Determine What You Want to Accomplish

Before you visit a Trust attorney, you need to determine what you want to financially accomplish with your estate after your death. This work is not hard to do. The starting point for most Trusts, the income of the surviving spouse, is discussed in the next chapter.

You also have the option of planning the end-value of your Trusts for your children and other heirs. If you have only one child, who will inherit your entire estate, you may (or may not) consider their inheritance of up to $2 million tax free, as a substantial enough sum for this one child to receive.

If you have several children plus grandchildren, you will want to increase the end-value of your Trust since it will be divided among so many.

REMEMBER:

YOU HAVE THE RIGHT TO STATE WHAT YOU WANT TO HAVE HAPPEN WITH THE FAMILY ASSETS YOU PLACE IN YOUR TRUST

YOU HAVE THE RIGHT TO:

1. **DETERMINE** the annual income your surviving spouse is to receive from the Trust.

2. **STATE** how the funds are to be invested.

3. **PROVIDE** for a higher end-value of the Trust for the benefit of your children, grandchildren and other heirs.

4. **PROVIDE** safeguards for the assets in your Trust for the protection of your family.

5. **PROVIDE** other important financial and management options available to you for inclusion in your Trust.

If you first consult standard Trust forms sold in stationery stores or over the Internet, they will probably not give you a document that will provide a satisfactory Trust for the needs of your family. The advice and considerations you need go beyond what are generally provided.

Some books on Trusts also provide standard forms. Are your key options in these forms? If you doubt this, compare these standard forms to the options in this book. [1]

Some banks may recommend Trust attorneys to help you. Banks have been the traditional professional managers of Trusts. Their marketing efforts, in the past, have been strongly tied to attorney referrals. These will be attorneys that the bank has worked with in the past and with whom they do business. This is no guarantee that these are the best Trust attorneys in your area.

Most Trust attorneys state that each Trust they prepare is tailored to individual needs. But, if the Grantors do not clearly state their objectives, the attorneys are limited in what they can provide beyond the legal issues relating to the tax code.

There are some Trust attorneys who will advise you of your Trust options as outlined in this book. Attorneys who do this generally have available to them one or more persons, trained in many of these financial options, who will work with you as part of a team to prepare your Trust. Very wealthy people pay for this type of estate planning. And, the fee they pay for this service is generally over $15,000.

If your estate is under $ 4 million, you can obtain the same basic benefits for your family by considering the financial options in this book.

---

(1)   It may be difficult, at first, to understand the legal wording of any Trust you review to determine what options are in that Trust. One quick test is to look for the income the person(s) named in the Trust are to receive. If the Trust reads that the person is to receive the "Net Income," it means that their annual income is reduced by about ten percent. You have the option of stating in your Trust that the person is to receive the "Gross Income," an option discussed in Chapter 14.

Other test questions are: does the Trust state the annual income the surviving spouse is to receive and how the assets are to be invested (see Chapter 7); does it provide the greater of $5,000 or 5% in addition to the income from investments (see Chapter 10); and does it address the many other important financial options presented in this book.

A friend who has established a Trust, may recommend the attorney who has prepared his, confident that he has a Trust that will properly provide for his family.

Such recommendations are often based on the fact that the Trust was prepared at a reasonable cost or that the preparer was a "nice person." A good Trust that will adequately protect and provide for your family and has been prepared based on your needs is expensive - but worth the cost. You can substantially reduce this expense by giving your attorney examples of what you want.

A review of your friend's Trust would more than likely reveal that it does not contain the options presented in this book. If these options are missing, your friend's Trust will be governed by Default Rules. These rules may impact the financial course of a Trust in a way not envisioned or understood by your friend or most Grantors. Protecting and providing for the family is one of the main objectives of a Trust.

You can plan for and provide for most of the important issues relating to your financial plan. You can make appropriate Directives in your Trust. Do not make the mistake of relying on the Default Rules.

As an example, if your wife is the surviving spouse and later in her life she is confined to a nursing home, would you want your children to visit her? Bring the grandchildren? Determine if she is being properly cared for? This would normally be done if the children lived nearby, But if they lived great distances, you can provide for the expense of these visits in your Trust.

Most brokerage firms also want your Trust business. All of the larger firms have established Trust operations. Their sales people will present the investment advantages of using their firm as your trustee. But the sales people in many of these firms do not understand the options you have and would want in your Trust. Few can help you determine the income requirements for your surviving spouse or advise you that Directives must be placed in a Trust to increase the value of it for your children.

Corporations normally look at their market opportunities coupled with their resources and capabilities. Once this has been determined, they set about to organize their company to capture these market opportunities.

In the brokerage industry there is a market opportunity to bring Trust business into their firms. But presently they compete for about 10% of the Trust business that uses professional trustees to manage Trust money. They have ignored the other 90% which they are in a strong position to attract using their firm's resource of a large and financially trained sales force.

Do not be fooled by the old and incorrect statement: "You cannot anticipate everything and therefore you should let the trustee make those decisions if and when these things come up."

An example is a couple who lived on the East Coast and had two daughters. Each daughter was married with children. One daughter lived in the Los Angeles area, the other in Denver. Their husbands worked but they were not wealthy.

Every other year the parents paid the airfare for their daughters, their husbands and their grandchildren to visit them for a week. They rented a seaside house for their visitors, near their own home, and spent part of each day with them.

However, if one of them passed away their Trusts had no provision to pay the expenses for their daughters and grandchildren to visit the surviving spouse, even though the Trust could grow in value to over $2 million. We do not know of any state's Default Rule that would allow the trustee to pay the travel and other expenses associated with these visits especially when the surviving spouse was ill or in a nursing home. Consideration for including this type of expenditure in a Trust is very important.

A trustee is not authorized to pay the travel and other expenses associated with such family activities or responsibilities unless you clearly state so in the Trust. A professional trustee handles the investments, but family members have a greater interest in determining if the surviving spouse is receiving proper care and attention in a nursing home or, if a change to another facility is required. In addition, think of the joy these visits can bring to the surviving spouse.

For this family that lived many miles apart, an attorney inserted into their Trusts authorization for travel and lodging payments for their daughters' families so they could visit the surviving spouse when ill or in a nursing home.

Review the material in this book. Especially note the illustrations for your attorney's use for each option presented and summarized in Part Four. The material offers important financial considerations and other options that may be in the best interests of the surviving spouse and the family.

CONCLUSION

Before you visit a Trust attorney, you must determine what you want to accomplish with your estate after your death. It is a revealing and rewarding process that only you can do.

If you are uncertain about what to expect in the way of services from a Trust attorney - think back on an early experience, that of buying your first home. You told the attorney the location of the house, the price you would pay for it, a mortgage and interest charges, and whether any items of personal property were to be part of the purchase (appliances, window treatments, etc.).

This is the decision work you do when buying a home, starting a business and when establishing your Trust. You determine what you want to accomplish.

A.   You must determine the income needs of you, your surviving spouse and other income beneficiaries from the Trust. Use Exhibit 1 and the instructions in Chapter 6.

B.   You must determine the desired end-value of the Trust for your children (see Chapter 8) and many other key financial and management options they have and can place in their Trusts.

C.   You must determine how best to provide for the spouse of a second marriage and your own children (see Chapter 12).

D.   You must determine the safeguards you want in your Trust and other options presented in this book and available to you.

E.   You must determine a very important but rarely stated objective: how to maintain a strong family relationship between and among the surviving spouse and the children.

Part Two

DISCOVERING YOUR FINANCIAL

and MANAGEMENT OPTIONS

We used to live in the house on the hill before John died.
But you'd be amazed how hard it is to live on an income
of a $1 million Trust under the Default Rules.

CHAPTER 6

Know Your Income Needs
(or be prepared to live on a lot less)

Introduction

This chapter presents the information you will need to give financial Directives in your Trust to provide the income required by you or your spouse. Over 95% of the Trusts reviewed do not provide an adequate income for the surviving spouse's needs. In fact the shortage can be $10,000 to $20,000 a year. This additional needed income could have been paid from the Trust if proper instructions had been given in the document. This chapter will show how this can be corrected. It is based on common-sense decisions and prudent financial judgment.

Read first about what causes the problem of an inadequate income. Then review our form that can be used to determine your income needs. It will help to plan and provide a sufficient income for yourself and your spouse. If you already have a Trust, this major financial option may not presently be part of it. To correct this, you may decide to revise your Trust. If you revise the income to be paid, you can at the same time add any other financial options outlined in this book that may also be missing from your Trust.

If you are planning a Credit Shelter Trust, the information that follows is your starting point.

First you determine the financial provisions that must be made to provide for the income needs of yourself and your surviving spouse. The next two important topics for your consideration will be in the chapters that follow. They are:

A.   How to help increase the value of the Trust for your children and how to give funds from the Trust to children during the lifetime of the surviving spouse (Chapters 8 and 9).

B.   In cases of second marriages with children from prior marriages, we will discuss how to adequately provide for your spouse financially while preserving ownership of the assets for your children (Chapter 12).

Other important issues will also be presented. The following material covers the most crucial of the financial issues you must decide. If a Grantor ignores this option, the result can be a very low income for the survivor, whether it is you or your spouse. Its omission is one that causes the most financial harm to the family.

IF YOUR TRUST IS LIKE MOST, IT PROVIDES A LOW AND INADEQUATE INCOME FOR YOU OR YOUR WIFE.

The example that follows is the approximate annual income (before state and federal income taxes) to be expected from most Credit Shelter Trusts that are silent as to income. Trusts, silent on this most important option, are generally silent on other vital issues. Grantors are not aware of the right everyone has to say what they want to financially accomplish through their Trusts. The amount of the Trust is the maximum amount allowed in 1998.

	ANNUAL NET INCOME PAID[1]					
Amount of Trust	**1st Yr.**	**5th Yr.**	**10th Yr.**	**15th Yr.**	**20th Yr.**	**25th Yr.**
$625,000	$19,516	$20,597	$22,719	$26,206	$31,937	$41,354

Note: The detail of the above estimated Annual Income Payments are in Appendix B - Chapter 6, Exhibit A.

In other words, placing $625,000 of family assets in a Trust yields an income of less than 3%, before state and federal income taxes, in the first year. This is a very low income. This is what will happen when you do not plan and clearly state the income needs of you, your spouse or your other Income Beneficiaries.

(1)   The above amounts for the spouse's estimated annual income are based upon many planning factors which can change and most probably will in the future. The factors used are: A 6% interest rate on good quality medium-term bonds; dividend payments of 1.3% on good quality growth stocks; fees and expenses of 1% based on the year-end value; and most volatile of all these planning factors, the future growth of stock prices.

The future growth of stock prices is very difficult to forecast over a short time period. While the long-term future trend has been for increased values, short-term periods have resulted in years of decreases. The judgement of future stock growth rests with the Grantor.

Because of these many future variables, the above amount should be rounded off to at least the nearest thousand and be given a variance factor, especially in the first five years or more, of a wide range. It was not done in order to preserve the source of the data from the Estate Planning Programs available to you on our Internet Site. You can enter the planning data into the Internet Programs and the exact same figures will result. This indicates that you are properly using the calculators. Once you know them, you can change the planning factors to review and compare the differences in the results.

Most surviving spouses need a higher income from the Trust than the example indicates.

Your Rights Under The Law.

You have the right to state in your Trust the amount of income to be paid to your surviving spouse or other Income Beneficiaries. You also have the right to state how the funds in the Trust are to be invested as well as many other financial and management rights required but left unstated in most Trusts.

The basic Trust law for the payment of a Trust income and the investment of Trust assets is that your trustee must follow the specific instruction you give in your Trust document. This is based upon the legal principle that these are your assets. What you clearly state in your Trust determines the trustee's duties and powers.

Unfortunately, most Grantors of Trusts never plan the income needs for those they love and want to provide for. States have Default Rules regarding this important issue of income to be paid and many other important financial options that Grantors neglect to address. You will recall from Chapter 2 that if your Trust is "silent"[2] on any issue that you could have given instructions about, it will be guided by the provisions of state Default Rules on that issue.

Many state laws regarding Trusts are called Default Rules. As mentioned earlier, "A Default is a failure, an omission of that which ought to be done."[3] Another definition of a default, under the law is: "failure to perform an act or obligation legally required."[4]

Everyone knows that if a person dies without a Will, the state will determine who is to receive their assets, even what percent each will receive and when they will receive it. But what most people do not know is that when they have a Will or a Trust, the state will still determine many issues, especially if they neglect to clearly say in their documents what they want to have happen.

(2) "Silent" is a legal term used when a Grantor neglected to give specific instructions on an issue or option in trusts.

(3) Black's Law Dictionary, sixth edition published by West Publishing Co.

(4) The Random House Dictionary of the English Language - College Edition.

You must plan how the assets in your Trust are to be invested and the annual income you and your spouse will need from your Trusts. You must clearly state in your Trusts your investment Directives, the annual income to be paid, increases for inflation and other economic considerations which you desire to provide for in your Trust.

This is important advice. If you follow the instructions given in this one section of the book, you can exercise the kind of financial influence on your Trust that will greatly benefit you, your spouse and your children.

First You Need to Plan the Income Needs From the Trust.

When you plan the income needs for you and your spouse that will be required from your Trusts, you must do so in today's dollars. This is the financial preparation you should do for yourselves in advance of your visit to a Trust attorney.

In previous chapters we presented how to properly use the services of an attorney - the work that you must do and the work an attorney does in representing you. The concept that applies in buying a home is the same when establishing a Trust. Be as prepared as possible.

Know what you want to accomplish before you visit an attorney. When planning a Trust, the most important issue you must determine is the annual income you , your surviving spouse or your other Income Beneficiaries will require from the Trust.

This is the most important starting point: the income to be paid. It is, unfortunately, ignored in most Trusts. Why? Because Grantors do not realize that this is an option they have. Grantors incorrectly believe that the income to be paid is controlled by Trust law and that they have no rights in this most critical issue.

There are very good Trust attorneys who will assist you in doing this work using a form similar to Exhibit 1, presented in this chapter. If you are fortunate enough to have a Trust attorney who will guide you in determining the income needs of each spouse, and other financial options, the additional legal expense will be minor compared to the benefits you will receive.

But, before you visit your Trust attorney you should determine the individual income requirements by using the one-page form, Exhibit 1 **"Income Needs of Each Spouse."** The Annual Income Need, on the form, is before federal and state income taxes.

You must decide and clearly state in your Trust that this amount includes increases for inflation and several other considerations. If you do not do these two things, the income you or your surviving spouse will receive from the Trust can be much lower than required. In some cases disastrously low and different enough from the current life style to cause shock waves.

This lower income will be caused by the Default Rules of the states that will govern the investments and the resulting income when a person does not use their option to give Directives in these two important areas of their Trust.

Knowing that you must clearly state the income to be received is the most important lesson to learn from this book. If you follow only the advice given in this section you will have accomplished a major change in your Trust that can benefit your surviving spouse and your children.

To help you in determining the income needs of you and your spouse that must be paid from the Trust, we will start with a completed form for the Wilsons, John and Mary.[5] To compare the differences in requirements for a husband and for a wife, we have combined each person's needs on a single form. See Exhibit 1 - Completed Form on Page 41 and review the information below on how the amounts were provided.

At the top of the form, "A" is stated the Current Annual Income Needed before state and federal income taxes. The starting point is generally your total gross income, before any adjustments to reduce it, on your tax return for last year.[6] The amount of income on our form, Exhibit 1, is $60,000. It could have been $35,000 or some other amount. No attempt was made to reduce current income needs resulting from the death of a spouse.

It is better to estimate a higher financial need. If after the form is completed, and the amount of income required from the Trust appears high, you can always review certain items and reduce them if needed. An estimate on the low side will not provide for the surviving spouse.

(5)   Because we review Trusts on a confidential basis, real names are not used in this book.

(6)   Information on how to adjust the Current Annual Income Needed and suggestions for completing the other items on this form are in Appendix C.

Next, in part "A - 2" the Sources of Income excluding that from the Trust are listed starting with Social Security and Pension payments each person will receive after the death of a spouse. In many cases, the wife receives a lower Social Security amount than her husband received during his lifetime.[6] In this example the amount each surviving spouse will receive is the same.

The amount listed as Pensions is lower for Mary. In this example her husband's pension of $30,000 would be reduced 50% after John's death. This is a very important item to consider. In some cases, the wife has died shortly after the husband retired. If the widower later remarried, his second wife, in most cases, would not receive even the reduced 50%.

Part "A - 2. c." of Exhibit 1 requires some planning as to how the family assets are divided in order to qualify for a Credit Shelter Trust.[7] If you plan to establish a Credit Shelter Trust or a Marital Trust, the assets you plan to place in your Trust must be in your name only and must become part of your estate at your death.

In the example, John and Mary owned stocks, mutual funds, CDs and saving accounts totaling $1,550,000 equally. They divided these assets equally so that each of them had $755,000 in their own name listed at their current value in A - 2. c. This means that each can fully fund a Credit Shelter Trust, without any appreciation of their current assets, up to the year 2004 when the federal estate-tax exemption increases to $850,000.[8]

(6)   The Social Security office in your area can give you an estimate of what the surviving spouse will receive. It can be about 80% of the amount their deceased spouse was paid if the survivor's work record indicates they would receive on their own a lower amount.

(7)   To qualify being placed in your Trust, assets must be in your name only. Joint accounts with right of survivorship will not qualify since upon your death, titles pass to your spouse. The value of assets that you own such as an IRA account or an Insurance policy that names another person as your beneficiary upon your death, cannot be used to fund your Trust. These amounts pass directly to your beneficiary.

(8)   As indicated in Section A - 2. c., $585,000 of their individual assets are in stocks and mutual funds. If stock and mutual funds owned by John and Mary increase in value at 5% a year, they will be able to fund a $1 million Credit Shelter Trust starting in the year 2006.

Exhibit 1 - Completed Form
INCOME NEEDS OF EACH SPOUSE

			By JOHN	*By MARY*
A.	**CURRENT ANNUAL INCOME NEEDED** **before Income Taxes** Excluding the cost of a new car and other items listed in "B" below . . .		$ 60,000	$ 60,000

A - 2 SOURCES OF INCOME excluding that
from the Trust:

a. Social Security	$ 12,000		$12,000
b. Pensions	30,000		15,000

A - 2. c. Other: List by name & current value

- Stocks & Mutual Funds, $585,000	$13,500		13,500
- CD's & Saving Accounts, $170,000	$ 8,500		8,500
Total Investments $755,000			
TOTAL INCOME	$ 64,000		$49,000
- Subtract total of "Sources of Income" from Annual Income Required		- $64,000	-$49,000

A -3   **TOTAL "A" INCOME REQUIRED FROM TRUST**   -$ 4,000 $ 11,000

B.   Additional Special Needs for Annual Expenses not included in the above:

		By JOHN	*By MARY*
B - 1	New Car costing $25,000 divided by 4 years =	$ 6,250	$ 6,250
B - 2	Travel & Vacations	$ 4,000	$ 4,000
B - 3	Family needs: assistance to children & grandchildren, Gifts, etc.	$ 3,000	$ 3,000
	Other: List		
	- HOME MAINTENANCE & PROVISION FOR MAJOR REPAIRS & APPLIANCES	$3,500	$3,500
B - 4	**TOTAL OF SPECIAL NEEDS**	$ 16,750	$ 16,750
	Convert Total for Special Needs to an amount prior to federal and state income taxes: If your top tax bracket is 20% in income taxes, increase by 25%; if your top tax bracket is 25%, increase by 33%; if your top tax bracket is 30% increase by 43%; and if it is 37% increase by 59%.		
	INCREASE	$ 7,200	$ 7,200
B - 5	**TOTAL FOR SPECIAL NEEDS**	$23,950	$ 23,950
B - 6	PLUS TOTAL INCOME REQUIRED FROM "A"	-$4,000	$11,000
C	**-TOTAL ANNUAL INCOME REQUIRED FROM TRUST IN YEAR IT WAS EXECUTED**	$ 19,950	$ 34,950

To complete section A, the Sources of Income (excluding the Trust) are added together and then subtracted from the Current Annual Income needed at the top of the form. Note: that the difference between what John needs from the Trust and what Mary needs is $15,000 - This is caused by the reduced amount of pension income Mary will receive if John dies first.

Next review Part B of Exhibit 1. In this section are items we may not purchase or spend funds on every year such as a car and extensive home repairs. Some of the sources of funds for these things may be our saving accounts and investments. List each item that you do not pay for out of your current annual after tax income.

In section "**B -1.**" New Car: There may be a difference between the amounts required by each person. Women want the safety of a new car.

Section "**B - 2.**" Long and expensive vacations might be taken every other year.

Section "**B - 3**" The amount is for the usual gifts you give for the holidays, birthdays and special events. It could be gifts for travel, etc. This section was not meant to include major gifts to children such as the $10,000 allowed per year or to pay the expense of a wedding, college tuition, etc. if other sources of funds were made available for these items.

If you own a home, major repairs can be expected. Appliances need to be replaced in any dwelling.

Line "**B - 4**" Total the amount of your Special Needs. Since we tend to think in terms of the actual purchase price of a car; the actual expense of vacation; the actual amount of gifts given to children; the above total is an after income-tax amount. To increase this to a before tax number, suggested percentage increases are given after line "B - 4.". The percentage used should be at your highest tax rate.

Line "**B - 5**" Total For Special Needs. This is the amount on Line "B - 4" increased by a tax rate explained above.

Line "**B - 6**" Place on this line the amount from line "**A - 3**" above.

Line "C" **This is the total of lines** "B - 5" and "B - 6." If this number is over $19,000 you should consider stating the amount in your Trust that is the income to be paid if you died the year your Trust was executed. This amount should also be increased annually for inflation. In our illustrations in this chapter we annually increased the amount required by 3%.

NOTE: The surviving spouse should have ample funds available. And, if possible there should be sufficient funds to buy gifts and pay for certain activities for the children and grandchildren. The goal is to maintain a strong family relationship unaffected by financial strain.

The Default Rules

Now that you have an understanding of how the Income Needs of Each Spouse was prepared in Exhibit 1, you also need to become aware of the following:

1. If you do not say precisely what the annual payments from your Trust will be to the Income Beneficiary, your trustee guided by the state Default Rules will determine what these payments will be.

2. If you do not say precisely what you want to have happen with the assets you place in your Trust, the state Default Rules determine how these assets are to be invested.

You have many Trust options. Each time you neglect to use one, you activate state Default Rules that then control the issue.

How do the Default Rules control the investments and the income payments?

A. For Investments:

If you do not say how the assets in the Trust are to be invested, Default Rules will require that approximately 50% of the assets be invested in Bonds and 50% in Stocks.

B. For Income to be Paid:

If you do not say how much annual income you or your surviving spouse are to receive from the Trust, the Default Rules will determine those payments. The results will be about 3% of the value of a Trust. Can you or your spouse live on an income from the Trust of $19,000 a year before state and federal income taxes? That's what it would be, based on current interest and dividend rates shown on the following pages.

The income your spouse will receive may also depend upon income received from other sources. This is particularly true if you gave your trustee, at their sole discretion, the authority to distribute or to withhold income. This is called the "Sprinkling Powers" and is presented as Option 3 in Chapter 8 (Page 69).

The important point to remember is that income payments to the surviving spouse are limited to the amount of income received. Our position is that the income needs may exceed the actual income received by the Trust. Therefore, the Grantor, when stating a higher annual income payment requires the trustee to take this additional amount from the principal of the Trust. Based on the estimates, this removal may come from the gains in the growth of the assets held by the Trust and thereby not cause a decrease in the value of the Trust.

Trust to Pay Net Income

Most Trusts state that the "Net Income" is to be paid to your surviving spouse or other Income Beneficiary. If you have a Trust, it probably says this. Why?

The "Net Income" provision reduces the income to be paid to the surviving spouse. In the majority of cases, as indicated in this book, the exact amount of annual income, increased for inflation is what should be clearly stated in the document that established the Trust. As the Grantor you also have the right to state that the "Gross Income" will be paid. For additional information on this option, see Chapter 14.

How the use of Net Income changed from early English law to its current use in the United Sates is very interesting.

Many of our laws come from England. Over four hundred years ago many of the wealthy gentry were the Lords and Barons who held vast lands. After their deaths, their Trusts stated: after provisions were made for: the payments to and upkeep for their overseers, servants and peasants who worked the land; reserves for repairs and purchase of the seed for next year's harvest and the grain and other feed for the livestock, what was then left over was "the net income" and was to be paid to the Income Beneficiaries.

We have modified this concept from English law. The legal rule in our country (based on the Uniform Principal and Income Act) is that if the Trust states "Net Income" is to be paid to the Income Beneficiaries, then half of the costs of managing, filing required annual reports with the federal and state governments and other expenses of the Trusts are charged against the Gross Income of the Trust. The other half of the Trust's expenses are charged against the principal of the Trust. The Net Income provision can reduce the income paid to the surviving spouse by as much as 10% a year. Additional information, including examples of why the selection of the Gross Income or the Net Income provision should be made by the Grantor of the Trust, is in Chapter 14.

With this information on Trust investments and net income, let's take a look at what happened to the Wilsons who established Credit Shelter Trusts because they heard they could save at least $235,000[9] in federal estate taxes.

John incorrectly believed that state and federal laws controlled his estate after his death and that he had no financial options. Because of this misconception, John first considered using a preprinted legal form for his estate plan. Later, he "shopped around" for an attorney who would prepare his estate planning documents for the lowest fixed fee. John selected an attorney based on the recommendation of a friend. John and his wife met with the attorney who agreed to prepare their estate planning documents for a fixed amount. In their meeting, the attorney asked the names of the children, their trustee and a few other items.

(9)   The savings of at least $235,000 in federal estate taxes is a result of a married couple combining their individual federal estate-tax exemptions. In 1998 each person has a $625,000 exemption. Combined for a married couple this amount is $1,250,000. But, if the first to die passed their estate to their surviving spouse, when that person dies the federal estate taxes on an estate of $1,250,000 would be $235,000. However, the first person who dies used their personal estate tax exemption, by establishing a Credit Shelter Trust with income payments to their spouse. The federal estate-tax savings of at least $235,000 are obtained. There may also be an additional savings in state taxes.

John never asked if he had financial options to consider. His emphasis was on the cost to prepare what he called "simple documents." A few weeks later John received drafts of the documents.

In reviewing them, John read many pages that continually referred to sections of the federal revenue code and other laws. He finally decided that all he needed to do with the documents was to determine that the names of his spouse, his children and the trustee were correct. Everything else, John incorrectly assumed, was controlled by various state and federal laws regarding Trusts. His assumption was a mistake. Like many other financially uninformed Grantors, he did not realize that he could and should exercise control of his money. He did not think of his Trust as an investment. John should have realized that he had many financial and management options that he should consider to properly provide for his wife, Mary, and for their children. If John had made these decisions and correctly expressed them in the Trust, it could have made a big difference to his wife and children.

The mistake of not being aware of the financial options was in part, the fault of John and his wife. They never asked what income the surviving spouse would receive from the Trust after the death of one of them. They were aware that if one of them died in 1998, $625,000 of their assets would go into a Trust and that this amount would increase to $1 million in the year 2006. And, they also knew that the surviving spouse could receive a lifetime income from the Trust.

John and Mary Wilson mistakenly assumed that a sufficient amount would be paid. They also assumed that what was written into their Trust was what was required by law. For the Wilsons these were incorrect assumptions and they remain incorrect for the rest of us. The question John and Mary needed to ask themselves was: "What income will the surviving spouse need from the Trust?" The Trust department of a bank could have told them the current interest rate on bonds and the average dividend percent on good quality growth stocks. With this information they could have quickly determined the amount of income that would be received and is shown below.

Because their Trusts did not state how the funds were to be invested, the State Default Rules will require that approximately 50% of the assets be invested in good quality medium-term bonds and approximately 50% invested in good quality growth stocks. Bond and stock funds would be selected for diversification.

If one of them were to die in 1998, then:

Type of Investment	Investment		Gross Annual Income	
	Percent	Amount	Percent[11]	Amount
1. Good Quality Medium Term Bond Fund	50%	$312,500	6.0%	$18,750
2. Good Quality Growth Stock Fund	50%	312,500	1.3%	4,063.
TOTAL		$625,000		$22,813

NOTE: If spouse is to be given
the "Net Income"[12] assume 1/2%
Reduction on year-end value of Trust   - 3,297
    NET INCOME FROM TRUST $19,516

The amounts that can be placed into Credit Shelter Trusts will increase to $1 million in the year 2006. But the income payments under the Default Rules will continue to be low.

John and Mary Wilson needed to determine if the income from their Credit Shelter Trusts would be sufficient for either of them to live on after the death of the other. Determining needed income is not complicated to do. By using Exhibit 1 "Income Needs of Each Spouse" John and Mary could determine the amount required from the Trust.

(11)   The Trust department of your local bank can provide you with the current interest rate of good quality medium term bond funds and the dividend rate from good quality stock funds. Bond funds with higher current interest payments are available. However, the risk is higher for these funds. The rates above are examples of those in 1998 for high quality bond funds.

(12)   A "Net Income" provision is found in most Trusts. A Grantor may believe that there will be little or no expense for their Trust since they are using a family member or friend as trustee. However, there will be expenses for annual tax reports to the state and federal government; legal and other professional services. A family member or friend who is trustee should evaluate the benefits of delegating the investment responsibility. The new Uniform Prudent Investor Act (Appendix E) relieves the trustee of legal liability if the investment decisions are properly delegated. If this is not done the Act places new requirements on the trustee that will probably add to the annual cost of the trusteeship. The assistance of a Trust attorney, especially in the beginning years of the Trust, will be needed. This is discussed in more detail in Chapter 14 and in Appendix "F."

This is a good point at which you and your spouse could each complete your own copy of Exhibit 1. Remove the copies, at the back of the book to use as work sheets. Make extra copies if needed. Simply follow the instructions for completing Exhibit 1 in Appendix "C."

Both John and Mary Wilson each followed this procedure. "Exhibit 1 - Completed Form" on Page 41, show their completed individual forms and their separate results. It was then that they discovered their Trusts did not properly meet the income needs of either one of them. Note the following in "Exhibit 1 - Completed Form:"

1.   Mary will need $34,950 in 1998 from her husband's Credit Shelter Trust if he died in 1998. But as indicated on Page 36, the "Net Income Paid" from a Trust controlled by the Default Rules will be $19,516 in 1998. This amount is significantly below Mary's needs.

2.   This shortage of income from the Trust for Mary Wilson will continue throughout her lifetime if her husband dies first. This is shown below. (Note: In four out of five marriages it is husbands who die first).

Years after Husband's Death	Trust Actual Payments[13]	Required Annual Payments[14]	Shortage
1st Year	$19,516	$ 35,000	$15,484
5th Year	20,597	39,393	18,796
10th Year	22,719	45,667	22,948

3.   John will need $19,950 in 1998 from his wife's Credit Shelter Trust if she died in 1998. And, as indicated on Page 41, even with trustee fees and expenses, the approximate Net Income appears to meet John's needs - at least in 1998. But this is not the case in later years. The increase in the cost of inflation could cause John Wilson to receive from the Trust less than he needs.

(13)   These are the amounts from Page 36 of this chapter. They represent the amount a surviving spouse would receive from a Trust whose investments and income are controlled by the Default Rules. The detail by year for these amounts are in Appendix B, Exhibit A for this Chapter.

(14)   These are the amounts that the trustee would annually pay Mary Wilson from a Trust that stated she was to receive $35,000 starting in 1998 and increased annually for inflation estimated at 3%. The annual detail is in Exhibit 2 on Page 57.

4.   Note that the only differences between John's needs from the Trust and Mary's needs is the pension payment. There would be a $15,000 reduction to his widow if John dies first. Mary is fortunate because in some cases the pension payments terminate upon the death of the husband. This is particularly true in many cases if a second marriage takes place after the husband has retired and is already receiving his pension.

Let's Look at the Revision of John's Trust for the benefit of Mary based on her Income Needs. Your Trust, May Require the Same Type of Revisions for Your Surviving Spouse

A.   John stated in his Trust that his wife was to receive $35,000 on the date his Trust was executed (1998) if he died in that year. And,

B.   That this amount was to be increased 3% each year starting in the next year and continuing each year during Mary's lifetime. This was an estimate of the cost of inflation.

John wanted a method to test the ability of his Credit Shelter Trust to provide this annual income to Mary. John wanted to know first if there would be enough funds in the Trust to provide the income, and what the value of the Trust would be during Mary's life. John also wanted to know what mix of bonds and stocks would best provide the income for his wife and then leave funds for their children upon Mary's death.

How this was done is presented in the next chapter.

CONCLUSION

1.   You must determine the income needs of you and your surviving spouse. To do this, use Exhibit 1 or some other method. Extra copies are in the back of this book.

2.   The amount required should be for the current year. Place this amount in your Trust. Next, increase it from that date for inflation. You may want to use an annual percentage, instead of requiring your trustee to apply official government data that is released after inflation for that period has occurred.

3.   Test the income requirements as presented in the next chapter.

CHAPTER 7

How to Test Your Financial Directives

Introduction

As indicated in prior chapters, a Grantor has the right to state many financial Directives in their Trust. As in John Wilson's case, in the prior chapter, once he learned that his wife would receive an income from his Trust that would be $20,000 less than her annual needs, he revised his Trust. These income requirements of his wife, compared to the income she would have received are shown on Page 57.

John's revision stated that his spouse was to receive $35,000 using as a starting date 1998. And, increasing that amount 3% a year for inflation from that starting date.

Since this new income requirement is more than 75% higher than his wife would have received from his original Trust, controlled by the Default Rules, John wanted a method to test the ability of his Credit Shelter Trust to provide this income to Mary during her lifetime.

A computer program was prepared to test the expected results. The program was designed to allow a Grantor to select the starting income their spouse would require; increase the income annually by a stated percentage; select and test various combinations of investments in bonds and stocks and assign reasonable forecasts of interest paid on bonds and dividends that might be expected from stocks. By using this program John and other Grantors can view the expected results based on the Grantor's forecast of the average annual increase in stocks over a this period of time. They would also have an estimate of the values of the Trust.

The Results of the Computer Program are Shown in Exhibits 2, 3 and 4.

Please take a few minutes to understand and review these pages. They show the plans of John Wilson for his wife, Mary. They indicate a method that you can use to plan the income needs of your surviving spouse and the estimated results based on the various planning assumptions you can make.

50

Each of these exhibits contains the same ten planning assumptions. They are shown below.

Starting Income from Trusts	**$ XX,XXX**	**Year**	**XXXX**	
Annual Increase	**X.X%**	**Percent in Stocks**		**XX.X%**
Starting Value of Trust	**$ XXX,XXX**	**Stock Dividends**		**X.X%**
Percent in Bonds	**XX.X%**	**Annual Increase**		**X.X%**
Bond Interest	**X.X%**	**Trustee Fees & Expenses**		**X.XX%**

The most important planning assumptions are at the top left. They are:

Starting Income From Trust*:* This is the starting annual income requirement to be paid to you or your surviving spouse from the Trust in today's dollars. This income was determined with the help of Exhibit 1, "Income Needs of Each Spouse" or by some other means that you use. It is one of the most important figures to be placed in your Trust as a Directive.

Next to this amount, on the right is the **"Year."**. Enter the year this amount will be required. In most cases the year is when the Trust is executed. Each time new projections are made, such as testing your planning assumptions 15 years later, enter the Year 2023, 15 years from now, as a reference date.

Annual Increase: This is the percent that the **Starting Income from Trust** is to be increased each year. This also is an important figure. All of the other planning assumptions that follow are used to test the ability of the Trust to pay the annual income required by you or your surviving spouse. As you review each exhibit you will see that this amount increases 3% a year for inflation. This may appear to be a small increase, but after ten years, the need for $35,000 has climbed to $47,037.

Starting Value of Trust: This is the amount of each individual's federal estate-tax exemption. In Exhibit 2, for 1998 this amount is $625,000. In Exhibit 3 and Exhibit 4 the amounts are $1 million.

Percent in Bonds: The decision on what to select is yours. The percentage used in the three examples in this Chapter is 25% in bonds. However, you can change this percentage as shown in other Exhibits in this book.

Interest Paid on Bonds: The actual percentage should be based upon current rates paid by good quality medium-term bond funds. Inquire about the interest paid on such funds from the Trust department of at least two banks.

Percent in Stocks: Again the decision is yours. The percentage used in the three examples in this Chapter is 75%[1] invested in stocks. Other Exhibits in this book use different percentages. If you have access to Estate Planning Program One, available from the Internet, recommend that you experiment by using many different percentages and compare their expected long-term results. Also realize that in the short-term, stocks have also declined in value.

Dividends Paid on Stocks: The actual percentage should be based upon the dividend rates you expect to be paid on good quality growth funds. Again, you can talk to the Trust department of your bank. The dividend rate in the exhibits of 1.3% may be a little high in today's market for good quality growth stocks.

Annual Stock Increase: This requires some knowledge of the stock market, its past history and your informed opinion of its current and long-term outlook. We have used in Exhibits 2 and 3 an 11% annual increase. This is based on the past history from 1926 through 1997.

However, in Exhibit 4 we used an 8% annual increase just to be able to illustrate that a lower stock growth can still provide the income that Mary Wilson, as the surviving spouse, requires. Also a lower stock growth can still increase the end-value of the Trust for the children. You should test several different estimates of the growth of stocks in the Estate Planning Programs prepared for this book and available to you on the Internet. See Appendix A.

Trustee Fees & Expenses: In our Exhibits 2, 3, and 4 we have used three quarters of one percent (0.75%) as the annual total for all trustee fees and expenses. In the Exhibits it is paid based on the annual year-end value of the Trust.

(1) You need to give serious consideration to the percentage of funds invested in good quality growth stocks. A Balanced Trust has 50% in stocks and 50% in bonds. A major reason for the 50% bond requirement was that bonds paid a higher income. Consider stating an exact amount of income that must be paid. This bypasses the Uniform Income and Principal Act that limits income distributions to income received. Growth of principal is not income under the Act. The new revised Act attempts to recognize, in some cases, part of the growth of principal as income. It also attempts to recognize part of the income, such as that from high interest paying bonds as principal that is not to be distributed. Use the Estate Planning Calculator to test various percentages of stock and bonds. When you are young consider a high percentage in stocks. Later in your life, you may want to consider reducing the stock percentage in your Trust since you or your spouse have a reduced life expectancy.

How the above Estate Planning Assumption Calculate the Yearly Detail Data Shown in Exhibits 2, 3 and 4 in this Chapter and in other chapters in this Book.

Once you have entered the above estate planning factors into the program the results are quickly calculated by very simple addition, subtraction and percentage amounts. The results are printed for you.. While there is a large amount of data presented, a review of the calculations made for the first year will help you to understand the results in the entire Exhibit.

1. The **Percent in Bonds** is calculated from the **Value of Trust**. In Exhibit 2 the Value of the Trust is $ 625,000 and the Percent in Bonds is 25%. The report prints out under **Bond Amount** $156,250 And, since this amount remains the same (bonds are not expected to increase in value), $156,250 is printed for each of the 25 years.

2. **Bond Interest** in Exhibit 4 is 6.0%. Therefore, 6.0% of $156,250 is $9,375. This amount is printed under the heading **Bond Interest.** And since the Bond Amount does not change, $9,375 is the amount of Bond Interest that will be paid in each of the 25 years on Exhibit 4.

3. The **Percent in Stocks** is calculated from the **Value of Trust.** In Exhibit 2 the Value of Trust is $625,000 and the Percent in Stocks is 75%. Therefore, 75% of $625,000 is $468,750. This amount is printed under the heading **Beg. Stock Amount** (Beginning Stock Amount) for the 1st year. The **Beg. Stock Amount** for each of the following years will change as presented below.

4. **Stock Dividend** in Exhibit 2 is 1.3%. Therefore 1.3% of $468,750 is $6,094. This amount is printed under the heading **Stock Dividend** for the 1st year. The amount of the **Stock Dividend** will change for each of the following years as presented below.

5. **Annual Stock Increase** in Exhibit 2 is 11%. Therefor 11% of $468,750 (the Beg. Stock Amount of the 1st rear) is $51,563. This amount is printed under the heading **Stock Increase** for the 1st year. The amount of the **Stock Increase** will change for each of the following years as presented below.

6. **End Stock Value** is obtained by adding the Beg. Stock Amount with the Stock Increase. In Exhibit 2, for the first year these amounts are $468,750 + $51,563 for a total of $520,313 printed under the heading End Stock Value for the 1st year. The amount of the End Stock Value will change for each of the following years as presented below.

7. **REMOVED from Principal** is obtained by first adding the Bond Interest and the Stock Dividend in the 1st year and then subtracting this amount from amount listed under the column **Total Income.**

NOTE: The amounts under the column Total Income are the controlling amounts in this program. The program is designed to pay out each year these amounts, that increase at 3% a year as John directed, to his surviving spouse.

Up to this point very simple math functions of adding, subtracting and obtaining the percentage amounts from the planning data that was entered in the program at the top, was done. These basic math functions will continue to be used in the following years, but a few additions are required to obtain the Beg. Stock Amount each year.

The amount shown in the column marked REMOVED From Principal only included the amount necessary to pay the Total Income to the surviving spouse. This was done so the Grantor could see the annual amounts that will be removed from the principal of the Trust and be given to the surviving spouse. The amount REMOVED From Principal did not include the amount to pay **Trustee Fees and Expenses** estimated at three quarters of one percentage (.075%) of the total value of the Trust

At the end of each year, the total value of the Trust is obtained by adding the **Bond Amount** to the **End Stock Value.** And then taking .075% of this amount as payment of trustee fees and expenses. This is shown below for the first year.

Bond Amount	$ 156,250	
End Stock Value	+ 506,250	
Total Amount	$ 662,500	times .075% = $ 4,969

The above amount for trustee fees and expenses is not shown on the report, But it is included when determining the following year's **Beg. Stock Amount** by adding the Trustee Fees and Expenses to the amount REMOVED From Principal required to pay Mary her Total Income each year from the Trust. This is shown below along with the computer calculations that establish the Beg. Stock Amount for each of the following years.

A. First year REMOVED From Principal
   to pay Mary her Total Income $ 19,531

B. Trustee Fees and Expenses   +   4,969
   Total Actually Removed from Principal $ 24,500

First year's <u>End Stock Value</u>	$ 506,250
Less: Total Actually Removed from Principal	<u>- $ 24,500</u>
Beg. Stock Amount, 2nd Year	$ 481,750

The above amount, $481,750 (results from rounding to the nearest dollar) is the amount listed under <u>Beg. Stock Amount</u> for 2nd year. And, since the beginning stock amount has changed, the amounts reported under the columns <u>Stock Dividend</u> and <u>Stock Increase</u> will change in each of the following years.

To refer back to John Wilson's last question -what is the estimated value of the Trust each year, based on the planning assumptions?, a summary of the value of the Trust in five-year increments is printed at the bottom of each exhibit.

To determine the value of the Trust in the interim years, add the <u>Bond Amount</u> to the <u>Beg. Stock Value</u> of the following year. The reason you add the <u>Beg. Stock Value</u> of the following year is that this amount has the Trustee fees and expenses removed.

You will note that Exhibit 2, is based upon the concept that the Trust is funded in the year 1998 and that the annual income paid to John's wife in 1998 is $35,000. This amount increases 3% each year for 25 years. Also note the amount of annual income to be paid to Mary in the 16th year is $54,529.

No one can predict how long John will live. Exhibit 3 is another "what if" exhibit to test the financial planning assumptions in John's Trust. It indicates the annual payments to be made to his wife, if John died 15 years later (in the year 2013) after signing his Trust in 1998. The **Starting Income From Trust**, at the top left, is $54,529 - the amount required in the 16th year of Exhibit 2. The **Starting Value of Trust** is $ 1 million, the amount permitted in the year 2006 and for following years.

The results in Exhibit 3 indicate that the payments for the total income can be from the Credit Shelter Trust.

Exhibit 4 is included because many people like to ask, "What would happen if the stock market's average annual increase over the projected 25-year period was less than the past history (1926 through 1997 of 11%)?" Exhibit 4 uses a 8% annual projection over the 25-year period. This is a 27% drop in history's past rate.

However, you must make your own projections and test them by using the Estate Planning Programs. These Programs are available to you on the Internet. The address is "http://www.ccmtrust.com/thebook." You need only enter a few variables and a report can be printed of the expected results. In addition to a Program for these exhibits, additional Estate Planning Programs are at this Internet site. They are easy to use and the instructions are in Appendix "A."

NOTE:

The Estate Planning Programs and the calculations that result and are used in this book are for instructional purposes only. Any calculations obtained need to be independently verified if they are to be used in actual estate planning.

As indicated in Appendix A, the transfer of the Estate Planning Programs to your computer should be checked to determine that they have been properly received. And, that the programs used in your computer are properly processing the data.

Exhibit 2
JOHN'S PLAN FOR THE INCOME TO BE PAID FROM HIS TRUST

Starting Income From Trust	$ 35,000	Year 1998	
Annual Increase	3.0%	Percent in Stocks	75.0%
Value of Trust	$ 625,000	Stock Dividends	1.3%
Percent in Bonds	25.0%	Annual Stock Increase	11.0%
Bond Interest	6.0%	Trustee Fees & Expenses	0.75%

Year	Bond Amount	Bond Interest	Beg. Stock Amount	Stock Dividends	Stock Increase	End Stock Value	REMOVED from Principal	ANNUAL Income
1	156,250	9,375	468,750	6,094	51,563	520,313	$ 19,531	$ 35,000
2	156,250	9,375	495,707	6,444	54,528	550,235	20,231	36,050
3	156,250	9,375	524,705	6,821	57,718	582,423	20,935	37,132
4	156,250	9,375	555,948	7,227	61,154	617,102	21,643	38,245
5	156,250	9,375	589,659	7,666	64,862	654,521	22,352	39,393
6	156,250	9,375	626,088	8,139	68,870	694,958	23,060	40,575
7	156,250	9,375	665,513	8,652	73,206	738,720	23,765	41,792
8	156,250	9,375	708,242	9,207	77,907	786,149	24,463	43,046
9	156,250	9,375	754,617	9,810	83,008	837,625	25,152	44,337
10	156,250	9,375	805,019	10,465	88,552	893,571	25,827	45,667
11	156,250	9,375	859,871	11,178	94,586	954,457	26,484	47,037
12	156,250	9,375	919,643	11,955	101,161	1,020,803	27,118	48,448
13	156,250	9,375	984,858	12,803	108,334	1,093,192	27,723	49,902
14	156,250	9,375	1,056,098	13,729	116,171	1,172,268	28,294	51,399
15	156,250	9,375	1,134,010	14,742	124,741	1,258,751	28,824	52,941
16	156,250	9,375	1,219,315	15,851	134,125	1,353,440	29,303	54,529
17	156,250	9,375	1,312,814	17,067	144,410	1,457,224	29,723	56,165
18	156,250	9,375	1,415,400	18,400	155,694	1,571,094	30,074	57,850
19	156,250	9,375	1,528,064	19,865	168,087	1,696,151	30,345	59,585
20	156,250	9,375	1,651,913	21,475	181,710	1,833,623	30,523	61,373
21	156,250	9,375	1,788,176	23,246	196,699	1,984,876	30,593	63,214
22	156,250	9,375	1,938,225	25,197	213,205	2,151,430	30,538	65,110
23	156,250	9,375	2,103,584	27,347	231,394	2,334,978	30,342	67,064
24	156,250	9,375	2,285,952	29,717	251,455	2,537,406	29,983	69,076
25	156,250	9,375	2,487,221	32,334	273,594	2,760,815	29,439	71,148

STARTING VALUE OF TRUST	$625,000
VALUE OF THE TRUST AFTER:	
FIVE YEARS	782,338
TEN YEARS	1,016,121
FIFTEEN YEARS	1,375,565
TWENTY YEARS	1,944,426
TWENTY-FIVE YEARS	2,887,626

NOTE: The key part of the income plan is that payments are based upon the income needs of John's spouse, Mary in 1998. In 1998, she needs $35,000 of income from the Trust, before state and federal income taxes. And this 1998 amount is being increased at a compounded rate of 3% a year.

Exhibit 3
JOHN'S PLAN FOR THE INCOME TO BE PAID FROM HIS TRUST

If John died 15 years after signing his Trust in 1998

Starting Income From Trust	$ 54,529	Year	2013	
Annual Increase	3.0%	Percent in Stocks		75.0%
Value of Trust	$ 1,00,0000	Stock Dividends		1.3%
Percent in Bonds	25.0%	Annual Stock Increase		11.0%
Bond Interest	6.0%	Trustee Fees & Expenses		0.75%

Year	Bond Amount	Bond Interest	Beg. Stock Amount	Stock Dividends	Stock Increase	End Stock Value	REMOVED from Principal	ANNUAL Income
1	250,000	15,000	750,000	9,750	82,500	832,500	$ 29,779	$ 54,529
2	250,000	15,000	794,602	10,330	87,406	882,008	30,835	56,165
3	250,000	15,000	842,683	10,955	92,695	935,379	31,895	57,850
4	250,000	15,000	894,593	11,630	98,405	992,999	32,956	59,585
5	250,000	15,000	950,720	12,359	104,579	1,055,300	34,014	61,373
6	250,000	15,000	1,011,496	13,149	111,265	1,122,761	35,065	63,214
7	250,000	15,000	1,077,401	14,006	118,514	1,195,915	36,104	65,110
8	250,000	15,000	1,148,966	14,937	126,386	1,275,353	37,127	67,064
9	250,000	15,000	1,226,785	15,948	134,946	1,361,732	38,127	69,076
10	250,000	15,000	1,311,516	17,050	144,267	1,455,783	39,098	71,148
11	250,000	15,000	1,403,891	18,251	154,428	1,558,319	40,032	73,282
12	250,000	15,000	1,504,725	19,561	165,520	1,670,245	40,919	75,481
13	250,000	15,000	1,614,923	20,994	177,642	1,792,565	41,751	77,745
14	250,000	15,000	1,735,494	22,561	190,904	1,926,399	42,516	80,078
15	250,000	15,000	1,867,560	24,278	205,432	2,072,991	43,202	82,480
16	250,000	15,000	2,012,367	26,161	221,360	2,233,727	43,794	84,954
17	250,000	15,000	2,171,306	28,227	238,844	2,410,149	44,276	87,503
18	250,000	15,000	2,345,922	30,497	258,051	2,603,974	44,631	90,128
19	250,000	15,000	2,537,938	32,993	279,173	2,817,111	44,839	92,832
20	250,000	15,000	2,749,269	35,740	302,420	3,051,688	44,876	95,617
21	250,000	15,000	2,982,049	38,767	328,025	3,310,075	44,719	98,485
22	250,000	15,000	3,238,655	42,103	356,252	3,594,907	44,337	101,440
23	250,000	15,000	3,521,733	45,783	387,391	3,909,124	43,701	104,483
24	250,000	15,000	3,834,229	49,845	421,765	4,255,995	42,773	107,618
25	250,000	15,000	4,179,427	54,333	459,737	4,639,164	41,514	110,846

STARTING VALUE OF TRUST	$1,000,000
VALUE OF THE TRUST AFTER:	
FIVE YEARS	1,261,496
TEN YEARS	1,653,891
FIFTEEN YEARS	2,262,367
TWENTY YEARS	3,232,049
TWENTY-FIVE YEARS	4,847,650

NOTE: The starting amount to be paid above, is $54,529. This amount is the value of $35,000 increased at 3% a year for 15 years. See 16th year in exhibit 3 on Page 57 - that amount is $54,529. If John died 20 years after 1998, the starting amount would be $63,214, from Exhibit 3 (the amount starting in the 21st year).

Exhibit 4
JOHN'S PLAN FOR THE INCOME TO BE PAID FROM HIS TRUST

If John died 15 years after signing his Trust in 1998
& STOCKS IN THE FUTURE ONLY INCREASED 8% A YEAR

Starting Income From Trust	$ 54,529	Year	2013		
Annual Increase	3.0%	Percent in Stocks		75.0%	
Value of Trust	$ 1,00,0000	Stock Dividends		1.3%	
Percent in Bonds	25.0%	Annual Stock Increase		8.0%	
Bond Interest	6.0%	Trustee Fees & Expenses		0.75%	

Year	Bond Amount	Bond Interest	Beg. Stock Amount	Stock Dividends	Stock Increase	End Stock Value	REMOVED from Principal	ANNUAL Income
1	250,000	15,000	750,000	9,750	60,000	810,000	$ 29,779	$ 54,529
2	250,000	15,000	772,271	10,040	61,782	834,053	31,125	56,165
3	250,000	15,000	794,797	10,332	63,584	858,381	32,517	57,850
4	250,000	15,000	817,550	10,628	65,404	882,954	33,957	59,585
5	250,000	15,000	840,500	10,927	67,240	907,740	35,446	61,373
6	250,000	15,000	863,611	11,227	69,089	932,700	36,987	63,214
7	250,000	15,000	886,842	11,529	70,947	957,790	38,582	65,110
8	250,000	15,000	910,150	11,832	72,812	982,962	40,232	67,064
9	250,000	15,000	933,483	12,135	74,679	1,008,161	41,940	69,076
10	250,000	15,000	956,784	12,438	76,543	1,033,327	43,710	71,148
11	250,000	15,000	979,992	12,740	78,399	1,058,392	45,543	73,282
12	250,000	15,000	1,003,036	13,039	80,243	1,083,279	47,441	75,481
13	250,000	15,000	1,025,838	13,336	82,067	1,107,905	49,409	77,745
14	250,000	15,000	1,048,312	13,628	83,865	1,132,177	51,450	80,078
15	250,000	15,000	1,070,361	13,915	85,629	1,155,990	53,565	82,480
16	250,000	15,000	1,091,879	14,194	87,350	1,179,230	55,760	84,954
17	250,000	15,000	1,112,750	14,466	89,020	1,201,770	58,037	87,503
18	250,000	15,000	1,132,845	14,727	90,628	1,223,473	60,401	90,128
19	250,000	15,000	1,152,020	14,976	92,162	1,244,182	62,856	92,832
20	250,000	15,000	1,170,120	15,212	93,610	1,263,729	65,405	95,617
21	250,000	15,000	1,186,971	15,431	94,958	1,281,929	68,055	98,485
22	250,000	15,000	1,202,385	15,631	96,191	1,298,575	70,809	101,440
23	250,000	15,000	1,216,152	15,810	97,292	1,313,444	73,673	104,483
24	250,000	15,000	1,228,045	15,965	98,244	1,326,289	76,653	107,618
25	250,000	15,000	1,237,813	16,092	99,025	1,336,839	79,755	110,846

STARTING VALUE OF TRUST	$1,000,000
VALUE OF THE TRUST AFTER:	
FIVE YEARS	1,113,611
TEN YEARS	1,229,992
FIFTEEN YEARS	1,341,879
TWENTY YEARS	1,436,971
TWENTY-FIVE YEARS	1,507,084

NOTE: It may be considered doubtful that the stocks over this 25- year period would only grow at an average of 8% a year. But it is likely that there will be periods of decreases in the value of stocks also.

On Page 48 it was noted that there would be a shortage of income for Mary Wilson's needs from her husband's Credit Shelter Trust if he died in 1998. The shortage was about $15,000 in the first year and increased to about $23,000 in the tenth year.

Listed below is the shortage if Mary Wilson's husband lived for another 15 years and was able to fund a Credit Shelter Trust, at his death, with $1 million in assets.

Years after Husband's Death	Trust Actual Payments[15]	Required Annual Payments[16]	Shortage
1st Year	$31,225	$ 54,529	$23,304
5th Year	32,956	61,373	28,417
10th Year	36,351	71,148	34,797

The above should clearly indicate that the problem will not disappear as the amount of funds that can be placed in a Credit Shelter Trust increase to $1 million in the year 2006. In fact, the problems just get worse. The shortage of annual income for the widow, Mary Wilson, increases every year.

An Additional Financial Revision John made in his Credit Shelter Trust for the Benefit of his wife, Mary, During Her Lifetime.

John stated that his wife could obtain an additional $5,000 each year from the Trust just by writing a letter to the trustee and requesting it. Under tax law, this currently is the maximum dollar amount she can request for no reason and under the Grantor's directive the trustee must pay it.

As you review Exhibits 2 through 4, please note that in every year the growth in the value of the Trust exceeds the total amounts (see Column under heading "Stock Growth"). Therefore, providing these additional $5,000 of unrestricted funds should not basically impact the value of the Trust.

(15) These are the amounts a surviving spouse would receive, 15 years later, from a Trust whose investments and income are controlled by the Default Rules. The detail by year are on Page 242 of Appendix B.

(16) These are the amounts that the trustee would annually pay Mary Wilson from a Trust that stated she was to receive $35,000 starting in 1998 and increased yearly for inflation estimated at 3%. The annual detail is in Exhibits 3 and 4 on Page 57 and Page 58.

The Grantor also has an option of stating that his surviving spouse can remove 5% of the value of the Trust each year, again just by asking for it. This option I do not recommend when a planned and reasonably calculated starting amount; indexed for inflation is stated in the Trust. This additional option of 5% annual withdrawals can deplete the Trust as discussed and shown in Chapter 10.

Your Trust should have the normal provision that provided additional funds from the principal of the Trust for the Income Beneficiary's needs at the sole discretion of the trustee. This provision can provide funds if needed. By placing a planned and reasonable amount to be paid in this year's dollars; indexed to inflation or increased a set percentage each year; and providing the ability to obtain an additional $5,000, just by requesting the money, your surviving spouse will receive a greater annual income than the Default Rules will provide.

As a Grantor of a Trust, you must indicate the actual annual income to be paid from the Trust. This income should include a reasonable annual increase in this amount to offset inflation and to make a provision for additional income just by asking for it.

If your Trust does not state an exact annual income, as of a certain date, to be paid to your surviving spouse, you should consider revising it to include those financial advantages.

Listed below are the changes in the federal law that slowly increase your amount of estate tax exemption to $1 million by the year 2006. Using the Default Rules, a spouse's annual income is listed[17] and the probable value of the Trust.

Year	TRUST	SPOUSE'S ANNUAL INCOME			VALUE OF TRUST		
		1st Yr.	5th Yr.	10th Yr.	15th Yr.	20th Yr.	25th Yr.
1998	$625,000	$19,516	$20,597	$22,719	$1,648,000	$2,497,000	$3,913,000
1999	650,000	20,296	21,421	23,628	1,714,000	2,597,000	4,070,000
2000	675,000	21,077	22,245	24,537	1,780,000	2,697,000	4,226,000
2002	675,000	21,077	22,245	24,537	1,780,000	2,697,000	4,226,000
2002	700,000	21,858	23,069	25,445	1,846,000	2,797,000	4,383,000
2003	700,000	21,858	23,069	25,445	1,846,000	2,797,000	4,383,000
2004	850,000	26,541	28,012	30,898	2,241,000	3,397,000	5,322,000
2005	950,000	29,664	31,308	34,533	2,505,000	3,796,000	5,948,000
2006	1,000,000	31,225	32,956	36,351	2,637,000	3,996,000	6,261,000

(17)   As indicated in Footnote (1), Page 36, the above amounts for the spouse's estimated annual income would normally be rounded off to the nearest thousand. However, to preserve the source of the date for use with "Estate Planning Program One," the exact amounts are used.

The assumption is that the Trust in each year states that the "Net Income" is to be paid and the total for all Trust expenses is estimated at 1% of the value of the Trust. If you have a professional trustee, the Trust expenses may be lower in the later years of the Trust.

These annual incomes, under the Default Rules, are very low for either survivor, be it John or Mary, compared to their calculated needs. It can be particularly low if the survivor is the wife. Remember that in most marriages the first to die is the husband. Perhaps your Trust is like John Wilson's original documents: the terms and conditions did not adequately provide for either he or his wife as the survivor.

If you suspect from what you learn here, that this is your situation also, start with the form on Exhibit 1 " Income Needs of Each Spouse". and complete it for you and your spouse. Extra copies of this form are in the back of the book. Then compare the results with the $19,516 of income shown on Page 36. If you need more than that amount, you should strongly consider revising your documents.

Summary of Key Points:

1.   From the example of an actual situation, Mary Wilson needed a much higher annual income than her husband's Trust would have provided. This is often true for most wives.

2.   By carefully completing Exhibit 1, "Income Needs of Each Spouse" a reasonable annual income for Mary can be selected for the current year.

3.   The Trust should state, payment of the amount that was calculated using Exhibit 1. Provision must then be made to increase this amount based on the cumulative increase in cost of inflation. It is also prudent to provide another slight annual percentage increase, say one percent, based on this reasoning: Official government inflation figures may not be truly representative of the increasing expenses of senior citizens - such as the cost of medical prescriptions.

4.   Even if it appears that the income under the Default Rules would be sufficient, as in the case of John Wilson, do not be misled by this quick assumption. The amount $19,950 in Exhibit 1, that John needed was for 1998. If his wife dies 15 years later, John would need $36,000 just to keep up with inflation. And John would not receive this amount because his wife's original Trust contained no provision for such funds.

If you look back to page 61, John would only receive $31,225 (the first year of income payments from a Trust of $1 million). This will produce a shortage in John's income from the Trust of about $5,000. And this shortage, compared to what he would need and could have had if this error was recognized, can become a $10,000 shortage in the fifth year and each year thereafter, the shortage will continue to worsen.

     5.   Consider the need for a provision for extra income. You can insert in the Trust the provision for the surviving spouse to ask for an additional $5,000 each year, if needed, and the requirement that it be paid to her. Note: $5,000 is the maximum dollar amount allowed under current federal tax law. There is also a provision under current federal tax law that allows the Grantor to state that the Income Beneficiary can annually withdraw as an alternative 5% of the value of the Trust. But, this is not recommend when the Grantor states an amount indexed to inflation.[18]

     6.   Recommend that you consider overriding the Default Rules to require a higher percentage of the assets in the Trust be invested in good quality growth stocks. The balance can be invested in good quality medium-term bonds.

John and Mary Wilson made several other changes in their Trusts that were financially advantageous. We will discuss these in later chapters of this book.

With the understanding you now have of your rights and the need to state in your Trust the income your spouse or other Income Beneficiaries are to receive, you are now ready to proceed with the following chapters. These will indicate important modifications that you may want to consider to strengthen the financial consequences of your Trust.

Use The Estate Planning Programs

Exhibits 2, 3, and 4 of this chapter were developed by using the Estate Planning Program One. This Program is available to you on the

(18)   If the surviving spouse is given the 5% power in addition to directives that provide a substantial income the Trust, annual use of this 5% power could deplete the Trust. See Chapter 10 and the test using Exhibit 4 in this Chapter.

Internet. The address is "http://www.ccmtrust.com/thebook."[19] You need enter only a few variables and a report can be printed of the expected results. In addition to a Program for these exhibits, additional Estate Planning Programs are at this Internet site. They are easy to use and the instructions are in Appendix "A."

Once you have obtained these estate planning programs from the Internet, they can be stored in your computer, if you want to use them later without reconnecting to the Internet

(19) The Estate Planning Programs available to you at our Internet site are actually spreadsheet template programs that work with Excel © version 5.0.

CHAPTER 8

Increasing the End-Value of Your Trust
For Your Children

Introduction

As indicated in prior chapters, you can increase the end-value of Trusts by giving clear Directives in your documents to invest more of the assets in stocks. This chapter will present how you can further increase the value of your Trust for your children and other heirs. If providing funds to be given to your children during your spouse's life is also a consideration, suggestions are presented in the next chapter.

If as a couple you have assets valued above your combined federal estate-tax exemptions, there are several additional Directives you can give in your Credit Shelter Trusts. These Directives can provide the highest end-value for your heirs.

The Credit Shelter Trust holds the funds that can be inherited by your children and others without any federal estate tax. This amount for each individual Grantor is currently $625,000 in 1998 and will increase to $1 million starting in the year 2006.

It is possible, over the remaining lifetime of the surviving spouse, to have the value of such a Trust increase to over $10 million.

The general rule is:

> As you give Directives to increase the end-value of your Credit Shelter Trust for your children and other heirs, you decrease the income from the Trust for your surviving spouse.

When the income to the surviving spouse is being reduced, a safety net should be in the Trust to provide additional funds if the surviving spouse needs them at some future time. This "Safety Net" is shown in Chapter 10, "Extra Money if Needed From the Trust."

Parents with one child may think that increasing the end-value of the Trust is not important. Their child will probably obtain a sizeable estate, of up to $2 million tax free, upon the death of both parents. For parents of a larger family increasing the end-value of the Trust is more important particularly when they want to provide as much as possible for the children and other heirs.

A Surviving Spouse with Little or No Need of Income from the Trust

Robert, age 66, and Jane Mathews, age 65, have a current net worth of about $2.4 million. They have four children and seven grandchildren. Robert receives a generous pension and upon his death, Jane will continue to receive a major part of it. The following is a listing of their assets.

Home - Jointly owned with right of survivorship		$350,000
In Jane's name:		
Stocks & Mutual Funds	$ 550,000	
CDs, Bonds, Savings Accounts	250,000	
Sub Total		800,000
In Robert's name:		
Stocks & Mutual Funds	$ 800,000	
CDs, Bonds, Savings Accounts	250,000	
Sub Total		1,050,000
Other Assets:		
Life Insurance, Face Value payable to Jane	$200,000	
Cars, Jewelry, home furnishings, etc.	50,000	
Sub Total		250,000
Total		$ 2,450,000

Included in the above assets is a total of $1,350,000 in stocks and stock mutual funds. This value is estimated, at a conservative annual growth of 8% a year, to increase to about $2,000,000 in five years and about $2,900,000 in ten years. If all the other assets did not increase, including the value of their home, their estate in ten years would be worth about $4.0 million and subject to large estate taxes. To mitigate this - Robert and Jane Mathews planned to annually review the growth of their estate and consider additional estate planning strategies. (These strategies are discussed in later chapters.)

The Mathews' current goal is to increase the end-value of their Credit Shelter Trusts for the benefit of their four children

Their prior estate planning documents included Living Trusts to avoid probate and to take advantage of their individual federal estate-tax exemptions. Their Living Trusts were properly funded. The balance of their individual estates passed tax free to the surviving spouse by the use of the marital deduction.

If Robert died in the current year, 1998, $625,000 would be placed in his Credit Shelter Trust. The balance of their assets would go to his wife Jane. As a result, Jane would have a net worth of $1,825,000 in 1998.

If Robert died ten years later, $1 million would go into his Credit Shelter Trust. After this deduction, Jane would have a net worth of about $3,000,000 based on the increase in their stocks from $1,350,000 to $2,900,000. The same basic amounts would apply to Robert's net worth, if Jane died first. Therefore, there was no need of income for the surviving spouse from the Credit Shelter Trust each had established.

Upon the death of the surviving spouse, a large state and federal estate tax would be due upon the death of the surviving spouse since that person would only have a federal estate-tax exemption of $1 million.

As a result, the surviving spouse would not want income from the Credit Shelter Trust. It would just add more funds to the already high estate taxes at his or her death. The living expenses and other needs would be paid from the earnings and growth of their capital. For family reasons, the Mathews did not want to leave the money from their federal estate-tax exemption directly to their children at death.

Each of the Mathews' Living Trusts were "silent" as to income and investments. Each Trust stated that the surviving spouse was to be paid the "Net Income" from the Trust.

The consequences of these silent Trust documents meant that the investments in them were controlled by Default Rules- the Principal and Income Act. If either Robert or Jane died after the year 2005, without revising their current Credit Shelter Trust, approximate end-values will be:

"DEFAULT RULES" - VALUE OF THE TRUST AFTER

Start	5 yrs.	10 yrs.	15 yrs	20 yrs.	25 yrs.
$1,000,000	$1,306,000	$1,810,000	$2,637,000	$3,996,000	$6,261,000

Note: The details of these estimated values are in Appendix B for this Chapter.

The Changes Robert and Jane Mathews had Made in Their Credit Shelter Trusts to Increase the End-Value for Their Four Children Were:

Option 1: They gave investment Directives to override the Default Rules. These Directives increased the percentage of investments in stocks to 100% from about the 50% (the amount designated by the Default Rule). By making this one change, Jane and Robert Mathews expected the following increases in the approximate end-values of their Credit Shelter Trust. The table below shows the dramatic results this one change might be expected to make.

Start	5 yrs.	10 yrs.	15 yrs	20 yrs.	25 yrs.
$1,000,000	$1,643,000	$2,701,000	$4,438,000	$7,293,000	$12,046,000

100% INVESTED IN STOCKS - VALUE OF THE TRUST AFTER

Increase Over
Default Rule

	5 yrs.	10 yrs.	15 yrs	20 yrs.	25 yrs.
- Amount	337,000	891,000	1,801,000	3,297,000	5,785,000
- Percent	26%	49%	68%	83%	92%

Note: The details of these estimated values are in Exhibit B of this Chapter in Appendix B.

A financial Directive to override the Default Rules is one thing parents can do to increase the end-value of their Trusts. There are other things that can be done also.

Option 2: The Mathrews included one in the form of a Directive on the income from the investments in their Trust. They replaced the current Directive in their Trusts that the "Net Income" which was to be paid annually to the surviving spouse. Instead they included a new Directive requiring that 100% of the trustee fees and expenses are to be charged to the income of the Trust. If there are insufficient funds from the income, [1] then any additional fees and expenses are to be charged to the principal of the Trust. [2]

(1)   A $1 million Trust invested 100% in stocks, paying dividends of 1.3%, will yield a Gross Income in the first year of $13,000. This Gross Income would be expected to increase to about $20,000 in the fifth year and to about $33,000 in the tenth year. Current fees of a bank serving as trustee, are about $11,000 for a $1 million Trust. There may be another $500 charge or more of bank charges for filing annual Trust tax returns.

(2)   Professional trustees will generally require this as a safety provision in the event the Gross Income does not fully cover expenses and fees.

If Option 1 and Option 2[3] are included, the value of the Trust, over the Default Rules could be additionally increased to:

100% INVESTED IN STOCKS & ALL FEES AND EXPENSES CHARGED TO INCOME - VALUE OF THE TRUST AFTER

Start	5 yrs.	10 yrs.	15 yrs	20 yrs.	25 yrs.
$1,000,000	$1,685,000	$2,839,000	$4,785,000	$8,062,000	$13,585,000
Increase over Default Rules					
- Amount	379,000	1,029,000	2,148,000	4,066,000	7,324,000
- Percent	29%	57%	81%	102%	117%

Note 1:   The details of these estimated values are in Exhibit C of this Chapter in Appendix B.

Option 3: After exercising options 1 and 2, above, there is a third option that the Mathews can use to reduce the taxes on the surviving spouse's estate. This option states how the income of the Trust will be distributed.

The option is based on this concept: If the income is distributed to a spouse, who already has a large taxable estate, the money will then be added to the value of the estate and will be taxed at a very high estate-tax rate when that surviving spouse dies. Or, if the surviving spouse has a large income from other sources and may not need all or part of the income from the Trust. In these cases, the trustee can give all or part of the income to the children, the spouse, or retain all or part of the income in the Trust.[4]

(3)   A Grantor has the option of stating how the fees and expenses of their Trust are to be charged to their Trust. The Grantor can state that the Net Income or Gross Income is to be paid to the Income Beneficiary. Or, that all expenses and fees of the Trust are to be paid out of income. The legal meaning in most states, if not all, of Net Income is that 50% of the fees and expenses of the Trust are to be deducted from the Gross Income. The remaining 50% of the fees and expenses of the Trust, with a Net Income provision, are deducted from the principal of the Trust. Additional information on this issue is in Chapter 14.

(4)   A legal term for this option when given to the trustee is "Sprinkling Powers."

There are two schools of thought on how this option should be stated. As indicated above, the most common form of Option 3, gives the trustee the power to distribute the income or to retain it in the Trust. One of the reasons for this recommendation is the potential tax advantage of holding the income in the Trust.

But this potential tax advantage can have several shortcomings when the income is held in the Trust instead of being distributed. This is particularly true regarding the children and other heirs named in the Trust.

A financial analysis of the benefits of retaining income in the Trust raises serious questions as to the validity of that concept. This analysis is presented in Appendix B. of this Chapter. In summary the analysis indicates that the value of funds held in the Trust for the future distribution to the children is not as great as allowing the children to have use of the funds in the current year.

The concept only has value when the children who receive the funds in the current year will waste them, a thing they might not do in their later years.

The concept of withholding funds from the children fails when they use these funds for a worthwhile purpose. This could be paying off their home purchase; educating their children; investing the funds, etc.

There is another legal alternative - giving the surviving spouse the power to instruct the trustee on how the income from the Trust is to be distributed between and among themselves and the children and other heirs. If this alternative is used, all of the income must be distributed. None of the income is permitted to remain in the Trust.

This alternative supports the concept of .the surviving parent as the head of the family

Issues and Problems With the Common Form of Option 3.

The common form assumes that the decision not to distribute all or part of the income, is a very important power that must be preserved.[5] Therefore, the trustee must be given this power.

But on a practical basis, this common form of giving this authority to the trustee can have problems.

1. Any of the beneficiaries of the Trust can contest what the trustee decides. Therefore, the professional trustee must carefully document any decision to distribute income. The trustee must continually gather financial information from the children and the spouse before determining how much income, if any, each will receive each year. This additional work of a professional trustee may result in extra fees (taken from the Trust). Decisions to withhold income is almost always the safest course for a trustee.

2. In the case where a family member is trustee, the results can be damaging. At best it will create strains within the family. How does a son or daughter determine the proper allocation each year among their parent, their siblings and themselves? What documentation must the family member trustee obtain to properly make the annual decisions and document these decisions against later arguments and perhaps even lawsuits within the family.

3. High income tax rates on income held in the Trust.

Advantages in Giving This Authority to the Surviving Spouse

The surviving spouse is probably a better judge of what is right for their children and should be relied upon to do it.

The trustee is then relieved of the responsibility of gathering information and documenting decisions. The trustee will be following the instructions of the surviving spouse.

The only loss of options in giving this power is that the surviving spouse can not direct the trustee to hold any part of the income in the Trust. All of the income must be distributed each year when the surviving spouse has this power.

A contingent provision can be made if, later in life, the surviving spouse is no longer competent.

Consider giving authority to direct that the funds be distributed from a separate Trust for the benefit of any child or other heir based on the decision of the surviving spouse.

Doing this preserves the concept of the parent as the head of the family.

Conclusion to Option 3

Whichever of the two approaches you select for Option 3, I think you will agree that the strength of the Trust is enhanced by a Directive that considers the children and gives authority to include them as recipients of the annual income from the Trust.

This issue may not be important if Grantor uses Options 1 and 2 as shown in this chapter. The detail of Exhibit C of this chapter in Appendix B shows that a very small amount of income is available during the beginning years of the Trust. During the first five years of the Trust, the average annual income available for distribution was estimated at about $2,300. Over the next five years, the average annual income available for distribution was estimated at about $4,000

In the next chapter this same question arises. Who should have the power to distribute funds from the principal of the Trust during the surviving spouse's lifetime- - the trustee or the surviving spouse?

The "Safety Provision" for the Surviving Spouse

As you consider the above financial Directives in your Credit Shelter Trust that increase the end-value of the Trust for the children and other heirs, a Safety Provision for your surviving spouse deserves serious consideration.

Most Trusts have a general provision for the removing of funds from the principal of the Trust for the benefit of the surviving spouse. But this authority is at the sole discretion of the trustee. And, in the past, trustees have required extensive documentation before they agree to the payment of the requested funds. Other problems have also been encountered as indicated in Chapter 10.

To avoid delays or extensive proof of need, I recommend a "Safety Provision" that allows the surviving spouse to obtain additional funds if needed just by asking for them from the trustee. As discussed in Chapter 10, this power allows the surviving spouse to annually request from the trustee the greater of $5,000 or 5% of the value of the Trust. And, within a stated number of days, the trustee must pay the amount requested.

Except for the immediate need of the surviving spouse, this power would not be expected to be used. If one of the children needed money, we recommend considering that the funds be available first from the Trust as presented in the next chapter.

Summary:

1. To increase its end value for your children, your Trust should give a Directive requiring that all or a very high percentage of the funds in the Trust be invested in good quality growth stocks.

2. If your surviving spouse will have ample funds outside the Credit Shelter Trust, you might want to direct that all fees and expenses of the Trust are to be charged to the income. This will again increase the principal value of the Trust for your children and other heirs.

3. If your surviving spouse will have income needs mainly satisfied from other sources, consider providing for all or part of the income to be distributed to, or held in a separate Trust for the children, as well as giving the income to the surviving spouse. You can direct that these decisions can be made by the surviving spouse, not the trustee.

4. Finally, make sure your surviving spouse has a safety net: the power to annually request up to the greater of $5,000 or 5% of the value of the Trust provides this safety.

In the following chapter, ways to provide funds for your children from the Credit Shelter Trust are presented. Remember, you can give the power to distribute funds from the principal to your spouse, instead of the trustee.

CHAPTER 9

Helping Your Children During the Life
of the Surviving Spouse

Introduction

During your lifetime you can do many things to help your children. After you have sufficient funds for yourself and your spouse, you can start by giving annual gifts of $10,000 a year to each of your children and grandchildren. This amount can be doubled to $20,000 per recipient if your spouse also makes a $10,000 gift. Surplus funds can be made part of a Family Limited Partnership or other strategies for estate-tax saving that will be discussed in later chapters.

The key issue is that you must continually review your assets and their projected growth at least every three to five years. The projected values will give an indication of your need to plan now how you will manage these increased values. You have many choices when it comes to reducing your estate taxes in order to provide funds for your children and for your grandchildren.

Few people properly address the issue of giving funds from their Trust to the children while the surviving spouse is still alive.

Things to Remember When Planning Your Trust.

1. It is important to insure that there will always be sufficient funds available for the needs of the surviving spouse.

2. The increases in the federal estate-tax exemption to $1 million per individual ($2 million per husband and wife) means that larger amounts of family assets can be placed in Credit Shelter Trusts.

3. Senior citizens are living longer. The surviving spouses can be expected to live into their eighties and beyond. As a result, many offspring will reach retirement age before the surviving spouse dies. This means that the children may not receive any funds from the Credit Shelter Trust or the surviving spouse's estate until they themselves are in their sixties and retired.

4.   The new investment strategies available today will result in substantial growth in these Trusts. An increase can be expected from the original value of the $1 million Trust to over $5 million in twenty years. Most of the increase (held in the Trust) will not be required by the surviving spouse. Why not release some of these funds to the children during the surviving spouse's lifetime?

Steps to consider

Many Trusts are being rewritten based upon the new estate-tax laws. As part of this work, families with adequate funds are making the following changes to   provide funds for their children:

Option 1:   Giving some funds to the children upon your death.

Consider giving directly to your children, at your death, part of your federal estate-tax exemption. You can state that at your death $100,000 or some other amount of your exemption is to be given to each of your children.

If you died after the year 2005, and have two children, $200,000 of your $1 million federal estate-tax exemption would go directly to your children, tax free. The remaining $800,000 of your exemption would be placed in your Credit Shelter Trust.

Option 2:   Authorizing the distribution of part of the principal of the Trust to the children during the lifetime of the surviving spouse.

As you will recall in the previous chapter, the common authority to distribute part or all of the income of the Trust to the spouse and/or the children was given to the trustee. (See Option 3 on Page 69 in Chapter 8, "How to Increase the Value of Your trust for Your Children.") It was suggested that as an alternative, the surviving spouse, as the head of the family, could have this power. The same is true of the option we are discussing here - giving funds from the principal of the Trust to the children.

Past use of this authority to distribute principal was also given to the trustee, at their sole discretion. But do you want to give this authority to your surviving spouse or to the trustee who might be your son, your daughter, your friend or the employees of the Trust department of a bank?

Option 2: If you give this power to the surviving spouse there are certain issues to consider. Due to a technicality of the law, while the surviving spouse can have the authority to determine the distribution of both income and principal, it appears that the authority to distribute principal should be written separately from the authority to distribute income.[1]

The authority for income distribution was presented in the previous chapter. The surviving spouse can direct the trustee to distribute all or any portion of the income to any one or more of a group consisting of the children, other heirs and themselves. This amount can be paid directly to those designated or held in Trust for their benefit as the surviving spouse, in his or her discretion, may determine.

Note 1: The authority to distribute a portion of principal, not all, and it should be subject to certain limitations.

For example, distributions might only be authorized when the Credit Shelter Trust is above certain values. This is used to make sure the surviving spouse does not give away funds that may be needed later. An initial value can be selected and can be indexed to increase for inflation or increase annually at a certain percentage.

Option 3: You can state in your Trust that you, as the Grantor, want to have distributions made from the principal, again under certain conditions.

You can also state these conditions in absolute amounts. You can stipulate whenever the value of the Trust is over a certain amount or, when surplus funds are indicated that you want these distributed. A method is required to determine to calculate surplus funds in the Trust.. It is not difficult to do and should be clearly stated in your Trust.

You can also consider this requirement when any distribution of the principal of the Trust is to be made, it must be made equally to each child, but may be held in a Trust for one or more of the children as directed by the surviving spouse.

(1)   Consult your Trust attorney on this issue.

Summary:

1. Sufficient funds for the needs of the surviving spouse must always be available.

2. Consider giving at your death part of your federal estate-tax exemption to your children. The remaining part of this exemption would still be placed in a Credit Shelter Trust.

3. Consider stating that your surviving spouse can instruct the trustee to distribute part of the principal of the Trust to the children and grandchildren. You can restrict this distribution to amounts over a stated value of the Trust.

4. Consider stating that distributions from the principal are to be made equally among the children when the value of the Trust is over a certain amount or when calculations indicate that there are surplus funds that you want distributed.

5. Consider the ages when you want the children to receive these funds directly instead of holding them in a separate Trust for their benefit.

Remember, senior citizens are living longer. A surviving spouse can be expected to live into their eighties and beyond. As a result, offspring may not receive any funds from the Trust or the surviving spouse's estate until they themselves are in their sixties. Trusts can reach high values that the Grantor can estimate and which may not be required for the needs of the surviving spouse. Consider a method to release some of this money to your children.

CHAPTER 10

Safety Provision: Extra money When You Need It

Understanding the use of the $5,000 or 5% rule[1]

Introduction

In addition to receiving from a Trust an annual income from the dividends and interest payments, there is a standard provision (an option generally placed in Trusts). It provides for additional funds for the Lifetime Income Beneficiary (you, your spouse or another person). These additional funds are from the principal of the Trust and are released at the sole discretion of the trustee. This is another area misunderstood by most Grantors.

You have the option of making an additional provision that can greatly increase the annual income you or your spouse will receive. If the plan for the Trust is to increase the end-value by restricting income, this directive can act as a financial safeguard for the survivor. It can provide a substantial amount of funds when used.

In this chapter we will:

1. Explain the difficulties the surviving spouse has in receiving any extra money from the standard provision in most Trusts.

2. Inform you of the work a trustee should do in following your wishes as expressed in the standard provision.

3. Explain the legal liabilities a trustee can have by granting the survivor's standard requests without a proper investigation, documentation and reasons for granting the request for funds.

4. Indicate how you can provide extra funds to the surviving spouse (of up to five percent of the principal, each year) just by their asking for it. Most important, you can direct that the request must be paid by the trustee without any questions asked or justification required.

---

(1) Internal Revenue Code Section 2041 entitled "Powers of Appointment," subsection (b)(2) which defines a general power of less than five (5%) percent or the greater of that and Five thousand ($5,000.00) dollars as not being a taxable lapse of a general power.

THE STANDARD PROVISION IN MOST TRUSTS:

An example of the language that may be found in some Trusts authorizing the payment of extra funds to the surviving spouse is that trustee is authorized to pay out of principal such sums necessary or proper for Income Beneficiary's health, maintenance, education, support, care, comfort, well being and general welfare."[2]

The provision found in most Trusts gives the trustee the authority to "invade" the principal of the Trust and give the funds to the Lifetime Income Beneficiary (generally the surviving spouse). The reaction to these requests reveals two categories of trustees. Each has the same duties to perform and the same financial liabilities for mismanagement.

1.   There are the professional trustees, such as those in a bank or other professionals, with a knowledge of the law and experiences in this area.

2.   In the other category is a son, daughter, friend or relative who has limited experience and perhaps is a trustee in only this single instance.

The professional trustee is always concerned about balancing responsibilities to the Remaindermen (generally your children) and to the Lifetime Income Beneficiary (generally your spouse). These professionals are equally concerned about the valid needs for these requests as well as lawsuits by the Remaindermen for any action that could be considered improper or that favored the Income Beneficiary.

(2)   The above example has been used because it can give the impression that due to its very broad authority the trustee can provide funds for almost any need of the Income Beneficiary. This may not be the case because the IRS has established requirements called "Ascertainable Standards." The standards are a test to determine the validity of any payments by the trustee if the Trust is to maintain it special tax status. Review this with your Trust attorney.

Any request from the Income Beneficiary for funds from the principal of the Trust will result in the reduction in the value of the Trust. This will reduce the future income from the Trust and the value the Remaindermen will receive when the Trust is terminated.

Granting a request for even a relatively small amount, if removed from the principal of the Trust, will reduce the funds eventually given to the Remaindermen. It can be argued that giving a total of just $50,000 of the principal of the Trust to you or your spouse by the trustee will reduce the funds the Remaindermen could have received by $150,000 or more. If these funds were given, without a complete and documented evaluation of the need for them, according to the terms of the Trust, the trustee has a potential future liability.

To guard against such suits later from the Remaindermen, as well as determining the valid needs of the request, professional trustees carefully evaluate all requests for additional funds from the principal of the Trust by the Income Beneficiary. This is done to determine if the requested funds are necessary and proper according to the terms of the standard provision in a Trust for the Income Beneficiary's maintenance, education, support, care, comfort, well being and general welfare.

Most Trusts state that the above conditions must be satisfied for any "invasion" (reduction) of principal. The trustee must follow the Directives in a Trust.

As part of this evaluation, professional trustees will determine if you or your spouse have funds from other sources, to meet your needs. If this is the case and you do have other resources, the request for extra funds can be denied. The "other sources" Directive is often waived.

A professional trustee can be held financially liable for mismanagement or errors made in the handling of a Trust. The same applies to a family member or friend that you select to be your trustee, Professional trustees have years of experience in Trust management and they do it to the exact terms of the Trust. Since the majority of Trusts do not give specific instructions, the professional management is based on laws and court rulings on these loosely defined concepts found in most Trusts. And, generally the law does not favor the surviving spouse over the Remaindermen.

That is why this book recommends that you state in your Trust exactly what you want to have happen. When you do this, your trustee must follow your

Directives. The family member or friend you selected for this responsibility, as your trustee, must do as you direct and cannot be held financially liable for following the Directives you have clearly stated in your Trust.

Professional trustees, as well as individual trustees, would not want to provide extra funds to a person who is a compulsive gambler, an alcoholic, or a person who is making questionable use of these extra funds.

Sometimes after many years of marriage, widows and widowers experience great loneliness. This is especially true in today's modern world where family members no longer live in the same neighborhood or in the same city.

Many couples at retirement age move to new locations. Their children and other relatives are many miles away. True, there are newfound friends in these places chosen for retirement. But even then, new relationships can change after the death of a spouse.

Requests for extra funds have sometimes been made for purposes other than those made in the statement to the trustee. While few requests are made for hidden purposes, older people can be talked into making foolish investments and can lose a great deal of money through illegal schemes. The promoters prey on older people because many do have money.

A trustee has a duty, when the standard provision is in a Trust, to determine the valid need for extra funds requested by the Income Beneficiary. An individual serving as a trustee would be well advised to follow the procedures professional trustees use in evaluating and granting any such requests. Most important, the individual trustee must fully document how they determined to grant or deny such requests. A trustee who has to justify why an action was taken several years before, without proper documentation, can find that future legal and financial liability may be the result.

Banks, after making their investigation, generally have various levels of approval required before the request is granted. A request for a small amount, in which there is a documented valid need, can be approved by one or more Trust officers. Requests for larger amounts, perhaps over $10,000 may go to a committee. In some cases, these bank committees may have individuals from the community serving as members.

Suggestions have been made that the Remaindermen (generally your children) should be asked to agree in writing prior to the granting of a large request for funds from the principal of the Trust. This is not always something a trustee encourages nor will it relieve the trustee of their duty as directed in the Trust document. The issue of obtaining approval may be further complicated if one of several children object or if others are also Remaindermen or future beneficiaries of the Trust such as relatives, friends or charities. Trustees therefore determine their course of action very conservatively from their powers and responsibilities as stated in the Trust document.

Trustees also know that occasionally the Income Beneficiary's request is a veiled attempt to obtain funds to give to one of their children. If this type of request is approved by the trustee it will not only deplete the funds that provide income for the Income Beneficiary, but it will result in one Remainderman being favored over the other Remaindermen which may not be authorized under the terms of the Trust.

If the Grantor had considered that income or principal would be made available to the Remaindermen, it would have been stated in the Trust documentation.

The list of possible invalid reasons to invade the principal of a Trust with a standard provision is almost endless. How does a trustee deal with an Income Beneficiary who gambles away the home left to them or loses significant assets left to them outside of the Trust. Such assets were very likely meant to also provide for needs of the Income Beneficiary. The Grantor may have assumed that while not included in the Trust, these assets would be passed on to their children at the death of the surviving spouse.

These are just some of the many reasons why experienced trustees make a careful evaluation of requests for the invasion of principal from the Income Beneficiary.

When an Income Beneficiary asks an experienced trustee for funds from the principal of the Trust, the experienced professional trustee will do the following:

1.   Ask the Income Beneficiary to make the request in writing and to state the reasons why these funds are requested.

2.   At the time the request is received by an experienced trustee, the normal practice is to send a response asking the Income Beneficiary to provide the trustee with:

a. A complete financial statement.

b. Copies of recent income tax returns and other information.

Remember that your trustee has a legal responsibility. It is, as stated in the standard provision of most Trusts, to determine if the funds requested are necessary or proper for Income Beneficiary.[3]

Depending on what is submitted by the Income Beneficiary, the trustees may ask for an explanation of certain items submitted or for additional data.

Most banks ask for a current copy of the individual's financial statement and they have a standard form that they send requiring this information. An example of a brief financial statement from an Income Beneficiary could be:

ASSETS		LIABILITIES	
Current Assets:		Current Liabilities:	
Cash	$ 2,400.	Accounts Payable	$ 1,975.
Stocks & Bonds	18,500.		
Other Assets:			
Home, Market Value	$ 290,000.		
Car & Other Items	10,000.	Net Worth	$ 318,925.
Total Assets	$ 320,900.	Total Liabilities & Net Worth	$320,900.

Certification would be required indicating that the above is a complete and accurate financial statement. In addition to the above, trustees have also requested copies of recent tax returns. What does the trustee do with this information?

1. From the Tax Returns the trustee will:

   a) Determine the total gross income the Income Beneficiary receives.

   b) Check the accuracy of the value of stocks, bonds, CDs, etc. submitted on the financial schedule to the tax schedules of interest and dividends received.

   c) Determine the amount of claimed deductions for medical and other itemized items, if deductions are itemized.

(3)   The standard provision for providing funds requires that the wording will establish an "Ascertainable Standard" that will receive IRS approval.

d). Determine the amount of losses claimed, if any.

e) Determine if the interest on any mortgage listed in the financial statement was listed as a deduction on the tax returns.

f) Look for changes in the income and net worth of the Income Beneficiary from the tax reports.

In addition to the information submitted, banks have access to credit reports providing additional data.

It may be proper for the trustee to visit with the Income Beneficiary and to make suggestions on how to reduce future financial needs by budgeting and planning expenditures. The income beneficiary might be encouraged to sell their $290,000 home and then use part of the proceeds to purchase a smaller home or a condo with less expenses.

One bank sent a representative from a nationally known CPA firm to the Income Beneficiary of a Trust. The accountant wrote a report stating that other assets should be sold by the Income Beneficiary and the proceeds from these sales would cover their needs. There are often good estate-tax reasons to have the surviving spouse's estate diminished.

Professional trustees may have in their fee schedules additional charges for the work they must do to properly evaluate a request for extra funds.

All of the above actions the trustee may consider in evaluating a request for an invasion of principal. They are considered reasonable things for the trustees to do if the standard provision is used in your Trust.

SOLUTIONS TO THIS PROBLEM OF HAVING FUNDS AVAILABLE FOR THE SPECIAL NEEDS OF YOU OR YOUR SPOUSE.

Your first solution is to provide from the Trust enough funds from the annual income so that you or your spouse are not continually placed in a position of needing extra funds from the Trust. Remember, the reason most individuals set up a Credit Shelter Trust was to save up to $235,000 in federal taxes. They did not do it to reduce the annual income they think the surviving spouse would receive from it.

To help ensure that you or your spouse have a sufficient annual income from your Trust, consider the recommendations in Chapter 6, i.e.:

a.   You can state in your Trust the income your surviving spouse is to receive.

b.   Obtain the highest reasonable return on assets by the investment Directives you give.

Next, you can anticipate certain events that you would expect to occur and have funds available from the principal of the Trust for these purposes.

Examples: - A wedding in the family.

- The need for a new car.

- Special training or education for family members.

- Needs that may apply to your family and that you wish to have funds available for from the Trust.

Do not become overly concerned with tax considerations that may complicate how smaller amounts of extra funds are distributed. A general recommendation is first to give the extra funds to the surviving spouse. That person can determine how these funds will be used. Chapter 8, covers how the surviving spouse can make funds available to one or more of your children, if that is your wish.

Remember that a strong continuing family relationship is one of your objectives. No one wants to place their surviving spouse in a position of saying to the children and grandchildren "wait until I die, then you will have money." Since parents are living longer, you may want to provide for the needs of children in their middle years.

Consider the Option of Allowing You or Your Spouse to Receive Extra Funds Just By Asking for Them From Your Trustee.

You have the right to state in your Trust that you or your spouse can receive a certain amount of the principal each year just by asking for it. Your trustee must give this amount to you or your spouse by the terms of the Trust. If you include the conditions, your trustee is required to do as you direct and is relieved of the responsibility for determining the validity and need of the requested funds. You or your spouse may then use these additional funds for any purpose.

In addition to the standard provision explained in the beginning of this chapter, there is another provision you can consider including.. In this new provision you can state that your trustee must pay to you or your spouse a certain amount, up to limits allowed by the tax code, when requested to do so.

If the option to obtain 5% of the Trust can be used anytime during the year the IRS, in the year the surviving spouse dies, can add 5% of the value of the Trust to the deceased person's estate. This could be done even through the deceased spouse never requested or obtained the 5%. This can cause extra estate taxes of over 50% of the amount the 5% represents.

To avoid this potential additional estate tax, attorneys draft the 5% provision to be available only at the end of each year. Therefore if the surviving spouse died in the prior months (January through November) the IRS cannot claim additional estate taxes from 5% of the value of the Trust. The full Trust amount, with the tax basis, can go to your children and other heirs.

A Credit Shelter Trust can start with $625,000 in assets in 1998. Five percent of this amount is $31,250. Starting in the year 2006, $1 million can be placed in a Credit Shelter Trust and 5% of that is $50,000.

As indicated in prior chapters, a Credit Shelter Trust properly invested can increase in value to well over $5 million and 5% of this would be $250,000. So concern about potential IRS claims that would tax this 5% amount are valid.

Also, the Grantor may want to restrict this annual claim by placing a limit on the amount that can be withdrawn under the 5% provision.[4] A Grantor could state, under the 5% provision, the maximum that can be annually withdrawn. This could be $25,000 or some other amount that would be less than 5%. A Grantor can reduce the allowed 5% to perhaps 3% of the total value of the Trust.

[4] This is the maximum amount federal tax code and rulings allow the Income Beneficiary to annually withdraw from a Credit Shelter Trust. This amount is not cumulative. If the provision is not used in a prior year it cannot be added to the authority in the current year to remove 10% from the Trust. Your attorney can advise you on this.

Use of the Option to Annually Remove the Greater of $5,000 or 5% of the Value of the Trust as a Safety Provision.

In Chapter 8, "Increasing the End-Value of Your Trust for Your Children," we examined use of this $5,000 or 5% power as a safety provision. This was done since a prime objective of the Credit Shelter Trust was to increase the value of the Trust for the Remaindermen. As a result of the Directives considered, the surviving spouse would receive a very small annual income from the Trust.

As a safety provision, we noted that if ever the surviving spouse needed extra funds, they could be made available by using the ability to obtain these funds. Hopefully it would never be used.

We do not recommend including the full powers in these Trusts where the surviving spouse needs a substantial income from the Credit Shelter Trust, provided for by the directives examined in Chapter 6. These directives provide a substantial amount of annual income. To increase this income, by removing, from the principal of the Credit Shelter Trust each year, an additional 5% a year could cause a rapid decrease in the value of the Trust and could in less than twenty years deplete all funds from the Trust. See page 246.

You can test this on the Internet calculator. Your first test should follow the conservative planning factors entered for Exhibit 4, in Chapter 7. Enter all of the Exhibit 5 planning factors into your program. Increase the "Annual Increase" by 5%. This will now produce an average annual increase of 8% in the starting Trust payments of $ 54,529. The results will indicate that the Trust will have no assets after 20 years. Nothing is left if the surviving spouse annually used this power.

Note: The details of this are in the Exhibit for this chapter on Page 246 in Appendix B.

If you want, you can reduce these powers to annually remove the greater of $5,000 or 5% of the value of the Trust. In the above example, where a high annual income was required from the Trust, you could give the surviving spouse the power to annually obtain up to $5,000 from the Trust. You can withhold the power to remove 5% of the value of the Trust.

The above example is another reason why the financial objectives of a Trust must be carefully planned and then the legal document prepared. There are very few immediate answers until the questions are carefully thought out. Then, the answers to the financial objectives of your Trust become clear and your attorney will be able to help you provide them.

One excuse for not doing this work is that no one can plan out everything - so, let the trustee handle these problems when they come up. By now you know that this is not the best answer.

Few Trusts properly consider the needs of the surviving spouse in the later years of his or her life. But you can project, with a strong degree of accuracy, what these needs might be. It can be anticipated that as the surviving spouse advances in age, medical needs increase. Nursing homes may eventually be required.

In many cases, family members no longer live in the same area. Sons, daughters and other family or friends can be hundreds of miles apart.

Provision should be considered in your Trust to pay the expenses for distant family members or friends to visit the surviving spouse in their later years to comfort them and ensure that they are receiving proper care.

A provision to make funds available for this contingency, when needed for these visits, can be placed into your Trust. Then, a son or a daughter could travel to visit the surviving parent regardless of how far away they lived. Grandchildren could also join in these visits.

This very important potential issue of the surviving spouse being in nursing home should be considered. I recently visited with an older couple, living on the east coast. When discussing their plans, the wife mentioned that if required, she would move to a nursing home in the area. They have two married daughters, one living in Denver and the other in California. Both have three children but limited resources for the expenses of visiting their mother.

The potential for the surviving spouse to become seriously ill or confined to a nursing home is real. It can be considered and provided for in the Trust document and it should be. A trustee cannot pay these expenses unless this is clearly stated in your Trust

You must provide well thought-out Directives, otherwise the trustee is limited to the Default Rules. In other instances, that a Grantor might believe the trustee will act, the trustee may have no authority unless stated in the Trust.

You may also hear objections about these powers that you can place in your Trust. In May, 1997, I[5] was a speaker at a meeting of the American Bar Association in Washington, D.C.

As part of the presentation on financial options in Trusts, the use of powers to permit the surviving spouse to annually obtain the greater of $5,000 or 5% of the value of the Trust was presented.

A few weeks later an individual who was not at the ABA meeting had received a copy of my charts. It was his opinion that no one should ever advise a client to consider giving the surviving spouse the annual ability to obtain the greater of $5,000 or 5% of the value of the Trust. He believed that the surviving spouse would have to pay 100% of the capital gains on the assets in the Trust.

This objection places tax concerns above the needs of the surviving spouse, regardless of the circumstances. If a person needs money, they would be willing to pay a capital gains tax on the funds they received instead of the alternative of not being able to obtain the funds.

His understanding of the tax laws relating to this option was only partially correct. If there is a gain in the funds received, there is a tax on that portion of the funds received from the Trust. In the beginning years of a Trust there may be no gains.

As an example: If the Trust started with $625,000 in 1998 and 5% were removed, the funds would came from principal and there would be no gains - therefore no tax.

If several years later, the Trust had increased to $850,000 and 5% was removed ($42,500), what would be a tax? The answer could range from nothing to a tax on the $42,500. The actual tax liability would depend upon the source of the funds paid out.

Taxes should not always be the reason for our every act. The authority to remove the greater of $5,000 or 5% of the value of the Trust is placed in a Trust to

(5)   Frank J. Croke speaking at the annual Spring CLE (Continuing Legal Education) and committee meetings of the ABA's Section on Real Property, Probate and Trust Law.

provide extra funds when needed. Part or all of the funds received may be subject to a tax. Capital gains tax rate is lower than the tax rate on ordinary income received from the Trust.

In Chapter 8 (" Increasing the Value of Your Trust for Your Children") we indicated that as you give Directives to increase the end-value of your Credit Shelter Trust for your children and other heirs, you decrease the income from the Trust for your surviving spouse.

Chapter 8 has options that may double the end-value of the Trust for your children. However, the income paid annually to the surviving spouse may be reduced to 1% or less of the value of the Trust. This was a plan to be considered when the surviving spouse would have an adequate income from other sources. As a safety provision we considered placing the "5 & 5" power in the Trust in the event, the surviving spouse would need extra funds.

When a second marriage Trust is established as shown in Chapter 12, we did not recommend using the full powers of this option. Other restrictions on the use of these powers are presented in other parts of this book.

CHAPTER 11

Taxation by State
and Local Governments

Introduction

More and more money is required by all of our federal, state, county and local governments. One out of every three workers is employed by them. To pay for this ever increasing expense at every level, governments tax every activity. Many of these taxes the average voter is not aware of, such as taxes on business. Many states now have an annual tax on Trusts. Large cities are attempting to tax Trusts. Such taxes have caused many banks to move their Trust operations out of these cities to avoid charging this tax to their clients.

Some states tax any Trust administered in that state even though the beneficiaries may not be residents. As a result, some banks have moved Trust operations out of those states.

You can protect your Trust from unreasonable state and local government fees, assessments, taxes, etc. by wording you place in your Trust. If your estate is very large there are decisions you can make that will help avoid excessive federal taxes.

Avoiding Unnecessary Annual City, County and State Taxes on Trusts

The best way to avoid taxes on Trusts by any city, county or state is to have in the documentation of the Trust the ability to change the state the Trust is governed by. A provision to do this should be in every Trust. This provision will also allow you to move to another state without the requirement for preparing new documents in your new place of residence.

Estate tax law is basically federal law. Every reference you will normally find in your Trust will be to sections of the federal law, regulations, etc. on Trusts. The only reference, normally found, to state laws and regulations is an article, generally toward the end of the document, that names the state whose laws shall govern the Trust. The state named is generally the state you currently reside in. This ties your Trust to the laws, including tax regulations, of that state. It also ties your Trust to the Default Rules and other statutes of your state that can cause results you may not want when you neglect to use your options.[1]

Because Default Rules can cause harm, I know several attorneys who place in their draft of the Trust document, a state Default Rule of investing without diversification. If a client reads the document they generally object to the rule and ask how they can change it.

It is very important that your document includes a provision that permits the Trust to be moved to another state's jurisdiction if this will be in the best interest of the Trust and/or the beneficiaries The reasons for doing this should be for any purpose deemed appropriate. This would allow the Trust to be moved to another state to minimize any tax imposed on it either now or in the future.

Also, if you move from your current state to another, you will not need to redo your Trust. If, after the death of the Grantor, the surviving spouse moves to another state, it may be best to change the jurisdiction that controls the Trust.

Ask Your Attorney About Inserting in Your Trust that the State that Governs the Trust Can Be Changed by a Letter or Other Instrument Filed with the Trust Records.

- Your current residence generally determines the state that controls your Trust. You want to be able to later move to another state and direct that this new state will control your Trust. You want to avoid having a new Trust prepared. This is done by an instrument filed with the Trust records.

- The reasons for this change may be for your tax benefit and that of others or for any other appropriate reason. Your trustee should also have the authority to do this.[2]

- This is applicable to any property held by the Trust.

Including the above article will allow you to quickly move your Trust out of any state and into one with a more favorable tax treatment towards Trusts.

(1)   Examples of State "Default Rules" and their problems are in Section G of the Appendix.

(2)   See Option 1, Chapter 24

Other Considerations

States do not normally tax residents of other states. An exception appears to be in Trusts when they are domiciled within the state and the Trust document is silent on this issue.

An example of such is the State of North Carolina. It's requirements are:

"The Trustee must file a state fiduciary income tax return for the Trust if the trustee is required to file a federal income tax return and:

    (1) The Trust derives income from sources within the state
OR

    (2) The Trust derives any income which is for the benefit of a resident of the state." [2]

Ask Your Attorney About Using in Your Trust Language that Clearly Indicates that State and Local Taxes are Not To Be Paid for Beneficiaries Not Living in the State.

- The Trustee is to investigate the legal requirement of filing state, or with other taxing authority within the state, Fiduciary Tax Returns, and paying taxes of any type.

- If taxes are to be paid for any Income Beneficiary or Remaindermen of the Trust who are not then residents of the state or of the domicile of the trustee, consider moving the Trust to another state.

Summary

1. The above financial recommendations in your documents will provide a means to quickly avoid any city, county or state fees, assessments or taxes you believe to be unfair.

2. And, equally important, these recommendations allow you to move your residence to another state without redoing your documents.

(2) Source: Form D-407A, General Instructions for North Carolina Fiduciary Income tax Return, Form D-407.

Chapter 12

Trusts for a Second Marriage

Introduction

Many second marriages include a prenuptial agreement. These agreements generally state that what each brings to the marriage will remain that person's property. They are meant to protect the assets of each partner and to allow each individual upon their death to pass their assets directly to their own children and other heirs.

However, later in the marriage, very often the partner with the most assets wants to provide after his or her death the same standard of living for the surviving spouse. This requires a higher income than their spouse with the more limited assets can achieve. In such cases, Trusts[1] are often established to provide this higher income. A Marital Trust can be used along with a Credit Shelter Trust.

Both types of Trusts, mentioned above, allow a person to place assets, tax free at their death, in them. The Trusts will provide an income during the surviving spouse's lifetime. Who will receive the assets in the Trusts, after the death of the surviving spouse, is stated in the Trust document when it was signed by the Grantor.

(1)   Insurance products could also be considered for part or all of the funds required. A life Insurance policy could be purchased on the life of the Grantor and held in a Irrevocable Life Insurance Trust. In discussions with the insurance executives, other forms of insurance, annuities, etc. are not currently available to provide the complete needs at reasonable cost. This is because:

The amount of funds required generally start at a lower amount than will be required at a later date as the age of the recipient increases. The starting date of the annual payments to the recipient are unknown (the date depends upon the date of death of the Grantor); the amount of annual payments to the recipient increases annually, by say 3% a year for inflation; and the ending date for the annual payments (the date of death of the recipient) is also unknown. Added to it is the fact that the excess funds, at the date of death of the recipient, are distributed to the heirs named by the Grantor and the Trusts may never be required if the intended recipient dies before the Grantor.

If an insurance type plan becomes available, compare the benefits and costs of the plan to your projected costs to fund a Trust as presented in this chapter.

To properly establish such Trusts with appropriate options requires time to make reasonable projections that need to be clearly documented in the Trusts. If you plan to do this, tests should be made of these Directives. They should include:

1). projecting reasonable needs for the spouse you wish to provide for, and

2). projecting the future value of your assets.

These kinds of Trusts also require frequent review. The review is to determine if the financial assumptions are still valid three or four years after they were established or last reviewed. Generally the financial assumptions were conservative, in order to ensure that adequate funds will be available to provide the income the surviving spouse will require. As a result, actual increases in the value of the estate can be greater than planned. When this occurs, it usually means that additional funds are available for the children with possible changes in the initial distribution of the Grantor's estate. The following material includes examples of how to develop a plan and to test the assumptions upon which the plan has been prepared.

To the surprise of many Grantors, the decision to provide for their surviving spouse is not in conflict with their wish to leave funds to their children. In most cases, a sizable amount of money can be given tax free to the children at the Grantor's death, while funds to provide the needed income for the surviving spouse are held in Trust.

This is the advantage of proper estate planning. It is not the case that all of a person's estate must be held in Trust if there is the wish to provide for the surviving spouse of the second marriage. Many of the same principles apply here that were presented in Chapter 6 "Know Your Income Needs" and in Chapter 7 "How to Test Your Financial Directives."

The Starting Point

In most situations, the worksheet, Exhibit 1 "Income Needs of Each Spouse' (see Chapter 6) is used as the starting point. Please note in this form that all the income the surviving spouse receives from his or her resources is deducted from the annual amount that spouse will need. Once an amount is determined as required from Trusts, the planning for how this will be accomplished starts.

Example 1: Second Marriages with $800,000 or more of Assets held by one Spouse

The first example will include a couple we call Henry and Margaret Bright. Henry's first wife died and several years later he remarried. He is retired and receives an annual pension of $40,000. If Henry's first wife had survived him, she would have received half of Henry's pension. However, Henry's second wife - Margaret, if she survives him, will not receive any part of his pension. At age 68, Henry has two grown children. Margaret, age 65, also has two grown children.

Henry owns, free and clear, the home they live in valued at about $125,000. He also has stocks currently worth about $ 600,000 and about $150,000 in CD's and bonds. His second wife, Margaret has CDs and bonds, in her own name valued at $250,000.

After carefully completing Exhibit 1, "Income Needs of Each Spouse", it was determined that Margaret would need, in 1998 dollars, $22,750 from Trusts Henry would establish. As part of the planning to determine the size of the Trust, an increase for the cost of inflation (estimated at three percent a year) was used.

The following table is a summary of the plan that was prepared based on the possibility that Margaret might live past age 100. Review in the table, column two, Margaret's ages and in column three the increasing amounts she will need.

Also look across to column six, the "Amount Required" to be placed in trust to provide the income payment to Margaret. The footnotes explain how these projections were made.

			Amount to Fund Trust, if Henry Died In			Estimated End Value For Henry's Children
Year	Margaret's Age	Trust Payment [1]	Year	At Age	Amount Required [2]	If Margaret lived to Age 100 [2]
1998	65	$22,750	1998	68	$ 450,000	$173,000
2003	70	26,373	2003	73	525,000	248,000
2008	75	30,574	2008	78	575,000	146,000
2013	80	35,444	2013	83	625,000	164,000
2018	85	41,089	2018	88	625,000	124,000
2023	90	47,633	2023	93	575,000	128,000
2028	95	55,220	2028	98	475,000	199,000

(1)   These amounts were obtained by increasing the annual income Margaret would need in 1998 by three percent for estimated annual cost of inflation.

Footnotes (2) and (3) on next page.

How Henry directed his Estate Planning Documents to Provide for Margaret and His Children from a Previous Marriage.

1. In 1998, the year the Trusts for Margaret were executed, Henry has a total estate valued at $875,000, including his home. His federal estate-tax exemption in 1998 is $625,000. Henry established a Marital Trust for Margaret with assets of $250,000. The Marital Trust included his home, valued at $125,000, and $125,000 of his securities. Henry then used his $625,000 federal estate-tax exemption to: a). give directly at his death, tax free, $300,000 to his two children and b). hold the balance of $325,000 of his securities in a Credit Shelter Trust for Margaret's benefit.

The result is a total of $575,000 that would go into these Trusts for Margaret. Of this total amount, $450,000[3] would be in securities and $125,000 would be the value of his home.

2. Henry directed the following:

a. Trustee is to invest 50% of the funds in both Trusts in growth stocks and 50% in bonds (a Balanced Trust under the Default Rules).

b. Trustee is to pay directly the real estate taxes and insurance on his home and deduct these amounts from the funds Margaret is to receive each year. Henry further directs that if Margaret wants to move from their home, the trustee will sell it and purchase for Margaret a new residence of her choice with the proceeds.

c. Trustee is to pay Margaret an income of $22,750, if Henry died in 1998, the year the Trusts were executed. If he lived past 1998, he instructed the trustee to increase the $22,750 by 3% a year for inflation.

(3) See Table of on prior page.

Footnotes from the preceding page:

(2) The annual stock increase estimate was reduced from the historical 11% annual gain to 8% for the above projections. This was done to be conservative in estimating the funds required for Margaret from Henry's Trusts. If the 11% had been used, less funds would be required. The amounts required to fund the Trusts were developed by using Estate Planning Program One, that is available to you on the Internet. Appendix A has an example of how the calculations can be performed to determine the amount of funding required for these types of Trusts.

d.   Trustee is to pay the annual income to Margaret first from the income of the Marital Trust; and next from the income of the Credit Shelter Trust. Additional funds if required, would be taken first from the principal of the Marital Trust. This was done for estate-tax purposes.

Henry intended five years later, in the year 2003, to review his financial position and his Trust documents. At that time he expected his stocks to grow in value from $600,000 to about $900,000. If this occurred, Henry's stocks would have increased at an average annual growth rate of about 8.5%, well below the historical rate of 11%.

Assuming no increase in value for his home, CDs, and bonds, Henry's total estate would then be worth $1,175,000 and his federal estate-tax exemption, in the year 2003, would be $700,000.

Henry planned revisions in his estate planning documents to include the following changes:

1.   To increase the securities in the Trusts required for Margaret to $625,000. This would provide the maximum funds required starting in the year 2013.[3] This assumes that inflation had increased at 3% annually over the last five years. Henry would in the year 2003 redo Exhibit 1 "Income needs of Each Spouse" the results of which might require minor adjustments.

2.   If Henry's total assets in the year 2003 had grown from $875,000 to $1,175,000, he would increase the amount to be paid to his children, at his death, from $300,000 to $425,000.

The above planned changes are important reasons why estate planning documents need to be reviewed at regular intervals. In this case, Henry's assets were estimated in 2003 to increase $300,000, based on his estimate of an average annual increase of about 8.5% for stocks. However, the value of the stocks could also have increased to over a million dollars if the stocks grew at their historical rate. Or, the value of the stocks could have decreased.

No one can accurately project the exact amounts that will be available five or ten years from now. One can project the general results expected and have a plan to frequently update the projections.

(3)   See Table on Page 96.

Note: the major changes in the year 2003 that Henry expected and that he could make in his 1998 estate documents were as follows:

1. He could increase the amount given to his two children, at his death from $300,000 to $425,000.

2. He could increase the securities in the Trusts for Margaret from $450,000 to $625,000. The Total Value of the Trusts for Margaret, including the home, valued at $125,000 in 1998, would be $750,000.

Henry also intended ten years later,[4] in the year 2008, to make a second special review of his financial position and his Trust documents. At that time:

He expected his stocks to have increased in value to about $1,350,000. If this occurred, Henry's total estate would then be worth $1,625,000 and his federal estate- tax exemption would be $1 million.

Based upon the projections in the increase of the value of his estate, Henry planned to revise his Trusts to accommodate a changing financial position.

He would increase the amount of his estate that would directly to his children from $425,000 to $875,000. The balance $750,000 would remain in the Trusts for Margaret.

His documents would state that the unused portion of his estate-tax exemption of $125,000 would be in stocks held in a Credit Shelter Trust. The balance of $625,000 would be held in a Marital Trust (of which $500,00 would be in securities and $125,000 would be the 1998 value of his home).

After the year 2008, when Henry would be 78 and Margaret age 75, Henry's assets could continue to grow. The first $125,000 of this growth would be given directly to his children tax-free, thereby using his full federal estate -tax exemption. After that, the taxes on his estate would then greatly increase. Henry would have several tax saving techniques that he could then use. The most common type is a tax-free gift of $10,000 to each of his children. Charitable Remainder Unitrusts could also be established that would provide a lifetime income for them individually. And, outright gifts to churches and charities can be made.

(4) He still intended to review his Trust every 3 to 5 years for other potential changes.

Henry's potential changes in his Trust documents could be on an attached schedule. Then, only the attached schedule would be revised. This is an important drafting technique that Henry's attorney could use for these Directives and certain other options, such as instructions for investing Trust assets.

However, it is important that an attorney be consulted when changes are to be made in an attached schedule.

Summary: First Example - Henry and Margaret Bright

1. **With proper planning, adequate provision can be made for both the wife of a second marriage and the husband's children from the first marriage.**

2. **But to do this a plan is required and should be completed before visiting an attorney.**

3. **Much smaller estates can also plan and obtain these benefits.**

Example 2:   Second Marriages with $2 Million or more of Assets held by one Spouse

The second example will be a couple called James and Helen Curnin. James' first wife died and several years later he remarried. His second wife Helen, age 58, has three grown children. James, age 64, also has three grown children. When James and Helen married, she had limited resources. A prenuptial agreement had been signed. James' current net worth is about $2.4 million.

James had taken early retirement. He and Helen travel extensively, have a home worth about $500,000 located in a private community with golf courses and a club. Their style of living might be considered affluent.

In addition to his home, James had assets of:
Growth Stocks and Mutual Funds $1,400,000
Municipal Bonds   500,000

Helen had been James' wife for about five years when he decided that he wanted to provide a continuation of their standard of living for her, in the event he died first. James was very happy in his second marriage. He felt that the prenuptial agreement would leave Helen with very little as his widow. James wanted to either leave her a portion of his estate or establish a Trust for her benefit during her remaining lifetime.

In talking with some golfing partners James learned that each of them had established a Credit Shelter Trust to take advantage of their personal federal estate-tax credit. Most of them gave their additional assets directly to their spouse and these would pass tax free. One of them had set up a second Trust, a Marital Trust, since his wife had limited financial experience and has no interest in managing money. James felt a Trust would be best for Helen. Before he could set up the right one, he needed an estate plan to be developed for him.

Developing an estate plan in second marriage situations requires the preparation of several separate forecasts of future needs as well as future values of current assets. The result of this work is an estate plan. Once you have completed this, your attorney will prepare the proper Trust documents taking into consideration tax issues. The work of preparing an estate plan may appear complicated but is not. The basic steps are shown below.

First - The Income Needs of Helen

Using Exhibit 1, "Income Needs of Each Spouse," it was estimated that James' wife would need $70,000 a year (before state and federal income taxes) from trusts that James would establish. This before-tax amount is required to maintain their permanent residence, their country club membership and other expenses. And this $70,000 projection was in 1998 dollars, so, it would be increased for inflation, estimated at 3%, plus an additional one percent.

Second - Funding the Trust

The following table is a summary of the plan that was prepared based on the possibility that Helen might live past 100.

Year	Helen's Age	Trust Payment [4]	Amount Required to Fund Trust, if James Died			Estimated End-Value For James' Children
			In Year	At Age	Amount Required [5]	If Margaret lived to Age 100 [6]
1998	58	$70,000	1998	64	$1,450,000	$365,000
2003	63	81,149	2003	69	1,600,000	100,000
2008	68	94,074	2008	74	1,750,000	82,000
2013	73	109,058	2013	79	1,875,000	127,000
2018	78	126,428	2018	84	1,950,000	143,000
2023	83	146,565	2023	89	1,925,000	66,000
2028	88	169,909	2028	94	1,700,000	83,000
2033	93	196,971	2023	99	1,300,000	145,000

A Common Concern - James' Children

James was concerned that if he established Trusts for Helen, his three children, currently ages 41, 39 and 38 might not receive any funds from his estate for another 25 or 30 years. Thirty years from now his youngest child would be 68 years old.

Once the above table was developed, the next set of projections for the Curnins could be prepared. They indicated that James could also leave substantial funds to his children at his death. This was accomplished as follows.

Estimating the Future Values of James' Estate

Each year James had removed some of his capital to cover his and Helen's living expenses. This year, James would sell about $25,000 of his stock for additional expenses.

Currently he has $1.4 million invested in good quality growth stocks. Even a low average annual increase of 8 % equals an increase in the value of his stocks of about $112,000. So the sale of about $25,000 of stocks should not materially decrease his holdings. And, while the stock market can experience periods of declines, in the long run its total return far exceeds other investments.

Footnotes from the previous page:

(4)   These amounts were obtained by increasing the annual income Helen would need in 1998 by 3% for estimated annual cost of inflation.

(5)   The annual growth estimate in the value of stocks was reduced from the historical 11% annual gain to 8% for the above projections. This was done to be conservative in estimating the funds required for Helen from James' Trusts. If the 11% had been used, less funds would be required. Investments are in a Balanced Trust(50% in bonds and 50% in stocks). Bond interest is 5.5% and dividend payment are 1.3%. Trustee Fees and expanses are 0.75%.

The amounts required to fund the Trusts were developed using Estate Planning Program One. The resulting amounts of "Trust Payments," in five-year increments, are summarized in Column three. The amounts required to fund these payments (Column 6, under the heading "Amount Required") can then be estimated after the annual income needed for the above time periods is known.

(6)   These amounts may be low based upon a conservative estimate of stocks increasing at an average annual rate of 8% over the next 42 years. The amounts could be substantially higher at the historic average annual growth rate of 11%..

This is especially true when inflation and high taxes on income are included in the analysis. In fact, James estimates that the $500,000 invested in municipal bonds yields, at best, a 1% annual return after the cost of inflation. And, he also realizes that because he is spending the interest he receives each year, the purchasing power of his money invested in municipal bonds is annually decreasing.

Once the income and expense plan for 1998 is prepared (and projections made of future income needs) a conservative forecast can be made of the future value of James' stocks. This forecast, shown below is first based upon a conservative 6% average annual growth of these stocks, after deducting what was to be sold annually for required living expenses. The column on the left side ("TOTAL ESTATE VALUE at 8% Net Increase in Stocks") is based on the historical average annual increase of stocks. This 8% stock increase is the net after deducting annual sales of stocks for living expenses. No increase was projected for the value of his home or the value of his municipal bonds.

	TOTAL ESTATE VALUE At 6 % Net Increase in Stocks [6]			TOTAL ESTATE VALUE at 8% Net Increase in Stocks [6]	INCREASING DIFFERENCE Between 6% and 8%
Year	Home & Bonds	Stocks	Total		
1998	$1,000,000	$1,400,000	$2,400,000	$ 2,400,000	
1999	1,000,000	1,484,000	2,484,000	2,512,000 . . . . $ 28,000	
2000	1,000,000	1,573,000	2,573,000	2,663,000	
2001	1,000,000	1,667,000	2,667,000	2,764,000	
2002	1,000,000	1,767,000	2,767,000	2,905,000	
2003	1,000,000	1,874,000	2,874,000	3,057,000 183,000	
2004	1,000,000	1,986,000	2,986,000	3,222,000	
2005	1,000,000	2,105,000	3,105,000	3,399,000	
2006	1,000,000	2,231,000	3,231,000	3,591,000	
2007	1,000,000	2,365,000	3,365,000	3,798,000	
2008	1,000,000	2,507,000	3,507,000	4,022,000 515,000	
2009	1,000,000	2,657,000	3,657,000	4,264,000	
2010	1,000,000	2,817,000	3,817,000	4,525,000	
2011	1,000,000	2,986,000	3,986,000	4,807,000	
2012	1,000,000	3,165,000	4,165,000	5,112,000	
2013	1,000,000	3,335,000	4,335,000	5,441,000 1,106,000	
2014	1,000,000	3,556,000	4,556,000	5,796,000	
2015	1,000,000	3,770,000	4,770,000	6,180,000	
2016	1,000,000	3,995,000	4,892,000	6,594,000	
2017	1,000,000	4,235,000	5,235,000	7,042,000	
2018	1,000,000	4,489,000	5,489,000	7,525,000 . . . . $2,036,000	

(6) Percent Increase in stocks is after sales of stocks as a source of additional income each year.

103

The projections use the future value of James' stock. The estimate on the left is based on the "6% Net Increase in Stocks." This is a conservative forecast and is used since this part of the planning is to ensure that sufficient funds will be available in the estate plan. Frequent reviews will provide for adjustments in the plan. If the stocks actually increase at the expected and higher rate, the additional funds can be used for many other things. However, the basic funding of Helen's Trust will not change.

Once the above projections on James Curnin's stockholdings are completed, an increasing difference can be seen between the projected amounts based on a 6% rate of increase for his stocks and the projected amounts based on the 8% increase. In 1999 the difference is $28,000. This difference increases greatly. In ten years it was $515,000. And after twenty years the difference is estimated at $2,036,000.

This is just one of the reasons why the financial issues in Trusts need to be frequently reviewed. Its very important that the proper wording be placed in the Trusts to provide trustees with a clear understanding of what is to be done.

In the past, many Trusts were prepared in very broad terms with extensive references to the federal tax code and to a minor extent the statutes of the state of residence. The results of specific financial plans were not stated in these Trusts.

These   tables provide helpful illustrations. The prior one   was accomplished by increasing the 1998 value of James Curnin's stocks by 6% and adding to these values a fixed amount, for his home, valued at $500,000 and his municipal bonds worth $500,000. The process was repeated using 8%, an increase more likely to occur.

The 6% annual increase was selected after assuming a conservative 8% average annual increase in the value of stocks over a twenty-year period. The difference of 2% would be equal to annual sales of stock for living expenses. The above table also listed an 8% annual increase based on stocks increasing at their historic rate of 11% and three percent of the increase would be sold each year for living expenses.

James' Estate Plan for his wife and children

We will use the lower estate ("At 6 % Net Increase in Stocks") of the "Total Value" of James Curnin's estate and combine it with the required amount to fund Helen's Trust ("Amount Required" from column six in the table on page 101).

Added to this will be James' federal estate-tax exemption during the next ten years. The result, on the next table, Page 106, is very interesting to review. It represents the summary of all the planning projections. It shows:

1. A conservative estimate of the total value of James Curnin's estate for the next twenty years.

2. It lists an individual's personal federal estate-tax exemption during this period. The Table indicates that James will be able to give his three children the full amount of his federal estate-tax exemption at his death starting in the year 2001. Remember that during the period 1998 to 2006, this exemption increases from $625,000 to $1 million.

3. The Table indicates that the balance of James' estate, after payment of his federal estate-tax exemption to his children, is initially planned to go into James' Marital Trust for Helen.

4. Column 5 indicates the amounts needed to fund the Trust during this twenty-year period. The amounts are from the Table on Page 106

5. The amounts in the last column "Extra Funds in Trust" can be used for many purposes. A plan should be considered for these extra funds. It could include:

   A. Using part of the funds to increase the Curnin's living expenses; giving gifts to churches and charities and giving annual $10,000 gifts to each of the children.

   B. Establishing Charitable Remainder Trusts to provide part of the income Helen will require during her lifetime. This would provide immediate tax benefits for James Curnin. These benefits are discussed in later chapters.

Carefully examine the data below that has been estimated for the next 20 years. At least every four or five years do a financial review and make appropriate changes. This is very important.

Year	Total Estate[7]	Federal Estate Tax Exemption To his Children[8]	Balance Remaining[8]	Securities Needed In Trust[9]	Remaining Funds[10]
1998	$ 2,400,000	$450,000	$1,950,000	$1,450,000	$ -0 -
1999	2,484,000	500,000	1,834,000		
2000	2,573,000	600,000	1,898,000		
2001	2,667,000	675,000	1,992,000		
2002	2,767,000	700,000	2,067,000		
2003	2,874,000	700,000	2,174,000	1,600,000	74,000
2004	2,986,000	850,000	2,136,000		
2005	3,105,000	950,000	2,155,000		
2006	3,231,000	1,000,000	2,231,000		
2007	3,365,000	1,000,000	2,365,000		
2008	3,507,000	1,000,000	2,507,000	1,750,000	257,000
2009	3,657,000	1,000,000	2,657,000		
2010	3,817,000	1,000,000	2,817,000		
2011	3,986,000	1,000,000	2,986,000		
2012	4,165,000	1,000,000	3,165,000		
2013	4,335,000	1,000,000	3,335,000	1,875,000	1,060,000
2014	4,556,000	1,000,000	3,556,000		
2015	4,770,000	1,000,000	3,770,000		
2016	4,892,000	1,000,000	3,892,000		
2017	5,235,000	1,000,000	4,235,000		
2018	5,489,000	1,000,000	4,489,000	1,950,000	2,039,000

(7)   Values used for Total Estate are based on a 6% net increase in stock, shown on page 103. No increase was projected for the home valued at $500,000 and the $500,000 held in municipal bonds.

(8)   Remaining Balance is after the maximum federal estate-tax exemption is given to James' children at his death. Exceptions: 1998, 1999 and 2000. NOTE: This includes the value of the home ($500,000) that is being made available to Helen.

(9)   From column 6 "Amount Required" in Trust for Helen from Table on page 101. Note: This is the amount of investable funds to produce the income Helen requires.

(10) Includes $500,000 deduction for the home. As this amount grows, other estate planning techniques need to be considered to reduce the estate taxes on these funds.

Conclusions:

1. As indicated in the summary table, above, funds can be available for a Trust for Helen. At the same time James' children can receive the full amount of the federal estate-tax exemption at the time of their father's death (exceptions in 1998 and the next two years when the amount given are less).[12] Again, it is not a case of either giving funds to the children at James' death, or holding them in a Trust for the surviving spouse. Helen's funds can be made available for her and James' children, if the financial aspects of the Trust are properly addressed.

2. James must give some thought to how he wants to use the surplus funds shown in the last column on the right.

How James directed his Estate Planning Documents to Provide for Helen and His Children:

A. James' 1998 Estate Plan:

1. In 1998, the year his estate planning documents were executed, James had an estate valued at $2.4 million. His federal estate-tax exemption in 1998 was $625,000. He established a Marital Trust for Helen that would contain $1,275,000 of the $1,450,000 in securities that would be required. The balance of the securities ($175,000) was placed in a Credit Shelter Trust. His home, valued at $500,000 was also placed in the Marital Trust. This left $450,000 of his estate that James will give directly to his children .as part of his federal estate-tax credit.

A. If James was to die in 1998, $450,000, tax free, would go to his children and $1,950,000 of his assets (including his home valued at $500,000) would be held in Trusts for Helen.

B. If James died a few year later, his children would receive the increase in his federal estate-tax exemption. The balance of his estate would amply cover the income needs in the Trust established for his second wife, Helen - see Table on page 106.

C. James also directs his trustees to pay directly the real estate and insurance on his home and deduct these amounts from the funds Helen is to receive each year. If major repairs are required on the home, the trustee is authorized to pay the costs of these repairs. Authority is also given to obtain a mortgage for these repairs. If Helen wants to move from their home, the trustee is to sell it and use the proceeds to purchase a new residence for her. Any surplus funds from the sale and purchase of a new residence would be added to the principal of the Trust.

This option given to Helen to have the current home sold and a new residence purchased was not confined to a single instance. James reasoned that Helen might, while still young, move to another location. And, later might move again to a home for retirement living.

B.   James Intended to Review the Financial Projections of His Estate Plan Every Three to Five Years.

James knows that he will have many financial options in the years following 1998. If his stock increases in value at a rate higher than 8% a year, he could consider many options during his lifetime. The key is knowing what these financial options are under the current laws.

The first option James thought he might consider was establishing a Charitable Remainder Trust during his lifetime and naming Helen as the second recipient of the income during her lifetime. If James did this, he would receive a large tax deduction in the year the Charitable Remainder Unitrust was established. The payments that Helen would receive from the Charitable Remainder Unitrust, after his death, would reduce the amount of funds required in Helen's Marital Trust.

Or, James could name one of his children as the second recipient to receive a lifetime income after his death. [11]

Later James would also review other options that would allow him to pass a greater amount of his estate to his children from his first marriage.

Charitable Remainder Unitrusts and additional options are discussed in other chapters.

(11)   A person may only name another person to receive the income from a Charitable Remainder Unitrust after their death. However, there is no restriction on the number of such Trusts a Grantor can establish.

Summary:

1. It is important to also develop an estate plan in second marriage situations. The plan requires the analysis of several forecasts:

    These would include the future needs of the second wife and the future values of current assets along with other techniques relating to estate planning. The basic steps were shown in this chapter.

2. When establishing a Trust for the second spouse, it is rarely a case of holding all of the Grantor's funds in Trust for the surviving spouse. In most cases, funds can also be given at the Grantor's death to his children or grandchildren from the first marriage.

3. Estate planning documents should not require a complete revision each time changes are made. Decreases or increases can be made in the amounts given directly to the husband's children and changes can be made in the amounts to be held in Trusts. But the documents should state that these issues are provided for in an attached schedule.

This means that based on the Grantor's financial review, only the attached schedule would be revised. This is an important drafting technique that attorneys should use for these Directives and certain other options, such as instructions for investing Trust assets.

In the two examples, Henry Bright and James Curnin, as Grantors, did not give Directives that would reduce any of the benefits their wives would receive if they were later to remarry after the Grantor's death. These would be restrictions they did not want to place on their widows.

CHAPTER 13

Marital Trust in Conjunction with a Credit Shelter Trust

This chapter discusses some of the (financial planning) options you have and should consider before establishing or revising your Trust. Before doing so, we will first look at what it is possible to do if you have sufficient additional funds to establish a Marital Trust.

First, what is a Marital Trust?

In addition to your state and federal estate-tax exemption, the assets you leave to your surviving spouse pass tax free to that person provided they are a United States citizen.

It is not necessary that your surviving spouse has control of these assets to qualify for the tax-free status upon your death. You can place some or all of these additional assets in a Marital Trust for the survivor. There is a requirement that all the income from this type of Trust be paid to your surviving spouse.

The interest and dividend income paid from a Marital Trust is taxed at the spouse's regular income-tax rates. Any distributions of the original principal from the funds placed in the Marital Trust are not taxed since these are funds your surviving spouse could have directly received, tax free at the Grantor's death. When your surviving spouse dies, the value of the Marital Trust can be taxed in her estate.

The Grantor of the Marital Trust controls who is to receive these assets at the death of the survivor, less any estate taxes, by stating in the document the names of the Remaindermen. Marital Trusts, combined with Credit Shelter Trusts are used in many second marriage situations as discussed in Chapter 12. Marital Trusts are also used when the Grantor believes that the surviving spouse is not capable of or interested in managing these funds.

In our example of Helen Curnin (Example 2 starting on Page 100) the amounts required to properly fund the Trust for her benefit during her lifetime exceeded the amount of her husband's federal estate-tax exemption. The solution was to place the required additional funds in a Marital Trust. After providing for Helen's needs, the excess amount of James Curnin's estate was to be given to his children at his death.

But in the example of Henry Bright (starting on Page 96) the funds for his second spouse would be held in both a Marital Trust and a Credit Shelter Trust. To illustrate this, let us assume that Henry Bright died in January, 2004. The table on Page 96 (and repeated below) indicates Margaret Bright would require a Trust with a value of $525,000 in securities plus the home valued at $125,000. The total in Trust for Margaret would be $650,000. Henry Bright's estate at the end of 2003 was projected to be $1,175,000. After reserving the funds for Margaret's Trust ($650,000), $525,000 can be given directly to Henry' children.

Year	Margaret's Age	Trust Payment [1]	Year	At Age	Amount Required [2]	Estimated End Value For Henry's Children If Margaret lived to Age 100 [2]
					Amount to Fund Trust, if Henry Died In	
1998	65	$22,750	1998	68	$ 450,000	$173,000
2003	70	26,373	2003	73	525,000	248,000
2008	75	30,574	2008	78	575,000	146,000
2013	80	35,444	2013	83	625,000	164,000
2018	85	41,089	2018	88	625,000	124,000
2023	90	47,633	2023	93	575,000	128,000
2028	95	55,220	2028	98	475,000	199,000

In this example, if Henry Bright died in January 2004. His federal estate-tax exemption would be $850,000. He would give directly to his children $525,000. This means that Henry has not used $325,000 of this exemption.

To preserve this unused $325,000 exemption, Henry's Trust documentation would provide for that amount to be placed in a Credit Shelter Trust for Margaret's benefit. The remaining funds required for Margaret's needs will be placed in a Marital Trust.

(1)   These amounts were obtained by increasing the annual income Margaret would need in 1998 by three percent for estimated annual cost of inflation.

(2)   The annual stock increase estimate was reduced from the historical 11% annual gain to 8% for the above projections. This was done to be conservative in estimating the funds required for Margaret from Henry's Trusts. If the 11% had been used, less funds would be required. The amounts required to fund the Trusts were developed by using Estate Planning Program One, that is available to you on the Internet. Appendix A has an example of how the calculations can be performed to determine the amount of funding required for these types of Trusts.

111

In order to be effective, Directives must clearly state how the funds in a Credit Shelter Trust are to be invested and how the funds in the Marital Trust are to be invested. Directives must also state the exact source of Margaret Bright's annual income. If the Directive states that any payment from principal must come first from the principal in the Marital Trust, this will allow the Credit Shelter Trust to grow in value for the future benefit of Henry's' children.

At this point, another important factor needs to be considered for Henry's' children. As indicated on Page 97 (footnote 2), the need for $525,000 to fund Margaret's Trusts was based on an average annual growth in stocks of 8%. This is a conservatively low estimate for Margaret's benefit but not for the benefit of Henry's children.

If the historical growth of stocks has occurred (11% annual average), Henry's children would have received $636,000 tax free at their father's death, in January, 2004, instead of $525,000. Directives can be placed in the Trust to provide additional funds for Henry's' children if the growth in stocks, after Henry's death, is also higher than 8%. The same calculations that established the required amount for Margaret are to be used to determine each year, after Henry's death, if there are excess funds in the Trust. Should this be the case, then the excess funds can be distributed to his children. These distributions should logically be made first from the Credit Shelter Trust since their will be no taxes when the distributions are made in securities.

At this point the need must be stressed for good estate planning prior to establishing the estate planning documents. What has been expressed up to this point is good common sense coupled with financial knowledge. It starts with the ability to ask the right questions.

1.   How much will Margaret need as income each year to maintain the Bright's current standard of living?

2.   How much of this income can Margaret provide from her own sources, Social Security, savings, etc.?

3.   What additional income is required from the Trust(s)?

4.   What amount of funds must Henry Bright place in Trust to insure that Margaret will have the additional annual income she will need?

5.   Is there a way to reevaluate the needs for the funds in the Trust, each year after Henry's death? If there are more funds in the Trust than needed, can they be made available to Henry's children?

These are simple, logically thought-out inquiries about life. You must do this - ask basic questions - when establishing Trusts for any purpose.

Suppose a Grantor had the basic information on how to provide for his second wife, but failed to ask the right questions. Perhaps he believed that in establishing a Trust, he had few if any options.

The Grantor's second wife was 65 years old. Together they estimated that she would require about $23,000 of income from a Trust in today's dollars. At the time it was prepared, all the Grantor's assets were placed in the Trust for his surviving spouse.

When the Grantor died, years later, his estate of $1.3 million went into the Trust. Nothing went to his children. To sufficiently provide for his second wife's anticipated needs, only $600,000 was required to fund a Trust for her. The remaining $700,000 of his estate could have been given to his four children.

The second wife, with a $1.3 million dollar Trust had a greater income than required. This had not been the objective of the Grantor. Such poorly planned Trusts can cause financial harm to the Grantor's children and can destroy the relationship with the stepmother.

A Marital Trust can provide the additional income your surviving spouse will need, while allowing your Credit Shelter Trust to greatly increase in value for your children and other heirs.

A Grantor may want to increase the value of a Credit Shelter Trust for children by using the techniques in Chapter 8. To do this, the Grantor might give a Directive that a high percentage of the assets are to be invested in good quality growth stocks and that all of the fees and expenses of the Trust are to be charged to the income of the Trust.

Total fees and expenses of a Trust have also been projected at 0.75%. This is based on the average value of the Credit Shelter Trust over the first 25 years at approximately $4 million. Over this 25 year period, total annual fees and expenses average $30,000 a year. As a professional trustee fee, this is a high. But we used it to depress the income from the Trust since all fees and expenses of the Trust were charged against the income. This procedure increased the amount of annual payments from the Marital Trust.

Once a Credit Shelter Trust has been funded, there can be assets not required or used for that purpose. A Grantor may decide not to pass these assets directly to the spouse for several reasons: perhaps family members will be given funds that the survivor will require later. There might be anticipated circumstances that could cause the loss of needed funds.

This concern of a Grantor that others might use undue influence to obtain funds from the surviving spouse also applies to other heirs of the Grantor. A 75-year-old widower might be able to leave, after taxes, $1.3 million to each of his married daughters. Suppose he had concerns that they would lose the funds they received in a short period of time. In such a situation, his estate planning documents could give each daughter $300,000 at his death. The remaining funds would be held in two individual Trusts of $1 million each.

The following example is another way to use a Marital Trust. The assumptions made are:

1.   The Income the surviving spouse will need from the Trusts in 1998 is $28,000.

2.   This amount needed in 1998 is projected to increase 3% per year.

3.   The Grantor will live until at least the year 2006. And at the death of the Grantor, $1 million will be placed into the Credit Shelter Trust.

4.   It was estimated that the surviving spouse would live until age 101.

From these planning assumptions we constructed the following summary Table, Exhibit 7. For ease of review, the amounts given are for every five years. The details by year are in Exhibit 7 of Appendix B for this chapter.

EXHIBIT 7

**High Growth in Credit Shelter Trust for Benefit of the Children Coupled with
a Marital Trust that Pays Any Shortage Based on Survivor's Stated Income Needs**

Year	Income Needs From Trusts	Income Paid From Credit Shelter Trust[4]	Shortage Paid Paid From Marital Trust
1998	$ 28,000	$	$
2003	32,460		
2008	37,630	17,197	20,438
2013	42,353	23,386	18,967
2018	49,098	35,811	13,287
2023	56,918	56,746	172
2028	65,984	92,024	- 26,040

Detail shown in Appendix B for this chapter

While not shown above, the total over this 36-year period that would be paid from the Marital Trust is about $410,000. But as shown in Exhibit 7-A, in Appendix B for this chapter, only $290,000 is required to fund the Marital Trust if the amount was invested in bonds paying 5.5% interest. This amount could be lowered if the funds were invested in stocks that paid a total return greater than 5.5%. When definite fixed obligations are required to be paid, a conservative analysis is preferred to indicate the required minimum amount for funding.

The objective of the Credit Shelter Trust was to increase its value for the Children by investing a high percentage in stocks (90%) and charging 100% of the trustee fees and expenses (0.75% in the planning assumptions) to income. Therefore, value of the Trust should be able to provide any shortage of income, if the funds in the Marital Trust are not sufficient

You can state in your Marital Trust that your surviving spouse is to receive the additional funds from the principal of that Trust whenever the income paid from it and the Credit Shelter Trust is below a certain amount.

As shown in Exhibit 7 and in the detail in Appendix B, the amount required to fund a Marital Trust need not be a very large amount if the differences are not great between the needs of your surviving spouse and what the Credit Shelter Trust will provide.

(3)   Planning Assumption number 3, on Page 114, that Grantor would live to at least the year 2006.

As an example, over $5,000 of interest might be earned in the first year based on an interest from short-term bonds and money market funds of 4%. This annual interest would decrease each year based on the reduced value, after annual payments to the surviving spouse.

By not calculating the value of the interest from the funds placed in the Marital Trust, a safety factor is created. This safety factor will allow a 20% reduction in the planned income to be received from the Credit Shelter Trust.

Also note in Exhibit 7, that the income needs of the surviving spouse have been increased for inflation.

The above Exhibit 7 is an example of one use of a Marital Trust funded with a small amount of money to aid your surviving spouse. Marital Trusts are considered when the surviving spouse may not be experienced nor interested in handling the investment of the funds that would be left to that person and to insure that the Remaindermen originally named inherit the Trust.

Using a Marital Trust to Provide for Your Surviving Spouse's Needs during their Lifetime and to Control Who Will Inherit these Funds at the Death of the Surviving Spouse.

There are many reasons why Marital Trusts are established. The most common are to control who will eventually receive the funds held in them.

Today there are many second marriages with children from prior marriages. It is common, when either one or both parties have substantial assets prior to the second marriage, that a prenuptial agreement is signed. These prenuptial agreements generally state that the assets each party has are theirs and that their upcoming marriage will not provide for a claim on the these assets.

However, in many cases the prenuptial agreement is modified by the Trusts that are later established in the marriage.

The first and most common modification is to make a home and funds available during the lifetime of the surviving spouse. If the assets of the Grantor exceed the federal estate-tax exemption, a Marital Trust is established for these assets to be held for the benefit of that survivor. At that person's death the assets in the Marital Trust go to the Grantor's children and other heirs.

If, after federal estate-tax exemptions, Grantor's assets are not sufficient to fully fund the required needs of the surviving spouse in a Marital Trust, then part or all of the funds placed in a Credit Shelter Trust are used.

Both Trusts, the Credit Shelter Trust and the Marital Trust, state who is to receive the final distribution of the assets upon the death of the surviving spouse.

Marital Trusts can also provide funds for the stepchildren, which is something that was probably not provided for in the prenuptial agreement.

Today people are living a longer and a healthier life. Those who started their working careers after World War II may be taking early retirement. Many of these people receive a monthly retirement check from a large corporation or from a government agency.

These retirees had the option of naming their spouse as the recipient of part of that income after their death. This option, in many cases, only provides for the current spouse, named in the retirement papers.

In a few cases married men who retired at age 55 or 60, lost their wives a short time later. If the man was to remarry, his second wife, on his demise, will not receive any portion of her husband's pension.

This indicates a greater need to provide for the surviving spouse in such a situation. A Marital Trust, in addition to a Credit Shelter Trust, can be an ideal way to provide for the second wife.

If the assets of the deceased person are left directly to the surviving spouse, that person has complete control of them. The surviving spouse can later make a Will change and designate who will benefit from these assets.

SUMMARY

To control the investments, the use of, and the final disposition of the funds of a deceased person, a Marital Trust can be used for assets when they exceed the amount of the federal estate-tax exemption.

A Marital Trust can also be used when the Grantor has concerns about the surviving spouse's ability to manage all of the assets that would be left to that person.

When the assets of a person have a high value, other estate planning techniques should be considered during the lifetime of both the husband and the wife. You will find several of these alternative techniques in this book.

Any individual or married couple with a substantial net worth should seek extensive advice on these various estate planning alternatives. They should develop a complete plan for their estate and give careful consideration to available options.

The above Exhibit 7 is an example of one use of a Marital Trust funded with a small amount of money to aid the surviving spouse. Marital Trusts are considered when the surviving spouse may not be experienced nor interested in handling the investment of the funds inherited.

CHAPTER 14

Paying the Gross Income, Instead of the Net Income

Introduction

Most Credit Shelter Trusts or Living Trusts (a Revocable Trust) contain the Net Income provision that will reduce the annual income to the surviving spouse. A Gross Income provision would give the spouse or other heirs a higher annual income from the Trust.

A Gross Income provision in your Credit Shelter Trust will annually provide about 10% more income to the surviving spouse or other Income Beneficiaries. This certainly is an option the Grantor of the Trust should be informed of and should be given the opportunity to select. Nothing is more out of date than the concept that all Trusts must have a Net Income provision.

What is the Difference Between a Gross Income and a Net Income Provision ?

A Gross Income provision requires the trustee to pay 100 percent of the income from dividends and interest on the investments in the Trust to the surviving spouse or other Income Beneficiaries. The fees and expenses of the trustee are paid out of the principal of the Trust.

A Net Income provision does not pay 100 percent of the income from dividends and interest on the investments in a Trust to the surviving spouse or other Income Beneficiaries. A Net Income provision requires the trustee to deduct from the dividends and interest on the investments in the Trust 50% of the fees and expenses of that Trust. And this, of course, reduces the annual income the surviving spouse or other Income Beneficiaries would have received. The remaining 50% of the fees and expenses are paid out of the principal of the Trust

Therefore, a Trust with a Gross Income provision will annually pay about 10% more income to the surviving spouse or other Income Beneficiaries than a Trust with a Net Income provision.

Married individuals who establish Credit Shelter Trusts do so to save $235,000 or more in estate taxes. They do not establish these Trusts in order to reduce the annual income to the surviving spouse. Unfortunately, the financial differences between the Gross Income and the Net Income provisions in modern day Trusts are not understood. These financial differences are explained in this chapter.

The financial and management options in a Trust have a very powerful economic impact on all the heirs and especially on the surviving spouse or other Income Beneficiaries.

Many Credit Shelter Trusts (in a Will or Living Trust) not only have the Net Income provision but are also silent as to how the assets are to be invested or how much income the surviving spouse is to receive from the funds placed in a Trust.

Unless they have ample assets and income available from other sources, a Gross Income provision can greatly benefit your surviving spouse, other Income Beneficiaries and many times, the Remaindermen named in your Trust.

Why Does a Trust Contain a Net Income Provision ?

Why do most Credit Shelter Trusts state that the surviving spouse is to receive the Net Income from the Trust? In most cases, the provision was placed in the Trust without any thought of the consequences.

Unfortunately few people ever ask why, but for the client who does, the answer may be that the Net Income provision is "standard." Grantors who asked why it is standard, may have been told that if all of the income of the Trust is paid to the surviving spouse, the $625,000 in principal (the maximum allowed in a Credit Shelter Trust in 1998) for their children would be reduced. This the Grantor may have been told since 100% of the expenses of the Trust will be paid out of the principal. This would be true if the Grantor gave a directive that 100% of the assets must be invested in bonds. But, at least 50% of the assets are invested in stocks which can be expected to increase in value.

Years ago this may have been so, but now it is misleading. The following sections will provide you with an understanding of the economic benefits of a Gross Income provision in your Trust.

The Benefits of a Gross Income Provision:

In this section we will show that:

1. A Gross Income provision will not reduce the $625,000 in principal for your children and other heirs.

2. A Gross Income provision will allow the trustee to provide the same initial income, when compared to a Net Income provision, for your surviving spouse while providing for a greater increase in the:

    a. value of your Trust for your children.

    b. future annual income for your spouse to offset inflation.

1. A GROSS INCOME provision will not reduce the $625,00 in principal.

TRUE ! In the previous chapters we indicated that the greater majority of Trusts are silent regarding investments. I must add that most "Living Trust" (a Revocable Trust) we have reviewed for clients and most Credit Shelter Trusts in Wills, reduce the annual income of the surviving spouse by including the Net Income provision in the Trust.

These Trusts that are also silent regarding investments are therefore considered Balanced Trusts. This means that about 50% of the Trust's assets will be invested in common stocks. The growth of the value of the common stocks, over a relatively short period of time, will result in 70% or more of the assets of the Trust in common stocks - bonds do not grow in value. Stocks, as a group, increase their dividends as the value of the stocks increase. As a consequence, the actual income paid to the surviving spouse will increase faster if the Trust starts with a higher percentage of stocks.

A valid conclusion is - In a Trust with a Gross Income provision, the actual annual income paid to the surviving spouse will increase at a greater rate than the annual income paid from a Trust with the Net Income provision.

Exhibit 8 contains the Trust classifications of a major U. S. bank. Next to each classification is the "Gross Income" and the "Net Income" that will be paid based on current dividend and interest rates[1]. The difference is that half of the trustee fees and other expenses of the Trust (such as the Trust department fees, Legal fees to advise a family trustee, CPA fees for the annual preparation of the federal and state tax returns that must be filed)[2] were deducted from the annual income received in a Trust with the "Net Income" provision.

With a "Gross Income" provision, none of the fees and expenses are deducted from the income of the Trust.

EXHIBIT 8
Trust Classification of a Major U. S. Bank
Applied to a Bypass Trust funded at $625,000 at Current Interest and Dividend Rates and for the Maximum Amount Allowed in 1998

TRUST	PERCENT		GROSS*	NET*
TYPE	STOCKS	BONDS	INCOME	INCOME
BONDS	0%	100%	$ 37,500	$ 34,375
INCOME	20%	80%	$ 31,625	$ 28,500
INCOME PRIMARY	30%	70%	$ 28,688	$ 25,563
BALANCED	50%	50%	$ 22,813	$ 19,688
GROWTH PRIMARY	70%	30%	$ 16,938	$ 13,813
GROWTH	80%	20%	$ 14,000	$ 10,875
EQUITIES	100%	0%	$ 8,125	$ 5,000

(1)   Current rates for high quality medium-term bond funds of 6% and 1.3% for dividends of high quality stock funds.

(2)   Trust fees and expense of 1% calculated on the starting value of the Trust.

Grantor has the option of stating "Gross Income" or "Net Income" to be paid to their surviving spouse.

NOTE: You may disagree with the above returns on stocks and bonds. But it is based on 1998 stated returns of the Trust departments of several large banks. Few can predict future interest rates and dividends nor the time of their death. It is better to use the options you have and place them in your Trust to ensure a higher income for the surviving spouse. And remember, the new Uniform Prudent Investors Act (UPIA) requires all trustees to invest in large security pools, such as mutual or index funds. Holding about 10 or so stocks is not diversification under this Act. See Appendix E.

A Word of Warning

There can be confusion when friends or relatives serve as trustees. If they are uncompensated the presumption can be that without trustee fees, the Net Income provision will pay the same amount as a Gross Income provision. It will not pay the same. There are other expenses in the administration of a Trust that should not be overlooked.

Most Trusts, with a trustee serving without compensation, state that the trustee can:

> " Engage attorneys, accountants, agents, custodians, investment counsel and other persons as deemed advisable, to make such payments therefore as deemed reasonable and to charge the expenses thereof to income or principal as equitably determined, and to delegate to such persons any discretion deemed proper;"

The above wording in a person's Trust encourages a non-compensated and generally inexperienced trustee to continually engage others for work to be paid for from the funds in Trust.

Most friends or relatives who agree to be a trustee have no knowledge of their legal and financial responsibilities. They would be well advised to seek the counsel of an attorney when they become trustees. Trust attorneys are well versed in the legal problems of and court cases against trustees who do not follow the law and do not document their actions as trustees. Appendix F describes in greater detail the responsibilities of trustees and a few court cases.

The expenses charged to a Trust, even with a trustee who is not compensated for his work, can be many thousands of dollars annually. This is especially true when a trustee wants to avoid any potential violation of their many legal obligations. The fees of attorneys whose advice is sought, the annual filing of state and federal trustee tax forms by a CPA and the CPA's fees, investment counsel fees and the cost of others engaged to provide professional assistance and services can be expected and will be charged to the Trust. In some cases these fees, in total, can be greater than the fees of a professional trustee.

And, if there are questions by the tax authorities or a suit to be defended, the expenses incurred in order to properly answer questions or to defend can be high. These costs are charged to the Trust.

If an action is started against a trustee, the trustee has the right to defend themselves with costs of the defense charged to the Trust.

These regular and normal expenses will be split and 50% of them will be charged against the income of your spouse in a Trust with a Net Income provision.

Furthermore, The new "Uniform Prudent Investor Act" (UPIA) places additional investment responsibilities on your family member or friend serving as trustee to document their investment plan The Act also relieves them of any liability for investments if the delegation of investment authority is properly given to a qualified investment professional. [3]

And the last phrase in the above paragraph referring to activities of trustees serving without compensation is:

" . . . to delegate to such person any discretion deemed proper,"

The above may appear to relieve a trustee of the responsibility by permitting such delegation, but it does not do this except under the provisions of the new Uniform Prudent Investor Act (UPIA).

(3)   If your state has approved the new Uniform Prudent Investor Act (UPIA), your family member or friend serving as a trustee in which the Grantor has not given clear and concise investment instructions would be well advised to engage a qualified investment advisor. See Appendix E.

You can delegate authority, but you can not delegate responsibility. The final responsibility, except delegated investment authority under the UPIA, rests with the trustee. And, the annual expense to the Trust for delegating investment authority will probably be the highest single expense item.

There is definitely a difference between a Gross Income provision and a Net Income provision even when your individual trustee is required to serve without compensation. Just the payment to an investment advisor can equal or exceed the annual fee of the Trust department of a bank.

The following examples indicate that there is a great difference between the income a surviving spouse, or any other income beneficiary will receive from a Trust with a Gross Income provision vs. a Trust with a Net Income provision.

The first example negates the usual statement that "the $625,000 of principal in a Bypass Trust (the maximum allowed in 1998) will be reduced if 100% of the expenses of the Trust's expenses are charged to the principal of the. Trust."

These examples are based on the history of stock prices and the average annual capital growth of the S&P 500 of about 11% [4]. For those not familiar with the S&P 500, and how it is used as a measure of the performance of your stock portfolio and the person who manages it, please see the information given on The S&P 500 in the Appendix. D.

Even if you have some knowledge of the market and the S&P 500 index, I recommend you review the material on it in Appendix D.

The following example indicates that even after annual trustee fees and expenses of one percent are charged to the $625,000 principal of the Trust, it could still increase.

The example also shows that the value of the Trusts would have increased even if the common stock gain was only two or three percent a year vs. their past history of an average increase of 11% annually.

(4)   In recent years the S&P 500 has increased at a much greater annual rate than 11%. However, we are using the historic growth rate.

	TRUST "A"	TRUST "B"	TRUST "C"
Percent Invested in Stocks	30%	40%	50%
Amount in Stocks	$ 187,500	$ 250,000	$ 312,500
Average annual Capital Growth of the stocks	$ 20,625	$ 27,500.	$ 34,375
Less: 100% of trustee fees & Charges (1% of $625,000)	- $ 6,250	- $ 6,250.	- $ 6,250
Net Growth of the Trust	**$ 14,375**	**$ 21,250**	**$ 28,125**
Growth Required to offset a 1% Trustee fee	3.3%	2.5%	2.0%

The above indicates that if 50% of the value of a $ 625,000 Bypass Trust was invested in stocks, it would only require an annual stock growth of 2% to offset Trust expenses of 1%. A 100% stock investment would only require a 1% growth to offset Trust expenses of 1%

The next two examples indicate the actual loss of income to your spouse in a Net Income provision. In these two examples, Trust "A' initially invests 30% of the $625,000 of the Bypass Trust assets in stocks vs. Trust "C" that initially invests 50% of the $625,000 of the Bypass Trust in stocks. Both Trusts invest the balance in good quality medium term bonds. The total expense of each Trust is 1%.

	TRUST "A"		TRUST "C"	
INVESTMENTS	AMOUNT	%	AMOUNT	%
- Stocks	$ 187,500	30%	$ 312,500	50%
- Bonds	437,500	70%	312,500	50%
Totals	$ 625,000	100%	$ 625,000	100%

ANNUAL INCOME	TRUST "A"	TRUST "C"
- Stocks (1.3%)	$ 2,438	$ 4,063
- Bonds (6.0%)	26,250	18,750
Totals	$ 28,688	$ 22,813
Less: 50% of the Trust expenses	-3,125	-3,125
"Net Income" to the Spouse or others	$ 25,563	$ 19,698

But what would the result have been if the Trusts had a Gross Income provision? The $3,125 would not have been charged against the income the surviving spouse was to receive. The amount paid would have been $ 28,688 for Trust "A" and $ 22,813 for Trust "C."

The additional $3,125 would be a 12% increase in income paid to the spouse in Trust "A." And a 16% increase in income paid to the spouse in Trust "C."

NOTE   I have provided for expenses in each Trust of 1% a year. For planning purposes, every Credit Shelter Trust should expect expenses and should provide that they will not decrease the income to the spouse or other Income Beneficiaries. This can be done by using the option of a Gross Income provision in the Trust.

The first example, in this chapter, indicates that a Gross Income provision will not reduce the principal of the Trust. This second example indicates that the surviving spouse or other income beneficiaries will receive additional annual income from a Gross Income provision in the Trust. Your Trust does not have to state that the Net Income is to be paid to your Income Beneficiaries. You have the option to state the Gross Income provision in your Trust. [5]

**There is no sound financial reason for
a Net Income provision in a Trust unless
the surviving spouse has sufficient income
from sources other than the Credit Shelter Trust.**

**A Net Income provision in a Trust
normally restricts income to the spouse!**

(5)   Reference: page 134, "A LAWYER'S GUIDE to ESTATE PLANNING, Fundamentals for the Legal Practitioner" by L. Rush Hunt, attorney, published in 1995 by the General Practice Section, American Bar Association

A GROSS INCOME provision will allow your Trust to provide the same initial income for your surviving spouse as a Net Income provision. The difference is that a Gross Income provision can provide for a greater increase in:

a.   The value of your Trust for your children.

b.   The future annual income for your spouse to aid in offsetting inflation.

At this point you might be somewhat confused, confused because all of your past advice has been that your Trust must use the Net Income provision with part of the Trust's expenses and fees paid from the annual income. And, if you selected the option that 100% of the income goes to your spouse, then the principal of the Trust, the $625,000 you are leaving tax free to your children, will be reduced.

But now you are being told that this advice is incorrect, and that the exact opposite can happen when you indicate an initial payment from the Trust to your surviving spouse. In other words, in this case, the value of your $625,000 Trust for your children can be greater with a Gross Income provision.

Let's continue by preparing a simple financial analysis of two different Credit Shelter Trusts. Each had the same objective of providing about $25,000. to the surviving spouse in the initial year of each Trust. And each of the Grantors of these two $625,000 Credit Shelter Trusts expects that this amount of income to the surviving spouse will increase each year to offset inflation.

The first Trust has a Net Income provision, the second Trust has a Gross Income provision.

In both Trusts, we will use an expected average annual dividend rate from a mutual fund of good quality growth stocks of 1.3% and an average interest payment from an intermediate bond fund of 6.0%. Both the Net Income provision Trust and the Gross Income provision Trust will be managed by a bank with a trustee fee of 1% or a non-compensated trustee who will incur expenses of about 1%.

Example 1.

For a Net Income provision to yield approximately $25,000. in the initial year for the surviving spouse it would be invested as follows:

31.9% in Stocks	$ 199,375	paying dividends of 1.3% =	$ 2,592
68.1% in Bonds	$ 425,625	paying interest of 6.0% =	25,537
Totals	$ 625,000		$ 28,129

Less: 50% of Trustee Fees and Expenses paid out of Income   -3,125

Payment to Surviving Spouse $ 25,004

Example 2.

Now compare the investment mix of a Trust that has a Gross Income provision, below. This Trust has the same objective of providing in the initial year of the Trust about $25,000 to the surviving spouse.

42.6% in Stocks	$ 266,250	paying dividends of 1.3% =	$ 3,461
57.4% in Bonds	$ 358,750	paying interest of 6.0% =	21,525
Totals	$ 625,000		$ 24,986

No payment of Trustee Fees and Expenses from Income   - 0-

Payment to Surviving Spouse $ 24,986

In comparing the two examples above, the major differences are:

a.   To obtain the same income of about $25,000 to be paid to the surviving spouse, the Trust with the Gross Income provision allowed the trustee to invest 42.6% of the Trust in common stocks. In the Trust with the Net Income provision, only 31.9% could be invested in common stocks. The reason for this is that a greater percentages of bonds, with higher interest payments, is required to offset the 50% charged against the income of the Trust for fees and expenses.

b.   The $3,125 in trustee fees and expenses charged against the income to the surviving spouse in the Net Income provision Trust are not charged against the income in the Gross Income Trust. The $3,125 will be charged against the principal of the Trust.

Next, look at the expected end values of each to determine which Trust had the greatest increase at the end of the year. Remember, $625,000 is the maximum amount you can put into your Credit Shelter Trust in 1998.

	EXAMPLE 1. NET INCOME PROVISION	EXAMPLE 2. GROSS INCOME PROVISION
Percent Invested in Stocks	31.9%	42.6%
Amount Invested in Stocks	$199,375	$ 266,250
Average annual Capital Growth of stocks at 11%	$ 21,931	$ 29,288
Less: trustee fees charged To principal	- $ 3,125	- $ 6,250
Net Growth of the trust	**$ 18,806**	**$ 23,038**

Note: No increase in value should be expected for Trust funds invested in bonds. They basically retain their face value.

In the first year of these trusts both Example 1 and Example 2 paid the surviving spouse the same amount of income. But the value of the trust, at the end of the year, for Example 2 is $4,232 greater than Example 1 as indicated below.

	EXAMPLE 1. NET INCOME PROVISION	EXAMPLE 2. GROSS INCOME PROVISION
Starting Value of Both Trusts	$ 625,000	$ 625,000
Increase in Value, End of Year (Based on Net Growth shown directly above.)	$ 18,806	$ 23,038
Trust Value, End of First Year	$ 643,806	$ 648,038

The above only tells part of the expected results. As shown above, the Gross Income provision pays the same amount to the surviving spouse in the initial year of the Trust as the Net Income provision. And the Trust with the Gross Income provision has a higher end-value than the Trust with the Net Income provision. What needs to be considered too, is that the Trust with the Gross Income provision can also have a higher final value for the children and more additional income during the surviving spouse's lifetime than the Trust with Net Income provision.

Look at a comparison of the results years later of the above two trusts:

Key Measurements After	5 years	10 years	15 years	20 years
A. Value of each Trust:				
Gross Income provision	$800,470	$1,044,737	$1,436,170	$2,063,430
Net Income provision	771,068	980,205	1,323,889	1,888,684
Difference	$ 29,402	$ 64,532	$ 112,281	$ 174,746

While the value of the Trust, shown above is greater for the children, a more important measurement is the income difference to the surviving spouse.

Key Measurements After	5 years	10 years	15 years	20 years
B. Annual Income to Spouse:				
Gross Income provision	$ 26,793	$ 29,683	$ 34,314	$ 41,734
Net Income provision	25,754	27,164	29,483	33,292
Difference	$ 1,039	$ 2,519	$ 4,831	$ 8,442

Review carefully the above comparisons in relation to your Trust. There is a significant difference for the surviving spouse and the heirs from using the Gross Income provision.

If you disagree with the projected growth percentage of the common stocks or the dividends and interest paid, make any reasonable changes in the percent growth of stocks, dividends and interest payments, and do it equally in both Trusts The results will still favor the use of a Gross Income provision.

Note: The Detail of the above estimated value of Examples 1 and 2 and the annual income to the spouse are in Appendix B for this Chapter. And, you can test this concept with various interest rates, percent growth of stocks and dividend rates on Estate Planning Program Two. See Appendix A.

A GROSS INCOME provision can allow your Trust to provide the same initial income for your surviving spouse as a Net Income provision while providing, over 10 or 15 years, for a greater increase in:

   a.   **The future annual income for your spouse to aid in offsetting inflation.**

   b. **The future value of your Trust for your children.**

131

A Gross Income provision Trust that pays the same initial annual amount to the surviving spouse as a Net Income provision Trust will have a higher percentage invested in stocks.

The growth of a Trust with the Gross Income provision can be greater, after 100% of the trustees fees are charged to the principal of the Trust than the growth of the Net Income provision where 50% of the trustees fees are charged against the principal and the remaining 50% will reduce the annual income to the surviving spouse.

WHAT TO PLACE IN YOUR TRUST TO PAY THE GROSS INCOME

You must clearly state in your Credit Shelter Trusts or "Living Trust" (a Revocable Trust):

A.   That the Gross Income of the Trust is to be paid.

B.   That all fees and expenses of this Trust are be paid out of the principal of the Trust. [6]

Therefore, today, knowledge of the financial differences between a Gross Income provision vs. a Net Income provision needs to be understood. This is especially true for Credit Shelter Trusts, one of the most frequently established Trusts today. These Trusts take advantage of an individual's lifetime federal estate tax shelter of $625,000. In 1998 and increasing to $ 1 million in 2006. If it were not for this federal tax credit, most of these types of Trusts would not be established.

The prime reason most people have for establishing a Credit Shelter Trust is to save $235,000 or more in federal estate taxes. One would also assume that an equal or more important consideration is to provide first for the needs of the surviving spouse.

(6)   Be careful of wording in other sections of your Trust that refer to payments to be made against income. An example in another section of Trusts that authorizes the trustee to hire attorneys, etc., it may also state to charge the expenses thereof to income or principal as equitably determined (i.e. 50% paid out of the income).

SUMMARY

Understanding the value of stating in your Trust that the spouse is to receive the Gross Income from the Trust is an important financial consideration. It can increase the survivor's annual income.

The Gross Income provision is considered for every Trust except when:

a.   The Trust states an annual income to be paid. See Chapter 6 and Chapter 12.

b.   There are sufficient additional funds from other sources to fulfill all of the income needs of the surviving spouse. See Chapter 8.

CHAPTER 15

Who Should be Your Trustee?

Introduction

Selecting your trustee requires careful planning and consideration of the work a trustee does. The work your trustee does is different from that of your executor.[1] The main responsibility of a trustee is the investment management of the assets in your Trust. Next, the trustee must know the laws regarding Trusts and properly administer the Trust according to these laws. And, annually your trustee must file state and federal fiduciary tax returns. These are the prime duties of a trustee.

The care for, advice and comfort given to your surviving spouse are best given by family members and friends. There is no requirement that only your trustee should do this for your surviving spouse. A professional trustee can provide some of this type of assistance, when nursing homes and other care are required for the surviving spouse. But again, family members can best handle this need and look to the trustee to pay the bills, if needed.

Yet, given the above, most Credit Shelter Trusts use a family member or a friend as their trustee. Why? Is it because the family member or friend has the training and experience in investments, normally devotes their time to this activity and can manage the investments better than a professional trustee?

The answer, honestly given in the majority of cases, is No, this is not the case.. We tend to use a family member or friend as our trustee because of the stories we have heard over the years about banks as trustees. At the time referred to, the

---

(1) An executor is a person appointed in a Will to carry out directives in the Will. These directives generally include burial instructions, the payment of debts, disposing of personal property and distributing the remaining assets as provided for in the Will. If assets are to be placed in a Trust, the Will names the Trust as the primary beneficiary and the executor gives these assets to the trustee. In addition, since a Will goes through the probate process, an executor is responsible for this and it is generally accomplished by hiring an attorney.

An executor's responsibility is to protect and preserve the assets of the deceased that are contained in the Will. The executor is not to invest these assets in securities other than in short-term investments that preserve the capital, such as savings accounts. A trustee does invest in securities and is governed by the directives in the Trust, Trust law and Trust case law.

banks were greatly restricted by law, in their Trust activities and in particular in their authority to invest in good quality growth stocks. Family members and friends are also used to avoid the fees professional trustees charge. These fees can be more than offset by the investment performance of professional trustees when compared to the investment expenses and results of family members as trustees.

But the case for a family member being your trustee should not be based purely on the expense of professional trustee's fees. These fees can be low sometimes less than one percent of the value of the assets

Hopefully the information presented in this chapter will alert you to the issues of current-day Trust management. This may help explain why some of the stories you have heard resulted from past laws that greatly restricted all trustees, including banks.

A BRIEF HISTORY ON THE LAWS ON INVESTING TRUST ASSETS

Most of the investment options a trustee has came about through changes in the types of securities approved by regulatory authorities for Trusts. Prior to World War II, bonds of high quality were to be held by trustees. In the thirties, high quality investment grade bonds paid a low interest rate of about 2.0% to 2.5%. Growth stocks were not held in Trusts unless the Grantor gave specific instructions, which rarely happened.

Many states had "legal lists" of securities a trustee could invest in. After World War II, a small portion of high quality stocks were approved for Trusts. Even then, many states' legal lists did not approve investing in mutual funds. The holding of stocks, as approved trustee investments, has steadily increased since then. Now about 50% percent stock holdings are considered reasonable and appropriate for a "Balanced Trust" to provide fairly for the Lifetime Income Beneficiary as well as for the Remaindermen.

Investing under the new Uniform Prudent Investors Act (UPIA) [2] is based on "modern portfolio theory" and requires wide diversification in stocks. Mutual funds and index funds can provide this diversification.

[2]   The new Uniform Prudent Investor Act (UPIA) rewards your family trustee by relieving them of future liability for investment results if a professional trustee is properly selected. See Appendix E, Section 9.

Stories that circulate about the low income a person received from a Trust were true and it can still occur today, at typical interest and dividend rates if a person does not use their options.

Very few Trusts had provisions for quickly and simply removing a trustee. Part of these changes that make it easier for the surviving spouse to remove and replace a trustee are the result of recent tax court rulings.

MYTHS ABOUT TRUSTEES

Separate laws and regulations do not exist for different kinds of trustees, one for professional trustees and another for those trustees who are family members or friends. The same regulations, laws, and case law apply for all trustees.

The courts do hold professional trustees more strictly accountable, such as banks, since they hold themselves out to the public as having greater knowledge in Trust management and investing.

A family member or friend serving as trustee must follow the laws for Trusts including the Default Rules of their state. This is why it is strongly recommended that a family member trustee seek the advice of a Trust attorney before acting as the trustee. The family member trustee must annually file tax returns for the Trust

KEY ISSUES THAT NEED TO BE PROPERLY CONSIDERED

1. How long will the Trust last?

Knowing how long a Trust will need to last is the first issue to look at when selecting a trustee. The issue is very important when the Grantor does not select the Trust department of a bank or a brokerage firm as their trustee. If a bank or a brokerage firm was selected, the question does not need to be addressed since these trustees can be expected to be in business during the full life of the Trust.

Many Grantors select a relative or friend to be the trustee of their Trust. One or more successor trustees were also named. Generally those selected as trustees and successor trustees were in their late fifties or older. There was no provision in the documentation for either the Income Beneficiary or the current trustee to name a successor trustee.

The following example would apply to most couples establishing Credit Shelter Trusts and clearly indicates that this important issue is generally not properly addressed.

Assume that a Trust was established when a man was 60 years of age and his wife was, for purposes of this example, 56 years of age. Based on a normal life time expectancy, the husband might die first at age 80 or older.

This means that the man's Credit Shelter Trust would become operative 20 years after he signed his Trust and designated his trustee. His wife might live until age 88 or 90 years of age. This indicates that the Trustee will be required for at least 35 to 40 years after the signing of the Trust.

Selecting a 55 year-old person as your trustee assumes that this person would be alive and be capable of serving as trustee when past the age 90. The incapacities of later years need to be considered.

Many Trusts name one of their children as trustee. Assuming that the son or daughter was age 30 or 35 when the Grantor was 60 years old, also assumes that the person named would be alive and be capable of serving as trustee when that person is past 65 years of age. Perhaps a reasonable assumption. But successors are also required. A bank could be the final successor.

When a successor trustee has been named, the same test applies. How old will the successor trustees be 35 to 40 years from now. Will they also be competent and able to serve during the life of the Trust?

Many Trusts do not have a provision for the surviving spouse or someone else to name successor trustees. One solution is to add a provision that allows your spouse to name the successor trustee. This recommendation is also in line with the other part of this issue, that your spouse or someone else should have the power to remove the Trustee (see Chapter 17).

An alternative recommendation is for the Trustee to be given authority to name their successor.

It may be possible to have the Income Beneficiary be able to terminate a trustee and name a new trustee. An alternative is for the surviving spouse to terminate the trustee and for one of your children (a Remainderman) to name the new trustee. One can also consider a provision, in the event the Income Beneficiary becomes incapacitated, for one of the heirs to have the authority to terminate the trustee and appoint the successor.

A brief summary of the duties and responsibilities of trustees is in Appendix F. It is very important that these items be discussed with the individuals the Grantor has named as trustees. Sometimes the person who had said they would serve as trustee, has asked not to be named a trustee after their duties and responsibilities were reviewed with them. And, in a many cases, after learning of the investment duties and responsibilities of their trustee(s), the Grantor changed who they originally selected.

2. Co-Trustees - issues and problems

Many Trusts use "Co-Trustees" such as a bank and a son or daughter or another relative of the Grantor. Perhaps this was suggested by the preparer of the Trust in response to the Grantor's desire to have a family member oversee the acts of the bank or brokerage firm serving as a trustee. Two family members may also be selected as Co-Trustees.

When you name Co-Trustees you are requiring that the trustees must act together - that both are in agreement as to the actions/decisions made in the handling of the investments in the Trust as well as other matters provided for in the Trust document. If one Co-Trustee does not agree, nothing is done.

When a professional trustee is selected as a trustee, along with a family member, it is generally the professional trustee who makes all of the investment recommendations. Before they are implemented, the professional trustee obtains the agreement, in writing, of the other Co-Trustee.

This at first may sound to the Grantor to be exactly what they want - a family member approving every action of the professional investment manager. Or, two family members being in agreement on all investment matters and decisions affecting your spouse, your children, and other heirs.

Rarely does a family member, as Co-Trustee, make investment recommendations to the professional investment manager serving as the other Co-Trustee.

Often the two family member Co-Trustees cannot agree to sell or buy a security. Then, nothing is done - which in itself is an investment decision.

As an example of this Co-Trustee problem, Mary Burns a niece was named Co-Trustee with a major bank in Florida. During the entire life of the Trust, about 10 years, Mary never approved any investment change recommended by the bank. Mary knew nothing about investments. She felt that the original stocks held by her Uncle Harry should not be changed. She did not want to be criticized by other nieces and nephews for selling and/or buying any securities after their aunt, Uncle Harry's wife died. Mary's thoughts were if Uncle Harry believed Pennsylvania Railroad, now bankrupt, was a good stock to own we will not sell it, despite what the bank recommends.

No Grantor wants a Mary Burns type of Co-Trustee. Yet bank Trust officers who attend my CLE (Continuing Legal Education) class continually state that they have these problems with about 5% of their Co-Trustee Trusts (but not as bad as the Florida bank had with "Cousin Mary"). A few banks have stated that their procedure is to advise the Co-Trustee that if this lack of cooperation is to continue, the bank will resign as trustee. In some of these cases, the courts would then select the replacement trustee for the bank since the Trust may not have contained a provision for selecting another bank as a replacement trustee

We could continue with many other examples of problems with Co-Trustees. The Co-Trustee concept many times is less efficient in the management of the Trust's investments. In too many cases, over time, this can result in investment losses in the Trust, reduced income to the Lifetime Income Beneficiary, and a lower value of Trust assets for the Remaindermen.

Consider a "Special Trustee."

You can provide in your Trust for a "Special Trustee(s)" such as family members or friends whose responsibilities are clearly stated in the Trust and are different from the traditional role of a trustee. These "Special Trustee(s)" would have responsibilities such as, caring for, advising and giving comfort to your surviving spouse or other Income Beneficiaries.

If a nursing home or other medical care is required for the surviving spouse or other Income Beneficiaries, this person would visit the nursing home to ensure that proper care was be given. This person would also have the Health Care Power of Attorney. Funds can be provided from the Trust for compensation for the "Special Trustee" and reasonable expenses could be automatically provided from the Trust for presents, travel expenses, etc. if needed.

3. The Work Trustees Perform.

Before you quickly decide who will be your trustee or co-trustees, first look at the work and any professional qualifications required by the work your trustee(s) are expected to perform.

A.   Management of the Assets in the Trust

The most important single thing a trustee does is to properly manage the investments of the assets placed in the Trust. This must be done carefully and by people with knowledge and experience in investing. It requires a great deal of time and is not a casual activity.

Because of past investment problems in Trusts, the new Uniform Prudent Investors Act (UPIA) was written. A copy of this new law is in Appendix E. Since this is a uniform act it has already become the law in many states and is scheduled for adoption by many other states. If your state has not adopted it, you can have written into your Trust key provisions of the Act that you want included in it.

You also have the right in your Trust to expand upon, restrict, eliminate or otherwise alter provisions of this new law (UPIA).

You should examine the Default Rules of your state which are separate from the provisions of the new Uniform Prudent Investors Act (UPIA) and consider those you want to override.

To clarify the above statements, let me use as an example the following:

A.   The Default Rules of most states require the trustee, when the Trust is silent as to how the funds are to be invested, to invest the assets into what is called a Balanced Trust that favors neither your spouse nor your children. This is generally interpreted as placing 50% of the assets in bonds and 50% of the assets in stock.

B.   You should give serious consideration to overriding this Default Rule. Consider placing a much higher percentage into good quality growth stocks. Consider stating the annual income to be paid to your spouse by using many other options available to you and presented in this book.

C.   The new Uniform Prudent Investors Act (UPIA) provides standards for investing the assets in the Trust. In Part 2 (your financial options) we only considered overriding the Default Rules of your state so far as they may indicate that 50% of the assets be invested in bonds, but not to override the investment concepts under UPIA.

A professional investment manager should be considered for the management of the investment duties of a trustee. As discussed in Chapter 17, you can give your spouse the right to replace this trustee.

Under Section 9 of the new Uniform Prudent Investors Act (UPIA), a family member or friend is motivated to hire such a professional investment manager. This law breaks new ground. It relieves the trustee of any future liability resulting from investments of Trust funds if the investment authority is properly delegated under the new law.

It is not sensible to name a family member or friend as your trustee just to save the small fee of a professional investment manager. Start recording the investment results of several professional trustees. Most banks publish this data and will give this information to you free.

Avoiding a small fee for a professional investment manager by naming a family member or friend as your trustee may not result in the saving of a management fee of a bank or other professional trustee. The provisions of Section 9 of the new Uniform Prudent Investors Act (UPIA) encourage your trustee to engage a qualified professional

I recommend you review this new law; and along with it, a few comments regarding it in Appendix E. Review also the types and fees of professional investment managers contained in Appendix H. You may want to reconsider your position.

B. Other Duties Of Your Trustee

Your trustee(s) has also been given the power to provide additional funds from the principal of the Trust necessary or proper for your spouse's maintenance, support, care, comfort, well being and general welfare.

How frequent and continuing will the need be to provide additional funds from the principal of your Trust?

If your Trust is like many it may not utilize your options to properly provide for the income your spouse requires. As a result, continual requests for additional funds will be made to your trustee.

If you have a professional trustee, the professional trustee will require full and complete documentation and justification of the request for additional funds. If a family member is a trustee, they may or may not quickly agree to the request for additional funds. Your family trustee will also be required to properly document the justification for agreeing to provide the additional funds.

There are many valid reasons for proper documentation of requests for additional funds. Professional trustees know this and the future legal problems that can occur by not doing so.

If you have a family member as your trustee, future legal and tax problems can result if payment of additional funds from the principal are made without proper justification. It can be very difficult years later for a family trustee to justify why they gave $50,000 out of the principal, without properly prepared documentation ten years before.

This is another reason why I recommend that a family member or friend consult an experienced Trust attorney immediately when the Trust is activated. Otherwise mistakes will be made by the trustee that can result in legal, financial and tax problems. For additional information on the duties of a trustee, see Appendix F.

Being available to the surviving spouse to answer questions and assist in the surviving spouse's needs is something Grantors like to think their trustee will do. As mentioned earlier this is generally done best by family members and friends. If needed you can provide for family members and friends to serve as "Special Trustee(s)," who have these duties and even make funds available to them.

Be careful in assuming that a professional trustee will be available to do this work or any part of it. Today professional trustees are investment mangers. A few banks still have in major locations a person in their Trust department who will try to assist the Income Beneficiary. However, this practice has been disappearing in the Trust activities of banks.

One very large bank has consolidated their smaller Trusts (those under one million dollars) into a major city and has given the beneficiaries an 800 telephone number to use for assistance.

Brokerage firms have recently entered into this business by establishing wholly owned Trust banks. While they have strong representation through their brokers, I have seen no indication of their using their large sales force to increase their Trust business among Grantors who do not use a professional trustee. Perhaps over 80% of the Grantors do not use a professional trustee.

Your surviving spouse should always have the authority to terminate a trustee, especially a professional trustee, and select a replacement. If your spouse should move, after your death to another state to be near your children, there should be the option of selecting a new trustee convenient to the new residence.

Generally, families rely on their children or friends to provide assistance to the surviving spouse. There is a strong need for this especially as the survivor advances in age. Medical needs increase. Nursing homes may eventually be required.

Few Trusts properly consider the needs of the surviving spouse in later years. In many cases, family members no longer even live in the same area. Children and other family members or friends can be miles apart.

Provision should be considered in your Trust to pay the expenses for those at a distance to visit the surviving spouse in their later years, to comfort them and ensure that they are receiving proper care.

CHAPTER 16

Limiting the Powers Given to a Trustee

- A Special Problem in Living Trusts

Introduction

A person's Trust will usually have articles on the various powers the Trust gives to a trustee. Included in these are references to statutes of the state. An example of this power may be stated as:

". . . absolute, discretionary power to deal with any property, real or personal, held in my estate as freely as I might in the handling of my own affairs, including the power to make tax elections available to my estate. Such power may be exercised independently and without prior approval of any court or judicial authority, . . . Without in any way limiting the generality of the foregoing and subject to (*State's Name*) General Statute, (*Section Number*), I hereby grant to my executor and my trustee all the powers set forth in (*State's Name*) General Statute, (*generally an additional Section Number*), and these powers are incorporated by reference and made a part of this instrument and such powers are intended to be in addition to and not a substitution of other powers conferred by law."

State statutes, such as these, contain very broad powers. Few Grantors every ask about them or read the sections in their state's General Statutes that are referred to in their Trust. They are available in most libraries and in the offices of attorneys. Acquaint yourself with them.

A trustee should not necessarily have the same authority an individual has when they are alive. General Statutes [1] of states are drafted to provide very broad

(1) As two examples, a trustee under North Carolina General Statutes can be empowered to:
> a. Invest in stocks or other securities as the trustee shall deem advisable, even though such investment shall not be of the character approved by applicable law but for this provision.
> b. To invest without diversification - to invest in one type of security or in one company.

This would allow the trustee to hold securities in a family owned or controlled corporation and even to purchase additional shares to maintain control. For additional information on these general powers given to a trustee, see Appendix G.

powers to cover every situation a trustee might be in, due to the numerous types of assets that can be placed in a Trust. This helps when the Grantor, may have required the trustee to hold assets with a high risk.

For most of us, the assets we leave in our Trust are of a type that should be conservatively handled, subject to the directives we place in our Trusts.

Trustees Should Not Usually Be Allowed to:

1. Hold securities in their own name or in a general escrow account that they directly control. If a bank or brokerage firm is not your trustee, your Trust can state that the funds are to held by some form of custodianship or at least an account in a brokerage house with monthly copies of reports sent to all beneficiaries. See safeguards for your assets in your Trust in Chapter 18.

2. Buy, sell and trade in securities of any nature, including short sales, or on margin.

3. Buy, sell and trade in commodities, commodity futures contracts and options on commodity future contracts.

4. Buy, sell, trade or deal in precious metals of any kind.

NOTE: The above powers are stated in Living Trusts for an individual handling their own assets while they were alive. However, if no provision is made to remove these powers in the event of the individual's death, they pass to the successor trustee.

The successor trustee was an individual who had never served as a trustee, as is the case with most Trusts. Would the successor trustee, in reading the Trust, believe that they were to make the above very risky investments? If the successor trustee consulted a Trust attorney, he would be cautioned not to do so. Professional trustees, such as banks, would have ignored the above authority. So why are these very broad and high risk investment powers retained in a Living Trust for a successor trustee - especially a family member with limited Trust experience?

A Special Problem in Living Trusts (Revocable Trusts)

Placing most assets into a Living Trust has been strongly promoted to avoid probate. Many people have done this.

When a Living Trusts is prepared, very broad powers are given in them to the trustee. The trustee in such a Trust is also the Grantor and the Beneficiary during his or her lifetime.

The Grantor of the Living Trust, through the Living Trust, had the power to borrow money and to pledge assets. However, if after the death of the Grantor the power is still required, then it should be restricted to those specific activities.

There should be limitations on the authority of the subsequent trustees. They generally should not have the right to exercise broad powers over the assets of the deceased individual. With a Living Trust the Grantor may trade on margin, deal in futures and speculate in commodities, etc.. Many other examples exist of broad powers that exist in a Living Trust that should not simply be given to the successor trustee after the death of the Grantor.

After the death of the Grantor these broad powers need to be eliminated in the documentation. They should also be curtailed when the Grantor is unable to act for himself.

However, in many Living Trusts these same powers remain after the death of the individual. For additional information on Living Trusts see Chapter 21.

CHAPTER 17

Removal of the Trustee -
Who Should Have This Power?

Introduction

Not too many years ago, a person designated as trustee in the Trust documentation was appointed for the life of the Trust. There was never a Trust provision in the document for a quick and easy method to terminate a current trustee and appoint a new one. The courts could remove a trustee, but strong proof was required of the need to do so. The process was very long and expensive.

The way to avoid such a problem is to include in your Trust a simple and quick provision for the removal of the current trustee and the appointment of a new trustee. Having this power in the Trust can help ensure that your surviving spouse and family will receive proper attention in their dealings with a bank, brokerage firm or other professional trustees.

When a family member or friend is the trustee, this removal power may be required later. The trustee may need to be replaced or forced to improve the management of the Trust assets and their other trustee duties.

A trustee's job is not easy. Laws must be obeyed, regulations adhered to and reports prepared for the beneficiaries and government agencies. There are penalties for trustees, both civil and criminal, who violate their fiduciary duties.

There is an old saying:
> "Whoever agrees to serve as trustee without compensation has never been a trustee."[1]

First - Your Surviving Spouse and Family Need To Be Able To Evaluate the Performance of Your Trustee.

No matter who your trustee is, your surviving spouse or any other person with the power of removal, they need a method to evaluate trustee performance.[2] The results should be discussed with the trustee.

(1)   Author unknown.

(2)   A suggested method to do this is in Appendix D.

A major part of the evaluation of a trustee is how well they are managing the assets in the Trust. Since the only assets in the majority of Trusts are funds invested in securities, an evaluation can easily be made using recognized benchmarks of performance.

You will find a suggested method for doing this in Appendix D. The person with the power to remove the trustee may be assisted in the evaluation by another family member.

Other Events that Require Authority to Appoint or Replace a Trustee

Your trustee can resign at any time. They may agree to be your trustee when the Trust is prepared, but in many cases, ten or more years can elapse before they are appointed. In addition, a family member or friend is often unaware of the full duties and responsibilities of a trustee [3] and usually that person has never seen a copy of your Trust and the value or the types of assets they will control upon your death.

Your trustee may serve for a very short time and then state that they cannot continue in that position. Trustees and successor trustees may relocate and not want to serve from their new location. Individuals, and this includes family members, do change as persons, during their lifetime. Sons and daughters have been known, years later, to lose interest in the family and lose contact with their parents.

If the work is extensive, such as the responsibility to oversee a business, especially without compensation, your initial trustee may use almost any reason to resign at the first opportunity. Those named as successor trustees who become aware of these difficulties may refuse to accept their appointment.

It is for all of the above reasons that in many Trusts, after all the family members or friends are named as successor trustees, an attorney has inserted the name of a bank to be the trustee. If this is not done, the court will appoint the trustee, something you want to avoid.

Below is an example of items to consider in your Trust for the removal of a trustee and the appointment of a new one. The recommendation below and alternatives are also contained in Chapter 24.

(3)   The Duties and Responsibilities of a Trustee are in Appendix F.

SUCCESSOR TRUSTEE [4]

The procedure for the removal of an acting trustee without court order and appointment of a successor trustee are generally as follows:

- The Grantor's surviving spouse is first choice to have the power to remove and replace the trustee and any successor trustee.

- This is generally done by giving written notice of such removal to the acting trustee.

- If the Grantor's surviving spouse is incapacitated and unable to legally act, then other individuals (usually children or other beneficiaries) should be given the power to remove and replace the trustee and any successor trustee.

- You may need to consider in your documentation a provision for a release for the terminated trustee. It may be possible to give the person who has the right to terminate the trustee, the power to give the release. Professional trustees will generally require this and may even go into a court to obtain it prior to releasing the Trust. The concern of professional trustees is that later they could be involved in a suit brought by one of the heirs.

(4) An attorney must be consulted to determine the proper wording for this and all of the other recommendations in this book, that you might want in your Trust. The Trust must be written to conform to the statutes, rules, regulations and case law of the federal government and your state.

CHAPTER 18

Safeguards for the Assets in Your Trust

The following financial requirement should seriously be considered for your Trust documentation:

> All funds and securities in the Trust are to be held by an appropriate custodian or at least be held in a brokerage account .

I[1] am an investment advisor registered with the SEC (Securities and Exchange Commission). As such, I am permitted to hold clients' funds in an escrow account. However, I have always chosen not to do so.

My clients' funds and securities are held with brokerage firms. Each client's account is in their name and is insured. Each month my clients receive a full and complete statement reporting on their account. I receive a copy of the statement from the brokerage firm also. This method is both efficient and safe. The client knows their funds are secure and prefer this method.

The monthly reports of the work the brokerage firms do for me and my clients are similar to what trustees must do. These responsibilities are listed below. Where appropriate, the words, trustee, Income Beneficiary and other heirs have been inserted.

The trustee should:

1.   Take physical possession of the funds and securities.

2.   Notify all appropriate parties and organizations that as trustee you hold the stocks, bonds, notes, etc. and that payments, reports, etc. are to be made to the trustee.

3.   Collect all funds, dividends, interest, etc. and immediately deposit these funds in a money market account or similar account to earn short term interest until the funds are paid to the Income Beneficiary or to be used for other authorized payments or investments.

(1)   Frank J. Croke as one of the authors.

150

4.   Provide a detailed copy of a transaction ledger to all the beneficiaries of the Trust at least quarterly if not monthly. [2]

5.   Provide to all the beneficiaries of the Trust a statement listing in detail all of the funds and securities in the Trust with their current market value at least quarterly if not monthly. [2]

6.   Prepare reports of each year's complete activity in the account for the preparation of annual state and federal fiduciary tax returns.

7.   Annually send the Income Beneficiaries a statement of their taxable earnings and tax payment withheld. Send copies to the state and federal government.

Why would any family member or friend, serving as your trustee, want to do the above work when the Trust departments of many banks will be the custodian and do this work for a reasonable fee? At the very minimum, a brokerage house will hold the cash and securities in an account for no fee.

One respected bank in our city charges one-tenth of one percent a year to be the custodian. They do have a minimum fee of $800.00 a year as custodian. Another bank, not really interested in acting as custodian, has a minimum fee of $3,000.00. So if you want to consider a bank as a custodian, ask about the fees charged by local banks. In your Trust give the ability to your trustee to change custodians. This will allow the trustee to change banks if the current one decides to greatly increase their custodial fees.

Stockbrokers will also serve as custodians and a fee may be charged. For no fee, brokerage firms may handle the funds and securities in an account at their local offices. This no-fee account will provide the first six required duties of a trustee listed above.

A family member, as trustee, can hire a CPA who will prepare and file the annual state and federal fiduciary tax returns. The CPA will also prepare and file the required forms for the reporting of taxable income.

(2)   Unless your clearly state these requirements in your Trust, your trustee is not required to give to your beneficiaries periodic statements on the value of the Trust, and the types of securities and other assets held in the Trusts. Your trustee may assume that you do not want them to have this information since the requirement to provide it is not in your Trust.

Brokerage firms, at the local branch level will do this work, without a fee, based on their expectation that when securities are bought or sold the transaction will be done through their firm.

If you select either a bank or a stock brokerage firm, they may require a copy of your Trust for review by their legal department.

Most Trusts exclude any consideration for requiring that all funds and assets of the Trust be held by a qualified third party.

In many cases Trusts that name a family member, a friend or anyone else as trustee state that:

1.   The trustee will serve without posting any bond.

2.   The trustee is not responsible to any court to report their actions and that such powers given the trustee may be exercised independently and without prior approval of any court or judicial authority.

3.   Granted to the trustee are all the powers set forth in General Statute and that these powers are incorporated by reference and made a part of this instrument and that such powers are intended to be in addition to and not a substitution of other powers conferred by law. [3]

You may have heard of someone invading the funds entrusted to them and using the funds for their own personal projects.

These cases are rare but often start with the person just borrowing the funds for a short time with the expectation of repaying it at a later date.

We may only hear about this occurring with an attorney because newspapers will report their disbarment and jail sentence.

---

(3)   Many state statutes are broadly written and provide for a trustee to operate basically without any checks and balances unless overseen by the Income Beneficiaries and other heirs. This is very difficult to do unless a custodian or a third party is required by the Trust to handle the assets for the Trust and to send reports to all the beneficiaries of the Trust as well as the trustee.

Who audits the Trust accounts when an individual is appointed as trustee? Some state statutes provide for bank checks to be drawn by the trustee and made payable to the trustee. It is stated in those same statutes that the bank or others receiving the checks are not bound to inquire whether the trustee is committing a breach of fiduciary obligations in transferring the money to themselves. A trustee can write checks on a Trust, held in his name, and deposit the money to his personal credit with no questions asked.

If a son or other family members or friends are given $625,000 in 1998 or $1 million in year 2006 as trustee with no requirements to safeguard the assets, who is to know what personal use they make of these funds?

A family member as trustee, in need of money, may rationalize that a large portion of these funds are to be his when his parent dies, so why not take part of his share now or at least borrow some?

Since no reporting is required by family trustees, who will know? If the income for the surviving spouse drops because of the reduced funds in the Trust, the family member trustee can use some of the remaining principal to keep the surviving spouse's payments from the Trust at the expected level.

If the taking of a small part of the Trust was so easy, why not take more later?

Even if the family member as trustee takes no funds from the Trust, family problems result when monthly or quarterly reports on the status of the Trust are not given to the other beneficiaries.

As an example, a woman complained that when she asked her brother, who was the trustee, for a written report on the value of the Trust, he responded, "Don't you trust me, everything is fine." But she and others have never had a report on the status of the Trust.

When a Trust is terminated, generally upon the death of the surviving spouse, the funds are given to those named in the Trust. If a Trust started at $625,000 and ten years later, at the death of the surviving spouse, the trustee states that it is now worth $800,000, what suspicions may arise if no reports have been given to the heirs?

153

Unless major distributions of principal were made to the surviving spouse, perhaps the Trust, ten years later, could be worth over a million dollars, not $800,000. There will always be questions. Such omissions destroy family relationships during the life of the Trust and after the funds are distributed.

Use of a custodian or a qualified third party and the frequent reports they will send to keep all the beneficiaries informed will avoid suspicions and alienating family relationships. These can develop when there is no regular accountability for all to read.

The normal practice for a trustee when terminating a Trust and distributing the funds is to obtain a signed release from the heirs. When this is done devoid of frequent past reporting on the Trust, suspicions generally result.

Once funds from a Trust are taken by individual trustees, the money is generally never recovered. It is very rare that the misappropriation of the funds ever comes to public attention or to criminal prosecution. Family members suffer their loss in silence.

Conclusion

Have your Trust attorney insert in the Trust (in legal form) wording that will require:

- The securities and cash of the Trust are to be held in a bank or in a brokerage firm designated by you in your Trust.

- That this bank or brokerage firm will send, at least quarterly, a report on all the activities within the Trust and the current market value of all securities to all beneficiaries.

- The approval for your trustee and successor trustees to remove and replace the bank, brokerage or qualified third party by giving notice of the their removal.

- All transfers of funds and securities are to be made between the bank or brokerage firm terminated and the newly designated bank or brokerage to hold these assets.

Why would any trustee want to do the work a Trust custodian or qualified third party will do? Why would a Grantor leave this simple safeguard procedure out of a Trust?

If a trustee objects to the above provision for a custodian or qualified third party you can appoint another trustee.

The statement that all custodians or brokerage houses send out have a complete audit trail, by date of every transaction that has taken place in the Trust.

If a dividend check is received on the 15th, the report indicates who it was from and the amount. When this dividend is deposited into the money market account, the report indicates the date it was deposited and the amount.

If income or principal payments are made to the surviving spouse or other Income Beneficiaries, the report indicates the amount paid, the date and the name of the person receiving these funds.

If securities are purchased or sold, the report indicates the date, names of the securities and the cost or proceeds. If a lawyer or CPA is paid for work done for the Trust, the date, amounts paid and the name of the attorney or CPA is given.

At the end, the report gives the market value of all securities held and cash or money fund balances on the date of the report. These ending market values and balances are the starting values for the next report.

Note: Brokerage statements do not necessarily properly distinguish between fiduciary accounting classifications of income and principal. However, when a Trust requires a stated income to be paid to the surviving spouse, increased annually for inflation, as discussed in Chapter 6, the amounts annually paid to the Income Beneficiary become the determining method of payment.

Part Three

ESTATE PLANNING AND

KEY DOCUMENTS TO CONSIDER

*Consider your Option to give your children money during the
lifetime of your surviving spouse.
See Chapter 19 and Option 12 in Chapter 25.*

CHAPTER 19

Removing Assets From Your Estate to
Reduce Estate Taxes

Introduction

There are many ways that you can give assets to your children and others to reduce your state and federal estate taxes. Most are very simple. Others may be a little complicated and must be done properly if they are to be allowed by the taxing authorities.

Should you consider removing assets from your estate? To determine your need to do so, first list the items you own and the estimated current market value of each. Next, make a reasonable estimate of their future values five and ten years from now.

When this is completed, compare the total value of your assets to the federal estate-tax table listed below. If the value of your estate, either now or in the foreseeable future, is over your exemption, you may want to consider removing assets from your estate.

As the table below indicates the percent of federal estate taxes quickly increases as your assets increase over your federal estate-tax exemption.

Examples:

1. If your estate in the future is expected to be $1.7 million, the table indicates that your assets over $500,00 of your exemption but not over $750,000 will be taxed at 37% by the federal government. To this you must add the tax rate of the state where you live. If your state tax rate is 7.5%, the combined state and federal estate taxes rate is 44.5%.[1] This means that of assets in your estate that are $500,000 over your estate- tax exemptions, your heirs will receive about 56 cents from every dollar. And this combined federal and state estate rate will continue to increase for assets that are over $750,000 of your estate-tax exemption.

Compare the value of your estate to the table of federal estate taxes on the next page. Start by determining your highest federal estate-tax bracket.

(1)   There is no deduction for state death taxes. Only a credit from a Table not keyed to your actual state.

2. If your highest federal tax bracket is 55% and your state tax bracket is 8%, then 63% will be your combined highest estate-tax rate. A top estate bracket of 63% means that $63,000 out of every $100,000 in this tax bracket will be paid in estate taxes. However, a gift by you of $100,000 will reduce your state and federal estate taxes by $63,000.

If you want to reduce your estate taxes, there are a number of things you can consider. The methods presented in this chapter are those most commonly used. There are other, perhaps more complicated, techniques. If you have a sizeable estate, you should consult frequently with a tax attorney. New tax laws and recent tax court rulings may indicate a need for you to consider new tax-saving actions.

Federal Estate Taxes (Using the Unified Estate and Gift Tax Rates)

Amount Over Your Exemption	But Not Over	Tax on Amount in Column 1 is	Plus, Percent Tax on excess Amount
0	$10,000	0	18%
10,000	20,000	$1,800	20%
20,000	40,000	3,800	22%
40,000	60,000	8,200	24%
60,000	80,000	13,000	26%
80,000	100,000	18,200	28%
100,000	150,000	23,800	30%
150,000	250,000	38,800	32%
250,000	500,000	70,800	34%
500,000	750,000	155,800	37%
750,000	1,000,000	248,300	39%
1,000,000	1,250,000	345,800	41%
1,250,000	1,500,000	448,300	43%
1,500,000	2,000,000	555,800	45%
2,000,000	2,500,000	780,800	49%
2,500,000	3,000,000	1,025,800	53%
3,000,000	10,000,000	1,290,800	55%
10,000,000	21,225,000	5,140,800	60%
21,225,000	. . . .	11,875,800	55%

Removing Your Home from Your Estate:[1] A Qualified Personal Residence Trust.

The permanent residence and perhaps a vacation home represent a significant portion of most estates. Removing all or part of them from your estate can substantially reduce your taxes that must be paid at your death. Yet you can continue to live in these places and transfer ownership at a discounted amount.

This can be explained by an example:

John and Mary Mahoney own a home with a current market value of $200,000. They also own a vacation home, valued at $100,000. Both properties are in their names as joint owners with right of survivorship. This means that whoever dies first, the surviving spouse will own the two properties outright. There will be no estate tax at the death of the first partner. When the second spouse dies, both homes will be subject to an estate tax at the then current market values.

The Mahoneys decided that they want to remove both properties from their estate. To do this they will transfer ownership to their children. If, however they make the transfer this year, they must use the current market values of their two properties. This is $300,000 and will reduce their lifetime federal estate-tax exemption by that amount. Such a high and unnecessary reduction can be avoided as shown below.

A method the Mahoneys can use to remove the homes from their estate is to deed their homes into Trusts for their children. The value used for gift tax purposes could then be as low as $105,000. The Mahoneys could also continue to live in their home and use their vacation property during the period of the Trust, say 10 years. Any increase in value of the current $300,000 will be out of their estate assuming the Grantors survive the term of the Trusts.

If they wish to remain in their home past the period of the Trust, they can make an agreement to pay rent to the children and continue to live there.

(1)   Since this opportunity to reduce your estate taxes is of interest to many people, a discussion paper on a Qualified Personal Residence Trust is in Appendix I. It was prepared by Alex Webb, Attorney and CPA with Webb & Craven P.L.L.C in Aberdeen and Wilmington, NC. It outlines the advantages, disadvantages and contains an example of the potential benefits.

To accomplish the transfer of a residence and gain the advantage of a low evaluation, an attorney experienced in "Qualified Personal Residence Trusts" must be consulted. The first thing the attorney will most likely recommend is that titles to the home and vacation property be changed from joint ownership with right of survivorship to tenants-in-common.

This change by the spouses will provide an additional "fractional interest" discount on the properties since it results in two separate individuals owning the properties. Their individual ownership becomes part of their individual estates and can now be passed on to whomever they designate. Each can now select a period of time for their part ownership to remain in the Trust before it passes to their children. This creates the first discount of about 15% on the current market values of $300,000 for their two homes.

The second and larger discount is based on the period of time that must pass before the children will own the properties. The general practice is for the wife to select a longer time period in which her part of the ownership will be held in Trust. The husband may select a time period two or three years shorter. This second discount could further reduce the discounted value of the home and vacation property to $105,000 for gift tax purposes.

If the Mahoneys kept the homes in the estate, these property values could increase in ten or fifteen years from the current $300,000 to $500,000 or more. But by properly establishing their Residence Trust, they may save $250,000 or more in state and federal estate taxes.[2]

There is a potential problem. If either Mr. Mahoney or Mrs. Mahoney dies before the ending date of their individual Trust, that spouse's share of the homes will be included in their estate, as it would have been if their Residence Trust had never been established. Therefore, you need to select a reasonable time period for both the husband's Trust and the wife's Trust. This time period would be based on the ages and life expectancy of each spouse when the Trusts are established.

---

(2)   This assumes that the Mahoney's future taxable estate will be about $3 million and that the current state and federal estate taxes will not increase. It also assumes that the federal estate tax on their estate, after a combined federal estate- tax exemption of $2 million (after the year 2005) for assets over $1 million will be 41%. See table on federal estate taxes on Page 160 and this will be increased by state taxes.

Using Life Insurance: Irrevocable Life Insurance Trust

You can set up an Irrevocable Life Insurance Trust to accept policies on your life and remove the proceeds from your estate. If this is not done, and the husband has life insurance policies the wife, who is generally the prime beneficiary, will receive the proceeds tax free if the husband dies. [3]

When the surviving spouse dies, taxes will be due on their estate if it exceeds his or her exemption. For a married couple, this is what estate planning is about - reducing state and federal taxes on estates after the second partner dies. This is accomplished by using the tax exemption on the estate of the first partner to die by deliberately avoiding the full use of the Marital Deduction.

If the wife were to die first, and the children were the contingent beneficiaries, the proceeds of the husband's life insurance would be added to his estate and would be subject to state and federal estate taxes.

To avoid this high taxation, the first thing to consider is transferring your current life insurance to an Irrevocable Life Insurance Trust. You must live for at least three years after the date of the transfer for the death benefits under existing policies to be excluded from your taxable estate.

Once you have established this Irrevocable Life Insurance Trust, additional life insurance can be purchased by the Trust. If the Trust purchases the policy there is no three-year waiting period for the death benefits to be excluded from your taxable estate.

The Irrevocable Life Insurance Trust must be the owner and beneficiary of your policies. The Trust would then provide for your spouse, children and other heirs according to the Directives you place in it.

Always use an attorney to establish an Irrevocable Life Insurance Trust. Until he has completed the Trust for you, do not purchase additional life insurance. When the Trust is completed, the Trust should purchase this new coverage with funds you give the trustee. This avoids the three-year inclusion period.

(3)   Exception: A surviving spouse who is not a U.S. Citizen. Consult an attorney on this issue.

Make Annual Tax-Free Gifts

Another method frequently used to reduce estate taxes is annual tax-free gifts. You and your spouse each can give $10,000, tax free, to as many people as you choose. If you have three children, together you can give $60,000, tax free, to them each year. If you have grandchildren, each of you can give $10,000 to each of them every year (a total of $20,000 to each grandchild).

You can make gifts greater than $10,000. But the amounts over $10,000 will reduce your estate-tax exemptions which may not be a benefit. There are certain types of gifts that can be given above the $10,000 that will not reduce your estate-tax exemptions. These include payments you make directly to schools for tuition and directly to the doctors and hospitals for the medical care of your children, grandchildren and others.

Keep in mind that if you established an Irrevocable Life Insurance Trust and must continue making premium payments, then some of your annual exclusion should be used to avoid having to use your estate-tax exemptions.

Charitable Remainder Unitrusts

Other alternatives are Charitable Remainder Unitrusts. People leave money to churches, charities and other qualifying tax exempt organizations in their Wills.

Often they are not aware that they can establish a Charitable Remainder Unitrust and receive a high income from it for the remainder of their life. If they establish such a Trust they can also designate that after their own death, a second person who can during their lifetime continue to receive the income.

This type of Trust has many advantages. Let's consider them step by step.

1. Increasing Your Annual Income

If you have assets that have greatly appreciated in value and now yield little or no annual income, you can obtain your first benefit from placing the assets in this type of Trust. These assets may be a home, other real estate, stocks, a valuable collection, etc.

As an example, review the results below of selling an asset now worth $100,000, with a cost basis of $5,000. First compare the amounts available for investing after a regular sale and payment of taxes to placing that asset in a Charitable Remainder Unitrust before it is sold.

	REGULAR SALE	SOLD in the TRUST
Sale Proceeds	$ 100,000	$ 100,000
Less: Cost Base	- 5,000	Zero
Taxable Gain	$ 95,000	Zero
State Tax (7.75% rate?)[4]	- 7,363	Zero
Gain after State Tax	$ 87,637	Zero
Federal Capital Gain Tax (20% Rate)	- 17,527	Zero
Gain After Taxes	$ 70,110	Zero
Plus: Cost Base	+ 5,000	Zero
Net Cash From Sale & Available for investment	$ 75,110	$ 100,000

As indicated above, there are no state or federal taxes on assets you donate to the Trust and which are later sold by the Trust. The next important issue is the expected annual income. Let's look at what happens if you invest the proceeds for income after a regular sale and payment of taxes compared to the benefits of the Charitable Remainder Unitrust .

	ASSET SOLD REGULARLY	Same ASSET SOLD From TRUST
Net Cash From Sale & Available for investment	$ 75,110	$ 100,000
Expected Annual Income:		
- Percent	6.0%[5]	8%[6]
- Amount	$ 4,507	$ 8,000

(4)   This tax will vary by state

Footnotes (5) and (6) on next page

The trustee is required by law to pay an amount equal to the percentage payout listed in the Trust document based on the market value of the Trust at the end of each year.

If the Trust's value increased to $104,000, in the following year, the Trust would pay the Grantor $8,320 (8%). If the Trust's value decreased to $90,000, the 8% payment would be decreased to $7,200.

Properly managed over time, the annual payments the Grantor receives, and a child receives as the second recipient, should increase when the annual payout percentage is between five and eight percent. You control how the funds are to be invested. You can be a co-trustee and you have the authority to appoint and remove the other trustee. Because these powers may have tax consequences in some certain circumstances, you should consult your attorney.

Most people who could benefit from such a Charitable Remainder Unitrust may not fully understand and appreciate the advantages and their control over the investments in such a Trust.

You can invest in good quality stocks that over time could produce a "total return" of about 12% .[7] The Grantor receives 8% and the balance (less any expenses of the Trust) goes to increase the value of the Trust. The Trust is not subject to taxes. Gains on sales of securities or other assets, are not taxed. If interest rates were to greatly increase, you could purchase for the Trust long-term bonds and CDs.

2. Reducing Your Estate Taxes.

The value of the asset placed in your Charitable Remainder Trust has been removed from your taxable estate. State and federal estate-tax savings can be over 50% of the amount of the assets placed in it. That means that for each $100,000 of assets contributed to this type of Trust, your estate taxes could be decreased by over $50,000.

(5)   The current interest on good quality medium-term bonds is about 6.0% or less. Thirty-year government bonds, CDs, and saving accounts are currently paying less than 6% interest.

(6)   You state in the Trust document the percent of annual income the Trust is to pay. The percentage must be 5% or more. A common percentage used is 8%. The trustee first pays the amount due from the interest and dividends received. Then the trustee removes from the principal any additional amounts required to obtain the annual 8% distribution.

(7)   Total Return equals the percentage growth in value plus the annual percentage of income.

A Charitable Remainder Unitrust can include a child as the second recipient of the income after the death of the parent. The parent who established the Trust could reduce their state and federal estate taxes by a large amount[8] for $300,000 of assets placed in this type of Trust. They can expect their child to receive an annual income from this Trust for the balance of that child's life.

Stated another way, if the parents left this $300,000 in their taxable estate and it represented an amount over their state and federal estate-tax exemption that would be taxed at 58.6%, the child would only receive $124,200 after estate taxes. To obtain a yearly income of $24,000 from an investment of $124,200 would require an annual return of 19.3%.

If the parent lived for ten or fifteen years after establishing the Charitable Remainder Trust and the value of the Trust increased 3% a year, the 8% income could have increased to $27,000 after ten years and to $32,000 after fifteen years.

3. Tax Deduction in the Year You Donate the Asset to the Trust.

Based on life expectancy tables, you also receive a tax deduction to be used to reduce your annual income taxes. This deduction starts in the year you make the donation. This might be as high as 50% of the value of your donation. You can deduct the contribution up to a limit of 30% of your Adjusted Gross Income. If you cannot use all of this tax deduction in the first year, you have a carryover that can be used in the next five years.

If you name a person in their thirties as the second recipient it will greatly reduce the tax deduction based on the longer life expectancy of the second recipient.

4. You Control the Charities That Will Receive the Funds

All of the funds must go to the charities you, the Grantor, designate. While the second recipient will receive the income during his or her lifetime, they cannot change the names or amounts to be given to each charity designated by the Grantor. Up until the time of the Grantor's death, the Grantor can change the name and amounts each will receive at any time.

---

(8)   The amount is determined by the ages of the recipients.

5. Parental Concerns About a Child's Proper Use of Their Inheritance

Parents with such concerns, when preparing their Wills, can establish a Trust with their after estate-tax assets. However, an interesting fact is the tax aspects when a Charitable Remainder Unitrust is established for such a child by a Grantor in a high estate-tax bracket. The funds placed in the Charitable Remainder Unitrust will reduce the taxable estate of the Grantor, provide an immediate tax credit in the year given, and can provide a higher income for the child.

A SECOND TYPE OF CHARITABLE REMAINDER UNITRUST

If the parents do not need additional income, but are concerned about a child being able to properly use their inheritance, there is a second type of Charitable Remainder Unitrust. It has some very interesting provisions that will allow the Trust to grow in value during the donor's lifetime.

In this second type of Trust, only the income from the Trust is paid to the income beneficiary. A person could establish this second type of Charitable Remainder Unitrust with assets valued at $25,000 and state the interest payout rate at say 7.5%. The child they are concerned about could be named as the second recipient.

In such a Trust, if the Grantor does not need this additional income especially during their working years, they can have different investment opportunities. The Grantor controls who is trustee. That gives the Grantor the freedom to invest the $25,000 in good quality growth stocks, such as the S&P 500 index fund, during their lifetime. At a 10% average annual increase in stocks, the Trust would grow in value and would be worth:

After	Amount
10 years	$ 65,000
15 years	100,000
20 years	170,000

At the death of the Grantor, the trustee then sells the stock in the Trust and invests in bonds.[9] If the parent lives for 20 years after establishing the Trust the

(9) The second recipient, at the death of the first recipient, may be allowed the authority to replace the trustee. This power will insure that the funds are now invested in bonds paying a higher interest. If there is a possibility that the second recipient may be unable to act, a guardian could be established.

168

estimated value of the Trust would be about $170,000. A 7.5% interest rate would provide the child with a taxable annual income of about $12,000. If interest rates on bonds were higher than 7.5%, the Trust includes a provision for make-up payments when they were lower than the 7.5%.

This make-up provision is very important. Any past shortage can be paid in years when the interest received by the Trust is greater than the percent stated in the Trust document. This includes the time when the assets in the Trust, during the Grantor's lifetime, were held in good quality stocks that paid less than 2%.

If interest rates again increase as they have in the past, bonds paying 10% or more could be purchased by the trustee. That would permit the full interest to be paid to the child until the entire "make-up" amount is satisfied.

Special Note

The same privilege would apply during the lifetime of the Grantor. At anytime, that person can have the Trust sell the stocks, invest in bonds and receive the make-up of any lost income should bond interest rates go above the 7.5% stated in the Trust.

This type of Trust established during the high income earning period of the first recipient would reduce taxable income if the trustee invests in good quality growth stocks that pay a low dividend. Later, when the Grantor of the Trust retires, the switch to bonds would provide additional income. A child could be the second recipient.

Family Limited Partnership

A Family Limited Partnership is another method that allows you to transfer to your children, each year, shares of limited partner ownership while you still maintain full control. This may be stocks, real estate, a business, or almost anything of value. This is the only technique where you can retain all the power of an owner, but not be taxed as an owner.

When a Family Limited Partnership is established, you and your wife become the general partners. Based on the fair market value of the assets in the partnership, you give limited partnership shares, each year, valued at $10,000 or less, tax free to each child.

Limited partners have no say in the management of the asset or profits paid out each year. You can give away 99%, as Limited Partnership interests over the years, and still maintain control as the general partners. Sometimes the general partner is a corporation for the protection of the parent.

If the assets in a Family Limited Partnership are increasing in value, the value of each annual gift of $10,000 Limited Partnership shares will greatly increase in future years.

Family Limited Partnerships that hold listed securities are easier to evaluate each year compared to partnerships holding real estate. Also, the value of the gift can be discounted since there is no market for these Limited Partnership interests.

Family Limited Partnerships, Life Insurance Trusts, Buy/Sell Agreements, etc. should only be done with good professional advice. Using these methods to reduce estate taxes, without a competent professional's advice, can later present severe problems with the tax authorities. If this happens, the goals and benefits you hoped to receive will be greatly reduced and even eliminated.

Include, if Possible, Your Children in New Business Ventures

Including your children and your other heirs in a new business venture can have many benefits. A good example that incorporated this idea was the purchase of an operating business

The business had substantial real estate and equipment. Mortgages and other loans were to be used in the purchase of the equipment. The buyer was advised to purchase the assets of the business, not the stock.

All of the real estate and equipment was placed into a limited partnership. The operating company (sales income, inventory and payroll expense, accounts receivable and payable, etc.) was in a corporation.

In the limited partnership, the children were made limited partners for 90% of the value of the partnership, the parent (the buyer) a 10% general partner. The total value of the limited partnership was over $ 4 million. But the debts placed on these assets was very high. Therefore, the $10,000 annual gift covered the cost of each child's share of their limited partnership interest.

The operating company, the corporation, leased the real estate and operating equipment from the partnership. The lease payments covered the debt payments and other expenses such as real estate taxes. Most of the profits of the partnership were sheltered by depreciation taken on the real estate and the equipment.

It was estimated that after ten years, the debt on the property would be reduced by over 60%. And, the real estate, initially purchased at about $ 3 million, would increase in value by at least $ 1 million (a part of this increase would be caused by inflation).

When the above happened, the original debts of the limited partnership were reduced from about $ 4 million to $ 1.6 million (increasing the value of the limited partnership by $2.4 million). This coupled with the estimated ten-year increase in the value of the real estate of $1 million yielded an equity in the limited partnership of $ 3.4 million.

The children's share, as 90% limited partners, was $ 3 million. Even after a capital gains tax, the children's share as a result of this planning would be substantial. Each of the children's share was in a Trust, prepared by an attorney. The Trust stated that only the income would be paid to the child starting at age 21. A third of the principal was to be paid to each child when they reached the ages of 25, 35 and 45.

In this situation the parent had definite control of the limited partnership. He could use the assets for other business ventures and not distribute them to his children and, as general partner, he could place new mortgages on the assets and have the tax-free use of several millions of dollars.

SUMMARY

Estate-tax planning starts with a review of the assets in your estate and their estimated future value. From these amounts you deduct your federal estate-tax exemption, currently $ 625,000 in 1998 and gradually increasing to $ 1 million by the year 2006.

For a married couple this amount can be doubled to $ 1,250,000 in 1998 and $2 million by 2006 by proper estate planning. This is the starting point to take advantage of these combined individual exemptions and using these exemptions in a Credit Shelter Trusts.

When there are substantial sums above your federal estate-tax exemption, a careful plan should be developed and experts consulted. Do not just look at one type of plan. Be prepared to explore other ideas.

But whatever you do, do something or your estate will be heavily taxed.

CHAPTER 20

Other Estate Planning Ideas & Potential Problems

Some estate planning ideas exist that may cause problems within the family or with the taxing authorities or both. When it comes to investing, many people think they are experts. The same is true on methods of avoiding taxes. People can make wrong judgments on both.

It would be a mistake to think that you can add the name of a child to a large asset, such as real estate, savings or securities accounts, to make it a joint account with right of survivorship. Doing this will not automatically allow the asset to pass free of estate taxes. The taxing authorities will require your child to prove their contribution to the asset and only credit them with this amount. The balance is added to the taxable estate of the parent.

Some Uses and Misuses of the Annual $10,000 Gift

The most common technique used to reduce your state and federal estate taxes centers around the ability each person has to give gifts of up to $10,000 every year to as many different people as they want.

When you give a gift it should be a "complete gift," i.e. the person you are giving it to has the full use of it for their own benefit, once you have given it. An exception is giving the gift to a minor. Then, it is held in some form of a custodial account until that person comes of age.

Potential Problems with Giving Gifts of up to $10,000 a Year to Minors.

The primary purpose of these gifts to minors is generally to provide funds for their college education. You must be careful of how these types of gifts are given to grandchildren.

By the time many children are 14 or 15, most have heard that there are funds for them when they are 18 for their college education. Many of these children start to plan to "do their own thing" by buying a new car; traveling and perhaps not attending college right away. In many cases, high school work starts to be neglected.

This can be the result of gifts made under the Uniform Transfer to Minors Act. It is quick, simple and without legal costs to establish. You just go to a bank or brokerage house and sign a form to open the account in the name of the child. On the account the letters "UTMA" (Uniform Transfer to Minors Act) appears after the child's name.

In many states the child receives the funds in these UTMA accounts when they are 18 years old.

An example of a misuse of a large amount of UTMA funds might involve a young boy who at 17 become a member of a "religious" group. Gifts given by parents and grandparents over the years to the boy grew to $100,000. The funds were in a UTMA bank account in the boy's name. His parents were concerned that when he turned 18 he would give the money to this group. A few months before his 18th birthday, his parents made an early withdrawal of the funds. They placed the money in their own name with the hope that their son would eventually leave the group.

But a few days before he turned 18, the boy picked up the family mail and saw a letter from a bank with his name on it. He opened it and saw a notice that a Certificate of Deposit had matured in his UTMA account. The letter asked if he wanted the $100,000 placed in a new CD?

Without consulting his parents, he visited the bank with the local head of this "religious" group and asked for the money.

The bank said the letter sent to him was a mistake, the funds had been withdrawn. With an attorney obtained by the "religious" group, the boy sued his parents The parents tried to delay a court ruling to return the funds to him by hiring their own attorney. They hoped that he would leave this group during the delay. The parents were willing to pay the legal fees, sanctions, interest on the money and other expenses associated with their delaying tactic. They knew that they would eventually lose in court and they did.

As a grandparent, if you have not given the grandchild's parents the maximum gift each year, it may be better to give these $10,000 gifts to them. Or, just put this money aside. Later, you can make direct payments to the college for the child's tuition costs, room and board, and books. Educational and medical expenses paid directly to the school or to a medical doctor are not included as part of your $10,000 a year limitation. When the grandchild starts college, you can still give that student additional money, up to $10,000 a year.

Think what an incentive that could be to maintain good grades. If you have the funds, as a grandparent, you will be able to tell the child that you will pay their full educational costs plus an allowance for all their travel and other needs. That could include the use of a car as long as they did their part by being a good student.

When you add the cost of college, paid directly to the school, and the $10,000 that can still be given to the student, this annual amount that grandparents can give during each college year can exceed $30,000 for each grandchild.

If the real purpose of these funds is education then the above may be a better plan than starting a UTMA account.

If you still want to give large gifts each year for a child's education or other needs, consult an attorney to learn of Trusts that can be established. Laws are continually changing. Attorneys have developed many new approaches to Trusts that have been upheld in the courts.

Giving a $10,000 Gift with Strings Attached

A few individuals have used various approaches to giving gifts with strings attached.

A parent has annually given an adult child $10,000 gifts. Those funds were deposited then by their children into their own checking account. Shortly thereafter, from such an account a check was written for $10,000 for deposit into a joint account with their parent. These checks are maintained by the child as proof of their contributions to a joint account. The purpose of this form of "money laundering" was for the child to be able to prove to the IRS, after the death of their parent, that a certain amount of the funds in the joint account with their parent belonged to them as evidenced by their canceled checks. They then try to argue that these funds should not be included in their deceased parent's taxable estate.

Gifts of $10,000 are sometimes given to adult children with the understanding that the funds would be used to purchase municipal tax-exempt bonds, held in the child's name. The tax-free interest was given back to the parents. If these parents were not so conservative and limited in their investment knowledge, they would realize, for many reasons, that this was not a wise act either. When parents have a combined taxable estate of over $1.2 million, there are better things they can do to help their children.

Using Your $10,000 Annual Gift to Buy a Home for Your Child.

Homes for children have been purchased with these annual $10,000 gifts. Parents might give their child and the child's spouse $40,000 in December and $40,000 in January for the down payment of $80,000 on a home. [1]

One must be careful as to what happens next. The parents should not provide the mortgage. [2] The child should obtain the balance of the funds for the purchase of the home from a regular mortgage lender. If the lender requires it, the parents could also co-sign the mortgage. The parents could continue in the following years giving $10,000 gifts to prepay the mortgage. [3] Each Child could then have a $200,000 home fully paid for in about five years.

Smaller gift amounts can be given for special purposes. You can give each child, when they start to work, annual gifts of $2,000 to be placed in their IRA. In the early years of work, it is difficult to save $2,000. If a grandchild worked in the summer, consider making a gift to match their earnings if they establish an IRA.

As the IRA table shows in Appendix B for this chapter, ten years of IRA contributions started at an early age produces a significant amount of money. Under the new IRA regulations, these funds can be used to buy a home and for other approved uses. Better yet, consider a conversion to a Roth IRA. You can as a parent or grandparent make a gift to pay the taxes on a conversion to the Roth IRA as well as to fund these accounts.

A few parents and grandparents, concerned about the child removing the money from their IRA, have given these funds on the condition that the quarterly statements are sent by the custodian to the parents' home. They required the child to agree not to change the address on the account or use these funds without first discussing it with their parents.

(1)   Each person can give a gift of up to $10,000 each year to as many people as they wish. The father gives $10,000 to his child and $10,000 to his child's spouse in December. The mother does the same for a combined total of $40,000 that year. This can be repeated in January, a month later, of the next year.

(2)   If the parents provide the mortgage, this act could be later questioned by the tax authorities and the mortgage amount could also be considered a gift that was above the $10,000 annual limit. Past mistakes such as low or no interest and other conditions and payment history have been questioned. Use a regular mortgage lender.

(3) '   The child should obtain a mortgage with no prepayment penalties.

Many firms, after a person has been employed for a stated time-period, provide a 401(k) or some other type of savings/retirement plan in which the employee may contribute a certain percent of their pay and the employer will also match part of this amount.

You can assist your child when they are eligible to enroll in these plans by your gifts to allow them to have the maximum amount deducted from their pay. Again the "time concept of money" shown in Appendix B for this Chapter will allow your annual gift, in the beginning years of your child's employment, to greatly grow for their benefit.

You Need a Financial Plan

On Wall Street they say, investigate before you invest. This also applies to estate planning and gifts. A few hours spent with an attorney who practices estate planning, plus the time you spend reading this book and making plans will provide many important financial and management benefits to your family.

Some people with assets of a large amount are not willing to let go of any portion of it during their lifetime. No matter how much money they have, they believe they may need it for medical expenses, nursing homes, etc. As a result, they eventually die with more money than they would ever need and their estate pays high taxes.

If they had been willing to make a financial plan or have a qualified person make it for them, they would have given annual $10,000 gifts to their children; perhaps invested money in a child's business; paid for private schools for grandchildren, etc. and would have probably had a better family relationship. Think of the joy they could have brought to others during a lifetime.

I have encountered people whose investable assets are mainly in tax-free municipal bonds. They have held these bonds for many years, some over twenty years. A few wanted their municipal bonds held in their Credit Shelter Trust. Some consider themselves "conservative" but it may be just limited knowledge. Alternative investments that will have a much greater after-tax return do exist and have a role in conserving assets and their purchasing power.

Frankly in many cases it is best not try to convince these people to sell their municipal bonds and invest for higher gains.

Why disturb the later years of a conservative person's life by criticizing them for holding large positions of their investable assets in municipal bonds, savings accounts, CDs, etc. If they have the funds they need to live on, let them enjoy the remaining years of their lives. Few will change no matter how well you present your case and it is their decision.

SUMMARY

To reduce your estate taxes, you can annually give up to $10,000 to as many people as you want. Together a husband and wife can give $20,000 a year to each child. Starting in 1999 that amount is to be indexed for inflation. It will take several years before a tax-fee gift reaches $11,000. The new tax law states that the benefits of adjustments for inflation will be announced in $1,000 increments.

A few of the many ways you can give these gifts up to $10,000 were shown, such as buying a home for your children and assisting them to own an IRA or a 401(k) account.

Charitable Remainder Unitrusts, Qualified Personal Residence Trusts and many other ideas were discussed in Chapter 19 to make substantial reductions in your estate taxes. An attorney can be of great help after you indicate what you would like to do. Tax laws are always changing.

As stated before, whatever you choose to do, do something or your estate will be heavily taxed.

CHAPTER 21

Living Trusts to Avoid Probate

Introduction

The important option of using a Living Trust as your primary estate planning document was placed last. This was done since many people start their estate planning with the establishment of a Living Trust into which is placed their Credit Shelter Trust, and perhaps a Marital Trust. Yet for many, this was done without any consideration of their many important options presented in the preceding chapters. They selected the Living Trust since it would avoid probate. This is a result of the numerous presentations being made on the benefits of this type of estate planning document.

It is only after you have developed a specific plan and know what you want to do that the proper type of estate planning document can be selected. Without a plan, the selection of a Living Trust will only provide the benefits of avoiding probate and perhaps saving about $235,000 in federal estate taxes, if both the husband and wife have a Living Trust prepared.

Assets that remain in your name will still go through the probate process. And, if the husband and wife have not divided their assets properly, the federal estate-tax saving is reduced and may not even exist.

A few may be confused and attribute another benefit to a Living Trust such as avoiding federal estate taxes. This is not correct.

The same Default Rules will control whatever type of Trusts are established in your Living Trust. Your surviving spouse will still receive the same low income discussed in Chapter 6 unless you use in your Living Trust the options presented in that chapter. None of the more than twenty major options, summarized in Part 4 will be available to provide for and to protect your family unless you consider each one of them and place those you want in your Living Trust.

LIVING TRUSTS

A Living Trust, sometimes called a Loving Trust,[sm] is a revocable[1] Trust and is prepared to protect your estate from probate. You do not save one cent of

---

(1)   A Trust in which the Grantor reserves the right to revoke the entire document; withdraw any property transferred to the Trust, or change any or all of the terms of the Trust.

estate taxes over a Credit Shelter Trust or other options available to you in a Will.. Avoiding probate is accomplished by changing the title of assets to the name of the Living Trust. Each asset's title must be properly changed to the name of the Trust in order to avoid probate for that asset. However, your ownership and all your rights to those assets in your Living Trust will not change.

As an example suppose there are many different stocks and bonds that you own and want to put into your Living Trust. When this transfer is completed the securities will avoid the probate process. If these securities are in your account at a brokerage house, you would notify the brokerage house to change the title of your account to the name of your Trust. This is the only act required. You must be absolutely sure it is done. Your following monthly statements should be in the title of your Living Trust.

Nothing else changes. You still have all the rights you had when the account was in your name. If you have check-writing privileges and a credit card with your brokerage account, you can still have them or obtain them. There is no tax event caused by the title change. The interest, dividends and capital gains are still reported to you each year and as usual, go on your tax return. The only difference is that the title of your account has changed

You continue to call your broker with your instructions when you want to buy or sell a security or have a check sent to you. The checks you write on your account or the credit card purchases you make are still signed by you. However, you sign as your trustee. Nothing else has basically changed.

This holds true if you want to remove some or all of the securities from your Living Trust. You can quickly do so just as you might have done before. If you want to make changes in any part of your Living Trust or even cancel it, you can also quickly do so.

This basically is the work required for each asset you own if you do not want it to go through probate. Avoiding probate is the major reason for establishing a Living Trust. Don't be fooled by any statements that a Living Trust avoids estate taxes. This is not true.

Before a married person transfers any assets to their Living Trust, that person must first have an overall plan on how the value of the assets fits into the combined estate-tax exemptions of both parties in the marriage. Couples with total assets of $1.2 million or more establish "Credit Shelter Trusts" within their Living Trust to save $235,000 in federal estate taxes. Often their assets are not properly distributed and placed in each person's Living Trust. If this is the case, they cannot take full advantage of the federal estate-tax benefits that the husband and the wife each have. Due to this mistake, their $235,000 federal tax saving may be lost.

Assets a married couple own that are held jointly with right of survivorship (such as their home) pass to the surviving spouse without going through probate. If your want to include your part of the property jointly held in your Living Trust, a change from joint to individual ownership must be made. Your individual ownership share must then be in the name of your Living Trust.

Other assets you own that name a beneficiary such as life insurance, IRAs and other retirement accounts do not go through probate.

Living Trusts can have many benefits. Living Trusts can also present many problems. One major cause of problems is that the very broad powers given to the Grantor during his or her lifetime are not reduced and restricted after the Grantor's death. Usually there is no provision in the Trust to do this once the Grantor has died.

In Living Trusts the Grantor's emphasis is on having the fullest range of powers to act during their lifetime. As an example, authority is given to the Grantor to:

1. Hold securities of any type in the Living Trust.

2. Buy, sell and trade in securities of any nature, including short sales, and on margin.

3. Buy, sell and trade in commodities, commodity futures contracts and options on commodity future contracts.

4. Buy, sell, trade or deal in precious metals of any kind.

Most Grantors of a Living Trust do not use these very broad powers to engage in high risk investments. But they are there if ever the Grantor wanted to use them. The problem is that none of these powers are removed in the event of the individual's death. As a result, these powers are passed to the trustee. If your trustee is inexperienced in Trust work and not properly guided, they may believe that you intended them to use these powers and engage in high risk investments.

The same problem exists with Trusts established in your Will. These Trusts, both in your Will or in your Living Trust generally state that they are to be governed by the state statutes which were discussed several times.[2] The state statutes give very wide authority to the trustee. Many of these wide-ranging powers in the state statutes can be controlled by the Grantor. This is done by clearly stating in the Trust what is permitted to happen after the Grantor dies.

A "Living Trust" is actually a "Revocable Trust."

After you establish this Revocable Trust called a Living Trust, anything you put into it you can remove at a later date. You lose no control over the assets.. You are the Grantor; the trustee; and the beneficiary of the Trust. Your tax identification number does not change. It is your Social Security number and remains so.

After your attorney prepares your Revocable Living Trust, make sure the assets you want to include in it are actually put in it. In many cases, a Grantor established a "Living Trust" and initially funded it with $10.00 in the attorney's office but then neglected to add any other assets. As a result, everything went through probate.

You add these assets to your Revocable Trust by having the title to each of them changed.

For assets in your name as *JOHN D. DOE*, the title would be changed to:

"JOHN D. DOE , REVOCABLE TRUST AGREEMENT
  Dated: Month, Day, Year
JOHN D. DOE , Trustee
FOR THE BENEFIT OF JOHN D. DOE
Street address
City, State and Zip code
Tax Identification No.: (Your Social Security Number)

Your attorney can help you with this and provide certificates for your use to change the title of each asset you wish to place into your Revocable Living Trust.

---

(2)   See Appendix G.

For real estate titles, your attorney can have the records changed to place their title in the name of the Trust. This is especially important and saves time and expense for property that may be located in another state.

After your death, many issues in your Living trust will be controlled by the Default Rules of your state just the same as they control the Credit Shelter Trust created in your Will.

There is basically only one benefit from a Living Trust. You escape probate for the assets you actually placed in the Living Trust. If you own property in another state, you avoid going through a second probate in that state.[3]

A Living Trust contains provisions found in other estate planning documents such as a power for another person to act for you as a successor trustee of your Living Trust when you are unable to do so. This power only relates to those assets in your Living Trust. Therefore, it is not a replacement for a Durable Power of Attorney that will apply to assets not in the Living Trust.

You first need to carefully plan what you want to have happen with your estate prior to having a Living Trust or any other type of Trust prepared.

Unfortunately many people have not done so and do not realize the many planning errors that can result in their Living Trust, and other estate planning documents.

(3)   Property owned in another state, after your death that is titled in your name must go through probate in that state. This can be avoided when the property is properly placed in your Living Trust. Consult your attorney on this.

183

CHAPTER 22

Durable Powers of Attorney, Pour-Over-Wills and Medical Directives

Introduction

The basic set of estate planning documents are listed and explained below. All are revocable documents. The term revocable means that the Grantor can change, modify or cancel these basic documents at any time

There is another set of estate planning documents that are irrevocable. Grantors who have executed such documents cannot change them. Of course there are indirect ways to terminate a few of them such as an ILIT (Irrevocable Life Insurance Trust). Usually, the only asset in an ILIT is an insurance policy. If you do not continue to pay the premiums to the trustee, the policy is either canceled by the insurance company or has a reduced value.

In addition to those mentioned above and discussed in this book, there are other types of Trusts. These are mainly used by people of great wealth.

The Basic Set of Estate Planning Documents - All Revocable

Will or Pour-Over-Will

Whether your decision involves a Will or a Pour-Over-Will, either document should be properly prepared with the assistance of an attorney in your state of residence. A Will appoints an executor of your estate and successor executors if the initial person so named is unable to serve. It states how your assets are to be distributed and if there are beneficiaries who are minors, it names trustees or guardians of the funds for those minors. A Will may name the trustee and successor trustees for any special Trust you established such as a Credit Shelter Trust and a Marital Trust. Terms and conditions for investing, managing and payments from these Trusts are contained in the prior chapters.

If you have a Living Trust, a Pour-Over-Will is also prepared since there are generally some assets still remaining in your name and not in the Trust. Though you may think that you have all of your assets in your Living Trust, a Pour-Over-Will provides protection in the event that such is not the case.

Both the Will and the Pour-Over-Will go through the probate process.

Durable General Power of Attorney

A Durable General Power of Attorney is an important document. It gives the person whom you designate as your agent very broad powers to act for you during your lifetime should you become disabled or incompetent. In these circumstances, the person you designate has the power to mortgage, sell or otherwise dispose of any real or personal property without advance notice to you or approval by you.

Each State has statutes that authorize and fully describe powers granted in this document. Since a Durable General Power of Attorney has such broad powers, it must be properly prepared, witnessed and notarized.

A place for safekeeping this type of document can be the safe deposit box of the law firm. Some attorneys I have dealt with offer to do this for clients and the reasons are good. One attorney, who offered this service, told me that the daughter of an elderly client attempted to sell her mother's home. He contacted the mother and determined that she was able to handle her own affairs. The daughter had decided that her mother should sell the large home and move to a smaller residence. The Mother did not agree. So, the daughter thought she could force this to happen if she had the Power of Attorney.

A "Durable General Power of Attorney" usually does not authorize anyone to make medical or other health care decisions for you. If you want this done, you must sign a "Heath Care Power of Attorney," discussed below.

Health Care Power of Attorney

The Health Care Power of Attorney is also an important legal document. You should be aware that it gives the person whom you designate as your agent very broad powers to make health care decisions for you when you are no longer capable of doing that for yourself.

The person named must act consistently with your desires, as sometimes stated in the document, or otherwise known to them. Unless you state otherwise, the person named has the same authority to make decisions about your health care as you would have done.

The person you appoint should be someone you know and trust. You should discuss this document with them. You have the right to revoke the authority given in the document. You do so by notifying the person you selected (your agent) or notifying your attending physician, the hospital, or other heath care provider, either orally or in writing of the revocation.

Important

1. The person(s) you have selected as your agent may need this document immediately in case of an emergency that requires a decision concerning your health care. You should keep the document where it is immediately available to those you have named. One solution is to give each person selected an executed copy of it. You may also want to give an executed copy of this agreement to your physician. Some people keep a copy in the glove compartment of their car when they travel.

2. If you are married and your spouse has established a Trust for you, consider including instructions in the Trust to pay the expenses of the person(s) you have selected for the responsibility of Health Care Power of Attorney. Generally a son or daughter is chosen as your agent. Years later, they may live hundreds of miles away. They could incur substantial travel and living expenses while making sure you have the best care. As your agent, they have access to your records; can obtain the opinions of other specialists and, if required, have you moved to a major hospital in another city for treatment. They should be with you at this critical time. The payment of their expenses for this activity should be in a Trust or other documents.

This document may be called by other names such as "Health Care Proxy" in New York State.

Living Will

A Living Will is another important document. Most states have recently passed legislation that supports a person's right to determine if extraordinary means should be used to maintain their life or if they wish a natural death. It addresses the issue of a person being in an incurable or irreversible mental or physical condition with no reasonable expectation of recovery.

The conditions for its use are if:

1.   You are in a terminal condition.

2.   You are permanently unconscious, or

3.   You are conscious but have irreversible brain damage and will never regain the ability to make a decision and express your wishes.

OTHER ESTATE PLANNING DOCUMENTS - IRREVOCABLE

These are documents that once executed cannot be changed. However, as indicated in the introduction to this chapter, there are indirect ways to terminate a few of them such as an Irrevocable Life Insurance Trust.

Many of these irrevocable trusts were discussed in greater detail in Chapter 19 "Removing Assets from Your Estate to Reduce Estate Taxes."

Removing Your Home from Your Estate (see page 161)

This is called a "Qualified Personal Residence Trust" (QPRT)

Using Life Insurance (see page 163)

This is called an "Irrevocable Life Insurance Trust" (ILIT)

Tax-Free Gifts (see page 164)

Charitable Remainder Trust "CRT" (see page 164)

Family Limited Partnership "FLP" (see page 169)

Grantor Retained Annuity Trust (GRAT)

This Trust allows you to transfer assets that produce a fixed amount of income to a Trust for a set number of years. The assets are in the Trust and at the end of the Trust term the assets go to the beneficiaries of the Trust. The beneficiaries are generally your children or other heirs.

You receive the income during the term of the Trust. If you die before the end of the Trust term, the assets in the Trust, at the current market value on the date of your death, go back into your estate and are taxed as part of your estate. The Trust is terminated. Therefore the Grantor should not establish an unreasonably long time period for the Trust.

The advantage of this type of Trust is that an effective discount is gained on the future value of the assets since your beneficiaries will not receive the value of the gift until the Trust terminates.

Types of assets placed in a Grantor Retained Annuity Trust are generally bonds or other types of assets that pay a fixed annual income.

Grantor Retained Unitrust (GRUT)

This Trust is similar to the "Grantor Retained Annuity Trust" described above. The difference is that the income from the assets placed in the Trust is not fixed. It generally increases as it would from a portfolio of stocks whose dividends gradually increase.

It is a more commonly used Trust than a Grantor Retained Annuity Trust (GRAT). It allows the Grantor to place stocks that are expected to appreciate in value, say over a ten or fifteen year period, into the Trust. The value of the assets placed in the Trust are removed from the Grantor's estate. The value of the inheritance is discounted since the children or other heirs will not receive the funds for a set number of years.

The Grantor receives the income during the term of the Trust. If you die before the end of the Trust term, the assets in the Trust at the current market value on the date of death go back into the estate and the Trust is terminated.

NOTE: In both the GRAT and the GRUT, above, if a Grantor dies during the term and the assets are put back in your estate, then any credit shelter used on the initial gift is also restored to your estate.

Charitable Lead Trust (CLT)

In this type of Trust the income from the assets placed in it go to a charity for a stated number of years. A Charitable Lead Trust also removes the assets from your estate and reduces estate taxes. At the end of the Trust period the assets then go to those you have named.

From the moment the Trust is established the assets in it are out of your estate.

There are other more sophisticated estate planning techniques for those with assets of many million of dollars. Consult an attorney who specializes in this area of estate taxes and asset protection.

If any of these techniques are used with offshore considerations again, you will require the services of an attorney who specializes in this. Do not simply rely on the services of someone employed by the provider of these offshore accounts and Trusts.

PART FOUR

OPTIONS TO HELP ACCOMPLISH

YOUR OBJECTIVES

Her Trust income was just to low
She had to let the limo go.

Chapter 23

Why These Options Should Be Considered

Introduction

If you are planning a Trust, the following financial and management options should be considered. These are the options not found in the preprinted forms sold on the Internet or at the stationers.. When you use these Trust forms, most of the very important issues you should consider for your family are missing. As a result, your Trust will be governed and controlled by the Default Rules of the state.

You cannot expect to find these options in Trusts prepared by an attorney when you, the Grantor, have not planned what you want your Trust to accomplish.

If you are not prepared, an attorney can only provide you with the basic elements for your Trust. He can make sure that the documents are legally correct, contain appropriate references to new and existing regulations, as required by Trust law, and are properly executed.

A Trust tailored to your specific needs is hampered by the public's misconception that they have no options and that with few exceptions all Trusts are the same. Because of this misconception the public shops around for an attorney who will prepare their estate planning documents for the lowest fixed fee.

State bar associations need to consider educating the public about their options. Most of the current bar association brochures on estate planning, Wills and Trusts do not address the many important options a Grantor has and the need for planning your Trusts. The omissions by the legal community in providing information on the numerous financial and management options a Grantor has reinforces the public's misconception of this most important issue.

Some of the options presented in the next chapter can apply to every Trust. Many are common to two types of Trusts, the Credit Shelter Trust and the Marital Trust. These types of Trusts are the foundation of estate planning. They can be used by anyone who has an estate that they wish to leave for the benefit of family and other heirs and to reduce estate taxes.

Additional types of Trusts can be used if your assets are over your federal estate-tax exemption.

We have gathered these options from throughout the book as a checklist. The list is followed by options for certain specific types of situations.

A Trust attorney must be consulted to draft the proper legal wording to accomplish your objectives. You must make sure that the wording in the attorney's draft preserves the intent of each option you select.

The laws that control your Trust are mostly state laws. These state laws that a Grantor needs to be first concerned about are Default Rules. Many of these Default Rules have been discussed in this book. Options you can consider to override them have been presented.

Limits and restrictions on your personal federal estate-tax exemption; generation skipping amounts; the 5 and 5 power and other tax-related issues are based on federal law, Treasury / IRS ruling, and federal tax court cases. State laws also apply in these situations. As an example, a Grantor's personal estate-tax exemption for a state is established by the state and may vary from the federal amount.

If you read a Trust, you will note extensive references to federal tax issues and citations to the federal tax code. It may appear that only a minor reference is made to the general statutes of your state of residence. This is important to know.

If you neglect to clearly state what you want in any vital area of your Trust, the provisions of local law (not federal law) apply.[1] Local law is state law. These state laws are "Default Rules" that we have discussed throughout this book. If your Trust is "silent" (a term the legal profession uses to mean that you neglected to clearly state in the Trust document what you want to have happen) then the statutes, regulations, and case law of that state will regulate your Trust.

Among the states, there are differences in some of the Default Rules in estate tax exemptions; annual taxes on assets in the Trust; who is allowed to witness your Will[2] and other areas of state Trust law.[3]

(1)   Review the section on "Laws Governing Trusts,"in Chapter 2 and in particular Page 15 - Under Federal Law,   ". . If a Trust is silent as to authorized investments, the trustee is guided by provisions of local law."

(2)   In many states an heir is allowed to witness your Will. This is not allowed in all states. If your Will was executed in a state that allowed your son or daughter as a witness, that Will may not be valid if submitted for probate in a state that did not permit such a witness.

(3)   One example is the "Uniform Prudent Investor Act," a new and important Act to protect the assets in Trusts. It is a Default Rule. It has not yet been adopted in several states. See Section E of the Appendix.

Chapter 24

Options that Should Be
Considered in Every Trust

We have recommended the following options in Trusts. At first it may not appear that there is neither a need nor a proper place to insert these options in special types of Trusts such as Charitable Remainder Trusts or a Grantor Retained Unitrust. Your attorney can help you resolve this.

The first option allows you to move to another state without the expense of rewriting your Trust. Most important, after your death the Trust is not locked-in forever to the laws, annual taxes, etc. of one state.

This can be important when you establish a Living Trust. The same recommendation of using Option 1 would apply to other types of Trusts, some of which are irrevocable, such as a Charitable Reminder Trust. Your Trusts always contains references to the statutes of a state whose laws cover many Trust issues. Some of those state laws either now or in the future may have disadvantages for your heirs. For this reason you always want to be able to change the state of jurisdiction that controls your Trust

OPTION 1 - The Ability to Change the State that Controls Your Trust

- Your current residence generally determines the state that controls your Trust. At some later date you may want to move out of the state and you should be able to direct that this new state of residence will control your Trust. This is done by an instrument, such as a letter signed by you, as trustee, of your Living Trust and filed with the Trust records. You can do this to avoid having a new Trust prepared.

- The reasons for this change may be for your own tax benefits, for your heirs or for any reason you deem appropriate. You as trustee of your Living Trust should have this authority. Later, after your death, it is possible that your surviving spouse may move to another state or a successor trustee may already be in another state. You want the option to change the jurisdiction of your Trust if it is of benefit to do so.

- Changing the state of jurisdiction is done by putting into your document the ability to do so. This will apply to any part of the property of the Trust, including real estate. States do not like to release control of real estate in their jurisdiction. But they may be forced to do so if the above option properly worded by your attorney is included in your Trust.

I am indebted to Alex Webb,[1] an attorney and CPA practicing in Aberdeen and Wilmington, North Carolina, for permission to use his material of the important option that follows:

Construction

The terms and provisions of this Agreement (TRUST) shall be construed, regulated and governed as to administration and as to validity and effect by the laws of the State of *(Name of State)*. To minimize any tax in respect to this trust, or any beneficiary thereof, or for such other purpose as it deems appropriate, the Trustee may in its sole and absolute discretion remove all or any part of the property of or the situs of administration of, such trust from one jurisdiction to another and elect, by an instrument filed with the trust records, that thereafter such trust shall be construed, regulated and governed as to administration by the laws of such other jurisdiction. Furthermore, if the trustee is changed to a trustee in another jurisdiction, then in the instrument of appointment, the applicable law may be changed to such new jurisdiction or remain the law of *(Name of State)* as the parties thereto elect.

OPTION 2   - To Safeguard the Assets in Your Trust and Maintain Strong Family Relationships.

As discussed in chapter 16, Option 2 should be considered in Trusts that use a family member or friend as trustee. If you use Option 2 -A (below) there will be custodian fees to pay to those who serve in this capacity. Such services can range from $1,000 to $3,000 or more per year for this service. Discuss with the potential custodian what the charges will be and what services are offered.

(1)   Alex Webb has suggested other important considerations for clients to place in their estate planning documents.

Option 2-A   If You Want a Bank or Brokerage Firm to Serve as the Custodian

- State in the Trust the name of the bank or brokerage firm you have selected to be the custodian of your Trust.

- Consider requiring that the custodian you select is to send, at least quarterly, a report on all the activities within the Trust and the current market value of all securities to your trustee, Income Beneficiary and all other heirs.

- You can give your trustee or others the power to terminate the current custodian and appoint a new custodian.

- You can instruct that all transfers of assets are to be made from one custodian to the other.

Option 2-B   If You Do Not Want to Pay a Custodian's Fee.

- State in the Trust the name of the brokerage firm[1] that you have selected to hold the account. You may name the specific broker you want to have the account (provided that the person is available when the Trust is funded).

- You can require that the brokerage firm you select is to send, at least quarterly, a report on all the activities within the Trust and the current market value of all securities to your trustee, Income Beneficiary and all of the other heirs.

- You can give your trustee or others the power to terminate the current brokerage firm and appoint a new brokerage firm.

- You can require that all transfers of assets are to be made from one brokerage firm to the other.

(1)   It is recommended that you use a brokerage house with SIPC (Securities Investors Protection Corporation) insurance for the funds and securities in the Trust.

OPTION 3 - Investment of Trust Assets

When securities are held in a Trust, the Grantor generally has a right to state what kind they will be. If the Grantor neglects to give this type of instructions, the Default Rules will most probably govern the selection and percentages of investments in types of securities to be held in the Trust. This could include the requirement of holding in the Trust 50% of the funds in bonds.

This issue of instructions for the investment of Trust assets is important and will be addressed several times.

- You can require that at least 75% or more of the investable assets be invested in good quality growth stock mutual funds, stock index funds and good quality stocks. Capital appreciation would then be the objective of the investments in the Trust.

- You can state that the initial amount of bonds, based on the initial allocation percentage should not be increased in amount as the total value of the Trust increases due to the growth in the value of the stocks.

OPTION 4 - Removal of Your Trustee and the Appointment of a New Trustee

When the surviving spouse is not the sole trustee, the Trust can contain a simple and quick provision for the removal of the current trustee and the appointment of a new one.

Your trustee can resign at any time. A trustee selected ten years ago may not be able to serve. Who will be the replacement trustee? Two or more names may be given in the Trust to assure that one will be available as a back-up trustee.

The procedure for removing the trustee and appointing a new one must be clearly stated in the documentation.

- In many cases the surviving spouse is given the right to do this. The current trustee is removed and the new trustee is appointed.

- In the event that the surviving spouse is unable to act, several others are named in order of succession.

- If none of the above are able to function there is generally a procedure used, such as a majority of the beneficiaries of the Trust acting to select the new trustee. Or you can name a bank as a back-up trustee. Whatever you do, stipulate some procedure in the Trust or the courts must appoint the new trustee.

NOTE: The above recommendations are made for Trusts in which the surviving spouse is not the sole trustee. In Trusts, where another person or entity is the trustee and you do not want your surviving spouse to have the power both to terminate and to replace the trustee, you can insert, as an alternative, the following.

- A. The Grantor's spouse can remove the trustee.

- B. The Grantor's son or daughter will appoint the successor trustee.

NOTE: If the authority is divided, the surviving spouse should generally be the one to initiate the process of terminating the trustee. The needs of your surviving spouse come first. That person should be given the opportunity to not only say that they want the current trustee terminated, but also they should have the authority to make it happen.

NOTE: **It is very important that you consult with an attorney on this issue. A trustee has certain rights and may object to the termination without first obtaining a release. Professional trustees, as a normal business practice may even go to court to obtain a release since they can later have a potential claim against them that could be expensive to defend, despite the fact that they did nothing wrong.**

Wording could be considered in the Trust that would permit a person, such as the one terminating the trustee, to sign a release based on their judgement at that time. Naturally, if the heirs felt something was improperly done, a release would not be signed.

OPTION 5 - Fiduciary Taxes (Annual State and Local Government Taxes on Trusts)

Governments at all levels, city, county, state and federal, are continually seeking new sources of tax funds. Estate taxes have become a major source of revenue for states and the federal government. In addition, annual taxes are imposed upon trusts by state and the federal governments. These annual taxes are at a high rate for gains in the assets and income held in Trusts.

Large cities and counties are also looking at trusts as an additional source of their annual revenues.

The best defense against these new and high state and local government taxes is a provision in your Trust. It clearly states that you want to avoid these taxes where possible and to do so are willing to move your Trust out of the local taxing authority's jurisdiction or even out of the state.[1]

You can instruct that:

- If the surviving spouse or any of my children do not live in the state or local government area that has a tax on the Trust, then the trustee is not to pay taxes on the income, gains or value of the Trust for those people who do not live in the area of the taxing authority.

- If the above is not possible, then you can instruct that the Trust be removed from that local government area or state.

    See Chapter 11 for additional information.

OPTION 6 - Compensation for the Trustee

This needs to be considered for trustees who are family members or friends. Being a trustee requires work and has very serious legal and financial penalties if this work is not properly done.

The person selected as trustee was chosen based upon their ability and experience to properly handle the investments in the Trust. If this job is done

(1)   This can be accomplished by using Alex Webb's draft of Option 1

carefully, the value of the Trust can be expected to increase. If the work is not done properly, the loss to the family can be great.[2]

In all other family enterprises the one who works in the family business is paid. Other members of the family share in the profits. Why should the family member or friend serving as trustee not receive compensation? That person will control a great majority of the fortunes of the family. They will be expected to put these assets to work, to increase the family estate. Should they be asked to do this very important job of trustee without any compensation?

Trusts have been executed that not only required handling the investments but also gave the trustee management control of an operating business. In this case the trustee was a cousin and was expected to serve as trustee without any compensation. The business had over 40 employees. They were all paid, but not the cousin who was to manage the business.

Everyone else who will work on matters connected with the Trust are to be paid. In fact most Trusts state that the trustee is authorized at their absolute discretion to engage attorneys, accountants, agents, custodians, clerks, investment counsel and other persons as deemed advisable, to make such payment therefore as deemed reasonable and to charge the expense thereof to income or principal as equitably determined, and to delegate to such persons any discretion deemed proper.

The above encourages a trustee to hire others. In an attempt to avoid legal and financial liabilities it would be wise for a family member or friend, serving as trustee, to do just that. When the above people are hired, their fees and expenses, in total, will most likely be higher than those a professional trustee would have charged.

Yet most Grantors still select a family member or friend as their investment manager to avoid paying a professional investment manager an annual fee of about 1% a year.[2] A fee of about $10,000 to manage $1 million of securities appears high to many Grantors.

---

(2)   Loses to the family result from lost investment opportunities as well as the lose in the value of current Trust portfolio holdings

(3)   See "Fees and Services of Professional Trustees" in Appendix H.

They expect a family member or friend to do this work for nothing, and in most cases make no provision for how this work is evaluated.

Perhaps these Grantors think "You get what you pay for" doesn't apply. Their reasoning is: "This is `Family' - my son or daughter is glad to work for the benefit of everyone in it with no compensation."   I suggest that Grantors think again carefully on this matter.

Who measures the results of the family trustee stewardship? If a bank, a brokerage firm or other professional trustee is used, given $1 million to invest, we would want to look at their performance. We would expect, on average, the $1 million Trust to increase in value $80,000 to $100,000 a year. Can we demand the same from an unpaid family member?

Most family members or friends serving as trustees would be well advised to hire competent professional money managers. The new Uniform Prudent Investor Act [4] encourages family member trustees to do this by relieving them of any legal liability for investment results when the delegation is properly made.

Grantors who have placed trustee responsibility on an unpaid family member or friend should reconsider their position and consider naming a professional money manager as the initial trustee. They then have a choice of who the first professional money manager will be. If they do not elect to do this, someone else may select the money manager under the UPIA or other authority cited above that allows a trustee to hire investment advisors.

OPTION 7   - Using Attached Schedules for Items that may be Changed as a Result of Future Reviews of Your Trust.

A Trust should be reviewed at least every three to five years. Items that may change should be placed in an attached schedule of the trust. These would include investment directives, income to be paid to the surviving spouse or other Income Beneficiaries, and perhaps the names of your trustee and successor trustees.

By doing this, the cost of revising the entire 20 plus page document can be avoided.

(4)   See Appendix E.

Chapter 25

Options That Should Be Considered When the Surviving Spouse Depends On Income from the Trust

Introduction

The majority of families are in this situation - the surviving spouse will need a substantial income from the Trust. Usually a major portion of the family wealth goes into a Credit Shelter Trust. This is done in order to save federal estate taxes. In many cases the surviving spouse would be better off if the funds were left directly to the surviving spouse.

My reason for stating this is that most Trusts do not provide an adequate income for the survivor. The Trust could have, but it did not.

An income of about 3% from a Trust is not adequate for most people. A before tax income of $19,000 is what will be received from a $625,000 Credit Shelter Trust under the Default Rules. If $35,000 is needed, $19,00 is not sufficient.

To override the Default Rules that will produce such a low income we recommend use of the following Option in the Credit Shelter Trust.

OPTION 8 - Income to be Paid to My Surviving Spouse or Other Income Beneficiaries

First, Determine the Income Needs of Each Spouse.

1. If your surviving spouse will have a sufficient annual income from their own income-producing assets or from a Marital Trust that will be established, skip this section and go to Chapter 26. "Options to Increase the Value of Your Trust for Your Children and Other Heirs."

2. If the surviving spouse will need an income from the Credit Shelter Trust, the husband and the wife should each complete their income needs using the Exhibit 1 "Income Needs of Each Spouse." Use the extra copies of Exhibit 1 at the back of the book. Make extra copies of Exhibit 1 if needed. Without an estimate of the needs of each spouse,

an income plan cannot be established. You must be aware of the potentially low income that results when the Trust is controlled by the Default Rules.

3. After the income needs of each spouse is determined, you can have your Credit Shelter Trust provide:

    - That your surviving spouse will have an annual income of a stated amount determined from Exhibit 1 or from any other source.

    - That this annual stated income will be increased for inflation[1] from initial date of the Trust. Example: If 15 years has passed since your Trust was prepared and inflation from that date has been a cumulative 58%, your trustee should do the following: Pay in the initial year of your death 1.58 times the amount stated when your Trust was executed.

    - This amount will increase each subsequent year based on the inflation rate of each subsequent year.

NOTE: This option generally requires that part of the payments of the required annual amounts to your surviving spouse will also be made from the principal of the Trust. The interest and the dividends will normally be insufficient to make these annual payments. See the Exhibits in Chapter 7.

Exhibit 4 was prepared with a low average annual increase of 8% in the value of the stocks compared to a history of about 11%. You can test out any starting amount of income, plus adjustments to other planning factors in Exhibit 4 by use of Estate Planning Program Two.[2]

4. The government's published inflation rate is on the low side, especially for senior citizens' pharmaceutical costs and other medical needs. If you wish to consider increasing the annual percentage amount over the government's published data, you can do so.

(1)   As an alternative, you can state an annual percentage increase. This was done for the Estate Planning Programs used in this book. The annual percentage increase selected was 3%. But you can change it in the Estate Planning Programs.

(2)   See Appendix A.

- As an example, you could add an extra one percent annual increase to the income requirements over the government's official inflation rate.

OPTION 9 - You Can Provide an Extra $5,000 a Year for You or Your Spouse, Just by Asking for it.

NOTE: $5,000 is the dollar limit, by federal tax law, that you can have your surviving spouse request and receive from the trustee without any approval by the trustee. You are also permitted to have your spouse request up to 5% of the value of the Trust even if over $5,000. We do not recommend giving the 5% option when you indicate a starting amount of income increased by inflation and perhaps an additional annual percentage increase. If you also gave the 5% option, in this situation, there is a risk that the Trust could be out of funds in twenty years or less.[3] Your attorney can explain this option to you. The federal government is considering increasing the dollar amount from $5,000 to $10,000. Your may want to ask your attorney about this.

OPTION 9-A Giving Your Surviving Spouse Each Year the Maximum Dollar Amount Permitted Just by Asking for it.

Discuss this option with your attorney. Instead of stating the right for your wife to ask for and will receive $5,000, a directive referring to the specific federal law or regulation that gives authority for the provision can be made. This will provide for higher amounts being available based on future changes in this section of the law.

OPTION 10 - Providing Travel & Living Expenses From the Trust

As stated in Chapter 15, families rely on their children or friends to provide assistance to the surviving spouse. There is a strong need for this as the surviving spouse advances in age. Medical needs increase. Nursing homes may eventually be required.

(3)   In Exhibit 4 in Chapter 7 the "Annual Increase" for inflation was 3%. To test out the ability of a Trust under those estate planning factors to annually withdraw an additional 5%, increase the "Annual Increase" from 3% to 8% to simulate annually removing an additional 5%. The result, using Estate Planning Program Two is that the Trust is fully depleted within 20 years.

Few Trusts properly consider added human requirements of the survivor's later years. We have mentioned earlier that in many cases, family members no longer live in the same area. Relatives and friends can be hundreds of miles away.

This very important potential issue of the surviving spouse being in a nursing home should be considered. Consider an older couple, living on the East Coast. When discussing their plans, the wife mentioned that if required, after the death of her husband, she would move to a nursing home in the area. They have two married daughters, one living in Denver and the other in California. Both have three children but limited resources for the expenses of visiting their mother.

Provision should be considered in your Trust to pay the expenses for distant family and friends to visit the surviving spouse in their old age to comfort them and ensure that they are receiving proper care.

A provision can be placed into your Trust to make funds available from it for this contingency. Then, a son or a daughter could travel to visit the surviving parent. Grandchildren could also join in these visits.

OPTION 11 - Home in Trust

In order to obtain an individual's maximum federal tax exemption a home may be placed in the Trust. Thinking ahead, provision should be made in the Trust for the surviving spouse to instruct the trustee to sell the present home and to purchase or to lease a new residence selected by or approved by the surviving spouse. This provision can be a continuous one.

A person may wish to move from a home to another residence; later move again to a retirement living home, etc. They may wisely decide to rent in a new location and buy later after they are familiar with the new locale.

Some retirement living centers require that a purchase agreement be signed stating that the owner will receive 90%, or some other figure, of the purchase price when the surviving spouse moves away from the facility or dies. The Trust should provide for acceptance of these types of conditions from quality retirement living centers.

All of these things are reasonable, are to be expected, and there should be provision for them in the Trust.

OPTION 12 - Providing Funds For Your Children From Your Trust

Parents are living longer. The funds in the Trust are expected to grow in value. At what point will there be a surplus of funds in the Trust over those required for the surviving spouse's needs?

- You can establish an amount, say $1.5 million or more, which funds are to be automatically distributed each year to your children and other heirs.

- You can give your spouse the right to dispense funds to your children whenever the Trust is over a certain amount. If your spouse is not the trustee, this is done by a provision that makes it possible for your spouse to instruct the trustee to distribute an amount designated either directly to the person(s) or to be held in Trust for their benefit.

This power discussed in the preceding paragraph should not normally rest with the trustee who is not the surviving spouse. The reasons for this position are stated in Chapter 8, starting with Option 3 and carried over into Chapter 9. In addition, the so-called tax advantages that are claimed are questionable and are presented in Appendix B for Chapter 8.

In summary, as long as the parent is competent, they should have this authority, not some other person or entity, just because they are trustee. In a situation where the surviving parent is no longer competent, it is recommended that annual disbursement to all the children and heirs be required of the trustee when the funds are over a certain amount, say $1.5 million.

OPTION 13 - Other Special Provisions for Your Trust

Do not be misled into thinking that you cannot anticipate everything so just let the trustee decide what to do.

Review Option 8 "Providing Travel and Living Expenses From The Trust" for family visits when the surviving spouse is ill or in a nursing facility. If the provision for travel and living expenses is not clearly stated in the Trust, there is no Default Rule, that we are aware of, that would permit the trustee to continually dispense these funds.

That being the case, think of other special instructions that you would want to provide for in the Trust. Start by carefully thinking about what may happen to your surviving spouse, children, and grandchildren. Every three to five years think about these potential issues as you review your estate planning documents. Become aware of changing family situations.

Options 10 and Option 11 are just two examples of items to consider. And, if you do not provide for these potential events, your trustee is not authorized to do these things.

If you have young grandchildren, think of the educational needs and development in their early years. Would you want to provide for private education, tutoring, summer camps, trips, etc. See Chapter 20.

Would you want to provide for these needs for your grandchildren in a special section of your Trust? Who would control and determine how these funds would be distributed? Would this person have the power to instruct the trustee to make the disbursements?

OPTION 14 - Consider a "Special Trustee."

If your spouse is the sole trustee, you may need a Special Trustee for certain responsibilities. If your spouse requires funds from the Trust, in addition to the greater of $5,000 or 5% powers discussed in Chapter 10, a Special Trustee is required to evaluate and approve the required funds from the Trust. Your attorney can advise you on this.

You can also provide in your Trust for other duties of a "Special Trustee(s)." These family members or friends whose responsibilities are clearly stated in the Trust can be different from the traditional role of a trustee. These "Special Trustee(s)" would have responsibilities to care for, to advise and to comfort your spouse or other beneficiaries.

You can have a special trustee[4] to evaluate the performance of the investment manager of Trust or the trustee that has the investment responsibility.

[4] A new term in Trusts is "Trust Protector" whose duty is to evaluate the performance of the trustee and that the assets in the Trust are protected.

If a nursing home or other medical care is required for the surviving spouse or other Income Beneficiaries, this person would visit the nursing home to ensure that proper care is given. This Special Trustee could also have the Medical Care Power of Attorney. Reimbursement funds can be provided from the Trust for reasonable expenses incurred by this person for travel, purchasing certain types of items, etc. if needed.

OPTION 15 - At What Ages are Trust Assets Distributed to the Children.

Young adults can make mistakes and lose what they inherit.

Many reasons can be given for the causes of these losses of the funds received such as bad investments, gifts or loans to friends or just plain foolishness.

A parent might state in his Trust that the children are to receive one-third of their share when they reached age 25; one-third at age 35 and the final one-third at age 45.

The parent might expect his children to lose the first third of the funds they receive and hope they would learn from that experience. It is possible that they will also lose the second third they receive when they are 35. Hopefully when they are 45 and receive the final third, they'll save a little for their old age.

It is interesting to consider the funds that would be received from this concept. As an example, if a child was age 25 and their share of the Trust was $1 million, they would receive $333,333 at age 25 and the remaining amount of $666,667 would be held in Trust.

Even if no specific Directives were given for investing the $666,667 to be held in Trust (therefore a Balanced Trust with 50% invested in bonds and 50% invested in stocks) and the income paid was the Net Income, the child would receive an income each year plus the benefit of the $333,333 they received at age 25.

When they reached age 35, their Trust could have increased in value to $1.2 million[5] and they might be expected to receive about $600,000 (half the value of

(5)   You can test this by using Estate Planning program Two, see Appendix A.

the Trust would represent the next third). Again the child would receive an annual income from the Trust plus the benefit of the $600,000 they received at age 35

When they reach age 45, their Trust could have increased in value to $1,100,000 and they would receive the full amount in addition to what they received in the past years.

This is a strong argument for distributing the funds from the Trust over an extended time period.

If your estate planning indicates that a sizeable amount of money from your Trusts may be available to your children, why not do give serious consideration to staggering the payments to them over many years? They will still receive an income from these funds that are invested by the Trust.

Ability to Change the Terms of the Distribution of the Trust Assets to the Children.

Credit Shelter Trusts and Marital Trusts provide that upon the death of the surviving spouse the funds in the Trust are distributed to the children and other heirs. There may be a requirement, based on the age of each child or other heirs that all or a portion of their share be held in Trust until they reach a required age - generally 21 years of age.

In most Trusts the terms and conditions of the distribution of the Trust assets are fixed in the document. Any future changes in the distribution would require a revision of the Trust while the Grantor is still alive or by obtaining a court order.

There are many reasons why there can be a need for changes in the terms and conditions of the distribution of Trust assets to the children. This need can continue after the death of the Grantor. The first consideration will then be the outright payment of the full share or will these funds be held in a Trust for the benefit of a child.

OPTION 16 - Changing the Method of Payment

Years after the Trust has been executed and after the death of the Grantor a child could have medical problems, a serious accident, become an alcoholic; become addicted to drugs. They could have a questionable marriage that could result in a divorce and a claim for half of their assets including the funds from the Trust. These are some of the numerous reasons why the funds from the Trust should now be held in a separate Trust (either for their entire life and then given to their heirs or held in the Trust until their later years). If this was done, the child receives only the income from the Trust or a stated amount similar to that provided under Option 8.

You can state in your Trust:

Distribution Upon Spouse's Death. [6] Upon the death of my spouse,

     1. The Trustee shall distribute all or so much of the then remaining principal and undistributed income of the Trust in equal shares to my surviving children, or their surviving issue, *per stirpes*, either outright or in a Trust, as my spouse may appoint by their last will making specific reference to this special testamentary power of appointment.

     2. If any part of the then remaining principal and undistributed income has not been effectively appointed by my spouse in accordance with their special testamentary power of appointment, then the Trust property not so appointed shall be distributed outright to my surviving children, or their surviving issue, *per stirpes*.

OPTION 17 - Changing the Share Each Child and Heir will Receive

In most cases the Grantor has stated that upon the termination of the Trust the assets are to divided equally among the heirs. However, there is another Option a Grantor has.

This option would permit the surviving spouse to change the distribution among the Grantor's children and other heirs. This power is called a "special power of appointment." Justification for this could be based upon one child having a substantial amount of funds later in life without the need any longer for funds in the Trust. Another child such as a daughter, with several children who lost her husband in an accident, may require additional funds.

(6)   This is another option not usually found in Trusts. The wording above is that of Alex Webb used with his permission.

You can sate in your Trust:

Distribution Upon Spouse's Death.[7] Upon the death of my spouse,

1. The Trustee shall distribute all or so much of the then remaining principal and undistributed income of the Trust outright to any one or more of my issue as my spouse may have appointed by their last will making specific reference to this special testamentary power of appointment.

2. If any part of the then remaining principal and undistributed income has not been effectively appointed by my spouse in accordance with their special testamentary power of appointment, then the Trust property not so appointed shall be distributed outright to my surviving children, or their surviving issue, *per stirpes.*

You can limit the amount of change of each person's share by stating, as an example, that each heir must either receive directly or have held in Trust for them, at least 50% of the funds they would have received prior to any change by the surviving spouse.

In the case of second marriages that do occur later in life, the recent spouse may have a short acquaintance with the children of the Grantor and limited knowledge of them. In such circumstances, the Grantor may not want to use Option 16 and Option 17 in their Trust.

OTHER IMPORTANT OPTIONS PREVIOUSLY DISCUSSED THAT SHOULD ALSO BE CONSIDERED

OPTION 1 - **The Ability to Change the State that Controls Your Trust**
See page 195

OPTION 2 - **To Safeguard the Assets in Your Trust and Maintain Strong Family Relationship Relationships**
See page 196

(7)   Printed with the permission of Alex Webb.

OPTION 3 - Investment of Trust Assets
      This option is very important. Recommend that you consider a
      Directive to invest a minimum of 75% in good quality stocks.
         See page 198

**OPTION 4 - Removal of Your Trustee and the Appointment of a New
      Trustee**   See page 198

**OPTION 5 - Fiduciary Taxes (Annual state and Local Government
      Taxes on Trusts)**
         See page 200

OPTION 6 - Compensation of Your Trustee See page 200

**OPTION 7 - Using Attached Schedules for Items That May be Changed
      as a Result of Future Reviews of Your Trust.**
         See page 202

    You may also have additional options that address special concerns for your
family.

Chapter 26

Options To Be Considered to Increase the Value of Your Trust for Your Children and Other Heirs

OPTION 18 - **Increasing the End-Value of Your Trust By Giving a Directive to Invest in Good Quality Growth Stocks.**

Chapter 8 indicated that as you increase the requirement to invest in good quality growth stocks you may, over time, greatly increase the value of the Trust.

Chapter 8 also addressed your rights to override the Default Rules that will require approximately 50% of the Trust to be invested in bonds and 50% to be invested in stocks. Bonds do not increase in value. Trustees do not speculate in bond futures in an attempt to make a large capital gain from a risky speculation.

Therefore the Default Rules will cause the Trust to lose the purchasing power of the funds invested in bonds. for future years. Stated another way, due to inflation, half of the initial Trust investment will decrease in value.

The Grantor has the option of directing the trustee to invest less in bonds and more in good quality growth stocks. On page 68 there was an example given of the potential results of investing 100% of the assets in stocks.
These results indicated a much higher value of the Trust over the Default Rules.

You can use Estate Planning Program One, see Appendix A, to test other combinations of investment directives such as 75% in stocks and 25% in bonds. Also test different percentages for annual increase in stocks. Do not go beyond the past history of an average annual increase of 11%. Be conservative, select a lower percentage as was done in Exhibit 4 on Page 59.

Also realize that the market can decrease and has many times over several years. This will result in losses for a Trust with a high percent of its holdings in stocks. This is particularly true over a short term which could extend to five years or even longer. The longer the Trust is in existence, the greater potential there is to obtain reasonable forecasted increases.

OPTION 19   **Give Directives to Charge 100% of the Fees and Expenses of the Trust to Income**.

Again review the material in Chapter 8. In that chapter this option was listed as Option 2. It indicated your right to have all of the fees and expenses of your Trust first charged to the income. The reason this was done was to again further increase the value of the Trust for your children and other heirs.

It was also done when the income the surviving spouse would need would be available from other sources.

OPTION 20   **Give the Surviving Spouse the Authority to Direct the Trustee on the Distribution of the Income From the Trust.**

In Chapter 8, this was listed as Option 3. As the chapter indicates this is not the traditional way this power has been given in the past. The trustee was given this power primarily due to a provision in the law that permitted the trustee to withhold the distribution totally or in part. The amount of income not distributed would then be invested by the trustee. This was after very high taxes were paid by the Trust to the state and federal government. In legal terms it is called the Sprinkling Powers.

The alternative of giving this power to the surviving spouse should receive serious consideration. Granted, all of the income must be distributed. None can be held in the Trust if the surviving spouse has the authority to direct the trustee on the income distribution.

Who knows best the needs of the children? This alternative reinforces the concept of the surviving parent as the head of the family. Review in Chapter 8 other issues and concerns of a son or daughter, serving as trustee, with this power.

OPTION 21   **Provide a Safety Provision for The Surviving Spouse to Obtain Income from the Trust if Needed.**

As stated in the beginning of Chapter 8:

> As you give directives to increase the end-value of your Credit Shelter Trust for your children and other heirs, you decrease the income from the Trust for your surviving spouse.

If you use Option 19 and Option 20, above, you can greatly increase the end-value of the Trust for your children. But the income will be very limited. In the example in Chapter 8, the surviving spouse was expected to have sufficient funds from other sources and would have no need of income from the Trust. But events can occur in the future that could change this situation after the death of the Grantor.

You have the option of placing the full "5 and 5" powers in the Trust as a safety provision. Hopefully it will never be needed. But if it is, the survivor can obtain the greater of $5,000 or 5% of the value of the Trust just by asking for it.

Chapter 27

Options To Be Considered for a Second Marriage Trust

Introduction

The objective of a second marriage Trust needs to be clearly stated. When completed, it becomes a guide and a tool to test the estimated results of the final plan. The following can be a starting point for objectives in a second marriage Trust.

1. To provide an income during the person's lifetime.

2. To use conservative financial assumptions in order to insure that adequate funds will be available to provide the income the spouse will require.

3. When actual results indicate that the Trust is over-funded, the surplus funds are to be distributed annually to Grantor's children.

The Starting Point for Objective 1. Above

The starting point is to first complete Exhibit 1 "Income Needs of Each Spouse" for the person you wish to provide for through the Trust.

Next, select an annual percent of increase for inflation. For planning purposes this increase is estimated. In our planning model we use 3%.

After a starting income in today's dollars is determined, plus an anticipated inflation rate, the planning for the amounts to fund the Trust over various time periods can be obtained by following the procedure outlined in Chapter 12. Additional information on how Estate Planning Program One was used to do this work is in Appendix B for Chapter 12. Additional information on Estate Planning Program One is in Appendix A.

OPTION 22   **Indicate an Amount to be Held in Trust to Provide a Lifetime Income for Your Spouse**

Using the techniques described, estimate the required amount to be held in Trust to provide a lifetime income for your surviving spouse or another Income Beneficiary. This procedure should be reviewed at least every three to five years since the amount required will usually change in that period of time. Review Chapter 12, "Trusts for a Second Marriage."

You may find an insurance program that can provide some of these results and combine the insurance program with this option. But evaluate the costs compared to providing 100% of the income from a Trust.

OPTION 23   **Require Your Trustee to Recalculate the Amounts Required at Least Once Every Two Years and Pay any Excess Funds to Your Children.**

You can state in your Trust how these calculations are to be made and designate those who are to receive the surplus funds. The surplus funds should first be distributed to your children from the Credit Shelter Trust.

By doing this, the tax on the funds received can be reduced for the recipients.

OTHER OPTIONS

Review the other options in Chapters 24 and 25, You can select from them options for this Trust that could also be appropriate

APPENDIX A

How To Use Your Internet Estate Planning Programs

Introduction:

These Programs are intended for CPAs and others who assist clients in estate planning. Many Grantors who have computers and like to use them for financial information and investing will find the Programs of value for their own estate planning concerns. Others who wish to review the details of the exhibits in Appendix B will find information on how the various Tables were prepared.

The calculations for each Program use simple mathematical factors such as percent, plus and minus. However, there is always the possibility that what was downloaded from the Internet was in error or that there are problems in your computer. Therefore, before you start using the data and calculations loaded into your computer, check the validity of the transferred data by manually checking the Program.

To do this, check the results expected by randomly selecting the factors that are used to obtain the results. Check your answers against those in the Program. The math functions for each Estate Planning Program are explained in this appendix.

Another benefit from this data checking exercise is that you will understand the interrelationship of the data used as input for each program.

There are two different Estate Planning Programs that you can access at the web site, " www.ccmtrust.com/thebook" Each one has a special purpose explained in this section. You will need to have installed on your computer Microsoft Excel Version 5.0 or higher.

After you have down-loaded the Programs into your computer, it will no longer be necessary for you to remain connected to the Internet. If you do not have a computer or access to the Internet, you can ask a friend who does to run these programs for you. You can also use the computers at your library, senior center, or other community organizations. Generally people are at these locations who can assist you.

Changing one or more of the planning assumptions at the top of each Program will allow you test many different alternatives and to select the ones you want to consider for your Trust. You can print out the results of each test.

INSTRUCTION FOR EACH OF THE ESTATE PLANNING CALCULATORS.

Estate Planning Program One

This Program was designed to allow you to select the starting income your spouse or other Income Beneficiary will require; to increase the income annually by a stated percentage; to select and test various combinations of investments in bonds and stocks; to assign reasonable forecasts of interest paid on bonds and dividends that might be expected from stocks. Based on your forecast of the average annual increase in stocks you can view the expected results of different rates of growth.

The Program is based on ten planning assumptions.

Starting Income From Trust	$ XX,XXX	**Year**	XXXX
Annual Increase	X.X%	**Percent in Stocks**	XX.X%
Starting Value of Trust	$ XXX,XXX	**Stock Dividends**	X.X%
Percent in Bonds	XX.X%	**Annual Increase**	XX.X%
Bond Interest	X.X%	**Trustee Fees & Expenses**	X.XX%

The most important planning assumptions are at the top left. They are:

Starting Income From Trust:[1] This is the starting annual income requirement to be paid to you or your surviving spouse from the Trust in today's dollars. This income was determined by using Exhibit 1, "Income Needs of Each Spouse" or by some other means that you use. It is one of the most important figures to be placed in your Trust as a Directive.

Next to this amount, on the right is the **"Year.".** Enter the year this amount will be required. In most cases the year is when the Trust is executed. Each

(1)   We are recommending consideration of stating an exact amount of income that must be paid. This bypasses the Uniform Income and Principal Act that limits income distributions to income received. Growth of principal is not income under the Act. The new revised Act attempts to recognize, in some cases, part of the growth of principal as income. It also attempts to recognize part of the income, such as that from high interest paying bonds as principal and not to be distributed. However, the revised Act does not solve the problems addressed in this book.

time new projections are made, such as testing your planning assumptions 15 years later, enter the Year 2023, 15 years from now, as a reference date. Also it is most important that you increase the <u>Starting Income From Trust</u> to the amount it would be in the future year.

Annual Increase: This is the percent that the **Starting Income from Trust** is to be increased each year. This also is an important figure. All of the other planning assumptions that follow are used to test the ability of the Trust to pay the annual income required by you or your surviving spouse. When you test the results, to insure that the data was properly loaded into your system, increase the starting income required by a percentage increase and check the results in the program. A 3% annual increase for inflation may appear to be a small increase, but after ten years, the need for $35,000 this year, increases to $47,037.

Starting Value of Trust: If you are using this amount for a Credit Shelter Trust, the amount entered is your individual federal estate-tax exemption for the year selected. These exemptions are shown by year in Chapter 2 of Appendix B.

If you are using this program to determine the amount that should be placed in a Trust for the spouse of a second marriage or for other Trusts for an individual, enter the amount you estimate might be needed. Then test the amount entered by reviewing the final values of the Trust during various periods of the expected life of the person you are providing for. In these instances, the amounts you enter are not related to the amounts of your federal estate-tax exemption. Information on planning the amounts to fund a second marriage Trust starts on Page 229.

The issue (of the amount to be placed in a Credit Shelter Trust and the amount to place in a Marital Trust) can be resolved after you know the total amount required and have obtained the advice of your attorney

Percent in Bonds: The decision on what percentage to select is yours. You should test the results of various percentages in combinations with stocks.

Interest Paid on Bonds: The actual percentage should be based upon current rates paid by good quality medium-term bond funds. Inquire about the interest paid on such funds from the Trust department of at least two banks. Again be conservative.

Percent in Stocks: Again the decision is yours. The percentage used in many of the examples vary from 50% to higher percentages based on the issues being discussed.   If you have access to this Estate Planning Program One, available from the Internet, you can experiment by using many different percentages and then comparing their expected long-term results. But you must also realize that in the short-term, stocks have also declined in value.

Dividends Paid on Stocks: The actual percentage should be based upon dividend rates paid on good quality growth funds. Again, you can talk to the Trust department of your bank. The dividend rate used in many of the examples was 1.3%. This may be a little high in today's market for good quality growth stocks.

Annual Stock Increase: This requires some knowledge of the stock market, its' past history and your informed opinion of its current and long-term outlook. We have used in some exhibits an 11% annual increase. This is based on the past history from 1926 through 1997.

But, we also used an 8% annual increase just to be conservative and still be able to illustrate that a lower stock growth may still provide the income the surviving spouse requires and perhaps increase the end-value of the Trust for the children. You should test several different estimates for the growth of stocks.

Trustee Fees & Expenses: In our Exhibits we have used three quarters of one percent (0.75%) and one percent (1.0%) as the annual total for all trustee fees and expenses. We have presented some information on trustee fees and services in Appendix H. In the Program, the trustee fee and expenses are paid based on the annual year-end value of the Trust. This includes the value of the bonds as well as the end-value of the stocks.

How the above Planning Assumptions in Estate Planning Program One Calculates the Yearly Detail Data Shown in the Program Results.

Once you have entered the above estate planning factors into the program the results are quickly calculated by very simple addition, subtraction and percentages. The results are printed for you.. While there is a large amount of data presented, a review of the calculations made for the first year will help you to understand and test the results.

Below is a sample of the information in the Tables with an explanation of how each was calculated.

Year	Bond Amount	Bond Interest	Beg. Stock Amount	Stock Dividends	Stock Increase	End Stock Value	REMOVED from Principal	ANNUAL Income
1	156,250	9,375	468,750	6,094	37,500	506,250	$ 19,531	$ 35,000
2	156,250	9,375	481,750	6,263	38,540	520,290	20,412	36,050
3	156,250	9,375	494,804	6,432	39,584	534,388	21,324	37,132

1. The **Percent in Bonds** is calculated from the **Value of Trust**. If you entered as the Starting Value of Trust $ 625,000 and the Percent in Bonds is 25% the program calculates that 25% of $625,000 is $156,250. The report prints out under **Bond Amount** $156,250 And, since this amount remains the same (bonds are not expected to increase in value), $156,250 is printed for each of the 25 years.

2. **Bond Interest**: If you entered 6.0%, then 6.0% of $156,250 is $9,375. This amount is printed under the heading **Bond Interest.** And since the Bond Amount does not change, $9,375 is the amount of Bond Interest that will be paid in each of the 25 years.

3. The **Percent in Stocks** is calculated from the Starting Value of Trust. If you entered the Value of Trust as $625,000 and the Percent in Stocks is 75%, the program calculates that 75% of $625,000 is $468,750. This amount is printed under the heading **Beg. Stock Amount** (Beginning Stock Amount) for the 1st year. The **Beg. Stock Amount** for each of the following years will change as presented below.

4. **Stock Dividend**: If you entered 1.3%, then that percentage of $468,750 is $6,094. This amount is printed under the heading **Stock Dividend** for the 1st year. The amount of the **Stock Dividend** will change for each of the following years as presented below.

5. **Annual Stock Increase:** If you entered 8%, then that percentage of $468,750 (the Beg. Stock Amount of the 1st rear) is $37,500.. This amount is printed under the heading **Stock Increase** for the 1st year. The amount of the **Stock Increase** will change for each of the following years as presented below.

6.   **End Stock Value** is obtained by adding the <u>Beg. Stock Amount</u> with the <u>Stock Increase</u>. Using the input data above, the End Stock Value for the first year would be $468,750 + $37,500 for a total of $506,250. printed under the heading <u>End Stock Value</u> for the 1st year. The amount of the <u>End Stock Value</u> will change for each of the following years as presented below.

7.   **REMOVED from Principal** is obtained by first adding the <u>Bond Interest</u> and the <u>Stock Dividend</u> in the 1st year and then subtracting that number from the amount listed under the column **ANNUAL Income.**

NOTE: The controlling amounts in this Program will appear under the column <u>ANNUAL Income</u>. The program is designed to pay out these amounts each year, increased at an annual percentage you select for inflation.

Up to this point very simple math functions of adding, subtracting and obtaining the percentage amounts from the planning data that was entered in the program at the top, was done. These basic math functions will continue to be used in the following years, but a few additions are required to obtain the <u>Beg. Stock Amount</u> each year.

The amount shown in the column marked <u>REMOVED. From Principal</u> only included the amount necessary to pay the <u>ANNUAL Income</u> to the surviving spouse. This was done so the Grantor could see the annual amounts that will be removed from the principal of the Trust and be given to the surviving spouse. The <u>Amt. From Principal</u> did not include the amount to pay **Trustee Fees and Expenses** based on your estimate of these fees and expenses.

At the end of each year, the total value of the Trust is obtained by adding the **Bond Amount** to the **End Stock Value.** The Program then takes the percent you entered into the Program for <u>Trustee Fees & Expenses,</u> calculates this amount and then deducts it from the ending value of the stocks. An example is shown below for the first year.

Bond Amount	$ 156,250	
End Stock Value	+ 506,250	
Total Amount	$ 662,500	times the percent of trustee fees & expenses. If .075% was used, the amount is $ 4,969.

The above amount for trustee fees and expenses is not shown on the report, But it is included when determining the following year's **Beg. Stock Amount** by adding the Trustee Fees and Expenses to the amount <u>REMOVED. From Principal</u> required to pay the Income Beneficiary's <u>ANNUAL Income</u> each year from the Trust. This is shown below along with the computer calculations that establish the <u>Beg. Stock Amount</u> for each of the following years.

A. First year <u>REMOVED From Principal</u> to pay spouse's <u>ANNUAL Income</u>	$ 19,531
B. Trustee Fees and Expenses	+ 4,969
Total Actually Removed from Principal	$ 24,500

Next, subtract this amount from the year's <u>End Stock Value:</u>

First year's <u>End Stock Value</u>	$ 506,250
Less: Total Actually Removed from Principal	- $ 24,500
Beg. Stock Amount, 2nd Year	$ 481,750

Note: The amounts are rounded to the nearest dollar amount for display. The exact amounts are carried forward in the Program.

The above amount, $481,750 (results from rounding to the nearest dollar) is the amount listed under <u>Beg. Stock Amount</u> for 2nd year. And, since the beginning stock amount has changed, the amounts reported under the columns <u>Stock Dividend</u> and <u>Stock Increase</u> will change in each of the following years.

A key question you must ask is what is the estimated value of the Trust each year, based on the planning assumptions? A summary of the value of the Trust in five-year increments is printed at the bottom of the program and an example is printed on the following page.

To determine the value of the Trust in the interim years, add the <u>Bond Amount</u> to the <u>Beg. Stock Value</u> of the following year. The reason you add the <u>Beg. Stock Value</u> of the following year is that this amount has the Trustee fees and expenses removed.

You will note that the initial results are based upon the concept that the Trust is funded in the year the Trust is to be executed and that the annual income to be paid to the surviving spouse is based on the income required in that year.

Few Grantors can predict how long they will live. To test what might happen years later, you need to program under <u>Starting Value of Trust</u> several different years and increase the starting income required. For example, select a period such as 15 years after your Trust is to be executed. If you select $35,000 as the amount your spouse would require in 1998 and this amount was to increase annually by 3% for inflation, the results should indicate that after 15 years your spouse would require $54,529.[2] This is the <u>Starting Income From Trust</u> 15 years later

Test this amount by entering it into a new set of planning assumptions as the **Starting Income From Trust**. The **Starting Value of Trust** of the Credit Shelter Trust could be $1 million, the amount permitted in the year 2006 and for following years, if you estimate this amount would be available.

The results should indicate that the <u>ANNUAL Income</u> can be paid from the Credit Shelter Trust based on your other planning assumptions. A first test is to review the summary data at the bottom of the Table. An example is shown below

STARTING VALUE OF TRUST	**$625,000**
VALUE OF TRUST AFTER:	
FIVE YEARS	**816,423**
TEN YEARS	**1,130,998**
FIFTEEN YEARS	**1,647,956**
TWENTY YEARS	**2,497,498**
TWENTY-FIVE YEARS	**3,913,161**

The Starting Value of Trust, $625,000 above, was the amount you entered into the Program. The potential results, based on your planning assumptions are shown in five-year increments. In the above example, the Trust continues to grow in value after the required annual payments are made to your spouse.

If any of the above amounts started to decrease, this a warning that your planning assumptions may not have been realistic.

As you enter data, always ask yourself "What would happen if their was a major decline in the stock market and especially immediately after my death?" You can make estimates of this.

To do this, assume a percentage drop in the market, after your death and after the funds have been invested according to your Directives. In the example below, it is assumed that the stock market drop will be 25%, the amount of your Credit Shelter Trust is $1 million and that you gave a Directive that 75% be invested in stocks.

Example of a 25% Market Decline:

Initial investment in stocks (75% of $1 million)	$750,000
Less: 25% drop in the stock market	- 187,500
Value of stocks after the drop	$562,500

Next, we need to estimate the additional amount removed from stocks to pay your surviving spouse the income required and to pay for trustee fees and expenses. During a market decline (the Program removes these amounts from stocks). If you estimated $40,000, the above value of the stocks ($562,500 less the $40,000) would decrease to $522,500. The value of the Credit Shelter Trust would now be:

Bonds (25% of $1 million)	$250,000	or 32.36%
Stocks	522,500	or 67.64%
Reduced Value	$772,500	

You can now test out the above by entering this new data into Estate Planning Program One. You also need to adjust other planning factors such as the Starting Income From Trust. In this example the initial Starting Income From Trust in 1998 was $35,000. After 15 years, the amount at annual 3% increase is now $56,529. This as also entered as the Starting Value of Trust.

Changes are also required in the planning assumptions for the starting percent in bonds and stocks. The new percentages are indicated above.[3]

You may want to also test a major market decline several years after your death. To do this you would enter your planning assumptions and review the results over the 25-year period and select various years later to test a market decline.

If one of your test periods was five years later, you would repeat the process above. To do this, first take the value of stocks five years later and apply a percentage reduction (to simulate a market decline); further reduce the value of stocks by additional amount for the income requirements to pay to your spouse and payment of trustee fees and expenses; and then recalculate the new percentages in bonds and stocks. Then enter your new planning assumptions into the Program.

(3)   The percentages have been rounded to the nearest one hundredth of one percent. However, if you want to have the exact dollar amounts, shown above, you will need to use the exact percentages to correct the minor dollar differences. In this example, the exact percentages for bonds is 32.36246% and for stocks, 67.63754%. If you enter these percentages as your planning assumptions, the amounts above will appear in your program. While it is not necessary to obtain this degree of accuracy in this type of forecasting, the exact percentages have been used in the following Table to show the above amounts in bonds and stocks.

Example of a 25% Market Decline Immediately after the Death of the Grantor and Investments Per Directive [4]

Starting Income From Trust	$ 56,529	Year	2013
Annual Increase	3.0%	Percent in Stocks	67.64%
Starting Value of Trust	$ 772,500	Stock Dividends	1.3%
Percent in Bonds	32.36%	Annual Increase	11.0%
Bond Interest	6.0%	Trustee Fees & Expenses	0.75%

Year	Bond Amount	Bond Interest	Beg. Stock Amount	Stock Dividends	Stock Increase	End Stock Value	REMOVED from Principal	ANNUAL Income
1	250,000	15,000	522,500	6,792	57,475	579,975	$ 34,736	$ 56,529
2	250,000	15,000	539,014	7,007	59,292	598,305	36,218	58,225
3	250,000	15,000	555,725	7,224	61,130	616,855	37,747	59,972
4	250,000	15,000	572,606	7,444	62,987	635,593	39,327	61,771
5	250,000	15,000	589,624	7,665	64,859	654,483	40,959	63,624
6	250,000	15,000	606,741	7,888	66,741	673,482	42,645	65,533
7	250,000	15,000	623,911	8,111	68,630	692,541	44,388	67,499
8	250,000	15,000	641,084	8,334	70,519	711,604	46,189	69,524
9	250,000	15,000	658,202	8,557	72,402	730,604	48,053	71,609
10	250,000	15,000	675,197	8,778	74,272	749,469	49,980	73,758
11	250,000	15,000	691,993	8,996	76,119	768,112	51,974	75,970
12	250,000	15,000	708,502	9,211	77,935	786,437	54,039	78,249
13	250,000	15,000	724,625	9,420	79,709	804,334	56,177	80,597
14	250,000	15,000	740,250	9,623	81,427	821,677	58,391	83,015
15	250,000	15,000	755,248	9,818	83,077	838,325	60,687	85,505
16	250,000	15,000	769,476	10,003	84,642	854,118	63,067	88,070
17	250,000	15,000	782,770	10,176	86,105	868,875	65,536	90,712
18	250,000	15,000	794,947	10,334	87,444	882,391	68,100	93,434
19	250,000	15,000	805,799	10,475	88,638	894,436	70,761	96,237
20	250,000	15,000	815,092	10,596	89,660	904,752	73,528	99,124
21	250,000	15,000	822,563	10,693	90,482	913,045	76,404	102,098
22	250,000	15,000	827,918	10,763	91,071	918,989	79,398	105,161
23	250,000	15,000	830,824	10,801	91,391	922,215	82,515	108,315
24	250,000	15,000	830,908	10,802	91,400	922,308	85,763	111,565
25	250,000	15,000	827,753	10,761	91,053	918,806	89,151	114,912

STARTING VALUE OF TRUST	$772,500
VALUE OF THE TRUST AFTER:	
FIVE YEARS	856,741
TEN YEARS	941,993
FIFTEEN YEARS	1,019,476
TWENTY YEARS	1,072,563
TWENTY-FIVE YEARS	1,079,655

(4)   See planning assumptions on prior page.

The Program allows you to estimate the potential ability of your planning assumptions to provide an adequate income for your spouse, and it can also indicate the potential end-value of the Trust for your children and other heirs.

You need to consider these potential end-values during the expected life of your spouse. Once the Trust obtains values above the need to support the annual income for your spouse, you can consider Directives to release these surplus funds to your children (see Chapter 9).

Using Estate Planning Program One for Second Marriage Trusts

In Chapter 12 second marriage Trusts were discussed. An example of the funds required to be placed in a Trust for Margaret Bright, who would need an income of $22,750 in 1998 dollars, was shown. The table on Page 96, indicated that her husband could obtain that income with $450,000 placed in a Trust in 1998. The following is how that amount was obtained using Estate Planning Program One.

The process requires a little trial and error to determine the funding amount. Conservative estimates should be used as shown below. The guide to this process are the amounts listed at the bottom of the Table and the amounts remaining in the Trust when Margaret's age is 101 (Goal was to provide for Margaret to age 100)..

Let's start by setting up the following data in the Program:

Starting Income From Trust	$ 22,750	**Year**	**1998**	
Annual Increase	3.0%	**Percent in Stocks**		50%
Starting Value of Trust	$ 600,000	**Stock Dividends**		1.3%
Percent in Bonds	50.0%	**Annual Stock Increase**		8.0%
Bond Interest	5.5%	**Trust Fees & Expenses**		0.75%

The Starting Value of Trust was a guess to start the process. Margaret in 1998 is age 65. We will be establishing an amount to provide for her to Age 100. Conservative planning assumptions have been used. The percent in bonds and stocks are 50% each. This is a Balanced Trust as indicated in the Default Rules. The annual increase in stocks over this 35-year period has been reduced to 8% instead of the history of 11%.

After we have entered the above data, the results at the bottom of the Table are printed below. Check your results using the Program. They should be the same as those shown.

Year	Bond Amount	Bond Interest	Beg. Stock Amount	Stock Dividends	Stock Increase	End Stock Value	REMOVED from Principal	ANNUAL Income
24	300,000	16,500	998,286	12,978	79,863	1,078,149	15,421	44,899
25	300,000	16,500	1,052,392	13,681	84,191	1,136,583	16,065	46,246

STARTING VALUE OF TRUST	$600,000
VALUE OF THE TRUST AFTER:	
FIVE YEARS	692,887
TEN YEARS	809,810
FIFTEEN YEARS	959,243
TWENTY YEARS	1,153,349
TWENTY-FIVE YEARS	1,420,518

The above results are for 25 years. Margaret in 25 years would be age 90. So we will need to test this amount for another ten years to determine if the Value of the Trust, after 25 years, will continue to provide for her in the next ten years. We do this by entering new data into the Program, shown below, from the above report.

Starting Income From Trust	$ 47,633	Year 2023	
Annual Increase	3.0%	Percent in Stocks	78.88%
Starting Value of Trust	$ 1,420,518	Stock Dividends	1.3%
Percent in Bonds	21.12%	Annual Stock Increase	8.0%
Bond Interest	5.5%	Trust Fees & Expenses	0.75%

As indicated from the first program, shown above, Margaret is to have an Annual Income of $46,238 in the 25th year. This amount needs to be increased by 3% to determine the Starting Income From Trust in the 26th year. A 3% increase requires the payment o$47,633 and this was entered above.

The new "Starting Value of Trust" $1,420,518 is the ending value shown after twenty-five years. Two additional adjustment are required for the starting percentages in bonds and stocks. Bonds have a value of $300,000 and represent 21.12% of the total value of the Trust at the end of the 25th year (the actual percentage is 21.11906% if you want the new starting bond amount to be $300,000).

Stocks now represent the balance. To obtain the Beg. Stock Amount in the 26th year, subtract the bond amount from the ending value of the Trust (this is required because the starting amount in stocks for the 26th year is not shown). The percent of stocks is now 78.88 (actual is 78.88101%).

We are now ready to look at the results for the next ten years. At end of that time, Margaret will have completed her 100th year.

Starting Income From Trust	$ 47,633		Year	2023			
Annual Increase	3.0%		Percent in Stocks		78.88%		
Starting Value of Trust	$ 1,420,518		Stock Dividends		1.3%		
Percent in Bonds	21.12%		Annual Stock Increase		8.0%		
Bond Interest	5.5%		Trust Fees & Expenses		0.75%		

Year	Bond Amount	Bond Interest	Beg. Stock Amount	Stock Dividends	Stock Increase	End Stock Value	REMOVED from Principal	ANNUAL Income
1	300,000	16,500	1,120,519	14,567	89,642	1,210,160	$ 16,566	$ 47,633
2	300,000	16,500	1,182,268	15,369	94,581	1,276,849	17,193	49,062
3	300,000	16,500	1,247,831	16,222	99,826	1,347,657	17,812	50,534
4	300,000	16,500	1,317,488	17,127	105,399	1,422,887	18,423	52,050
5	300,000	16,500	1,391,542	18,090	111,323	1,502,866	19,021	53,611
6	300,000	16,500	1,470,323	19,114	117,626	1,587,949	19,606	55,220
7	300,000	16,500	1,554,184	20,204	124,335	1,678,518	20,172	56,876
8	300,000	16,500	1,643,508	21,366	131,481	1,774,988	20,717	58,583
9	300,000	16,500	1,738,709	22,603	139,097	1,877,805	21,237	60,340
10	300,000	16,500	1,840,235	23,923	147,219	1,987,454	21,727	62,150
11	300,000	16,500	1,948,571	25,331	155,886	2,104,456	22,183	64,015
12	300,000	16,500	2,064,240	26,835	165,139	2,229,379	22,600	65,935

As the above indicates, at the end of ten additional years the value of the Trust would be:

Value of Bonds	$ 300,000
Ending value of stock (Beg. Stock Amount, 11th year)	1,948.571
Total Value	$ 2,248,571

The results indicate that if $600,000 was placed in Trust for Margaret in 1998, it would be more than needed. And, it would reduce Henry's ability to also leave some money upon his death to his children.

When your planning assumptions produce an end-value that is too high, try a much lower estimate, such as $400,000.. If you use that lower number and follow the above instructions, the result will indicate that an amount larger than $400,000 is required.

You will know that the amount needed to fund the Trust in 1998 will be between these two: the $600,000 that was more than required and the $400,000 that was less than required. The actual amount, using this method, and listed on Page 96 is $450,000. The Trust at the end of Margaret's 100th year will have a value of about $173,000.

CAUTION: Remember these amounts are forecasted estimates. Hopefully they were conservatively made. But there is no guarantee. It is your best judgement coupled with a planning tool.

Estate Planning Program Two

This program is used for a Grantor who wants the end-value of their Credit Shelter Trust to grow for the maximum benefit of their children and other heirs. This Program does not contain a planning factor for the "Starting Income From Trust" for the Income Beneficiary, generally the surviving spouse nor an "Annual Increase" in the starting income.

Program Two can also be used to forecast potential results under the Default Rules for a Balanced Trust. To do this, always start with 50% of the Trust invested in bonds and 50% invested in stocks.

Listed below are the planning factors you can change each time you run this program. The explanation for "Starting Value of the Trust," "Percent in Bonds," "Percent in Stocks," "Interest on Bonds," Dividend Percent" and "Annual Growth in Stocks" have not changed from those in Estate Planning Program One. You can review the use of each starting on Page 220 The mathematical calculations are also the same as shown on Page 223.

Starting Value of Trust	$ XXX,XXX	**Interest Paid on Bonds**	XX,X%
Percent in Bonds	XX.X%	**Dividends Paid on Stocks**	X.X%
Percent In Stocks	XX.X%	**Trustee Fees & Charges**	X.X%
Annual Growth in Stocks	XX%	**Charged to Income**	X.X%

Estate Planning Program Two does contain a new planning factor, your option of a Directive to state how the Trustee Fees & Charges will be Charged to Income or charged to principal. If you want to view the results of a Net Income provision in a Trust, charge half of the Trustee Fees and Charges to income.

If you want to increase the value of the Trust for your children, you can give a Directive to charge all of the Trustees Fees & Charges to income. To do this, use the exact same percentage of trustee fees and charges to Charged to Income . If you want to charge all the fees and expenses to principal, place zero.

NOTE:
The Estate Planning Programs and the calculations that result and are used in this book are for instructional purposes only. Any calculations obtained need to be independently verified if they are to be used in actual estate planning.

The transfer of the Estate Planning Programs to your computer should be checked to determine that they have been properly received. And, that the programs used in your computer are properly processing the data.

APPENDIX B

Detail of Chapter Exhibits & Additional Information

Introduction

Many of the Tables in this appendix came from Estate Planning Programs that you can access from the Internet and load into your computer. You can then change the input data to develop a plan for your family and other heirs that will become the foundation for your Trust. Instructions to access the programs are in Appendix A. Others, like the Table below for Chapter 2, indicate basic facts such as an individual's federal estate-tax exemption.

Chapter 2 - Basic Facts About Trusts

Individual Federal Estate-Tax Exemption

Year	Exemption Amount
1998	$ 625,000
1999	$ 650,000
2000	$ 675,000
2001	$ 675,000
2002	$ 700,000
2003	$ 700,000
2004	$ 850,000
2005	$ 950,000
2006	$1,000,000

A married couple by combining their exemptions through proper estate planning can double the amount of the above exemptions. A husband and a wife (if they die after the year 2005) can leave up to $2,000,000 free of federal estate taxes to their children and other heirs.

Chapter 6 - Know Your Income Needs

Page 36 of the text presented the data below:

Amount of Trust	ANNUAL NET INCOME PAID					
	1st Yr.	5th Yr.	10th Yr.	15th Yr.	20th Yr.	25th Yr.
$625,000	$19,516	$20,597	$22,719	$26,206	$31,937	$41,354

The details by year of a Trust with the Net Income provision controlled by the Default Rules are on the following page. Please review at the top of the page the eight planning items and the data entered for each.

Note:

1.   Since there are no Directives for the starting income to be paid to the Income Beneficiary (generally the spouse) from the Trust nor an annual increase of that amount for inflation, these two important options are missing. Therefore the annual payments to the spouse are listed under the column Net Income.   The amounts will vary dependent upon interest rate movements and Market conditions.

2.   The Grantor gave no Directives for any of these eight planning assumptions. The Starting Value of Trust is controlled by tax regulations (Credit Shelter Trust); Percent in Bonds and Percent in Stocks are controlled the by state Default Rules; Annual Growth in Stocks, Interest Paid on Bonds, Dividends Paid on Stocks are controlled by the Market; and Trustee Fees and Expenses are controlled by the Trustee; and last, the amount of these fees that will be charged against the income (50%) is established by the Net Income provision that the Grantor signed and probably never understood.

3.   Grantors who sign preprinted forms or obtain the lowest priced documents are not aware of the above happening or of their financial options for items above that they could have controlled by Directives.

If you want to review the explanation for each of the eight planning factors at the top of the next page, See Appendix A. An explanation of how the results were calculated is also in Appendix A.

Page 48, this data was also referenced again as footnote (13).

INCOME CONTROLLED BY DEFAULT RULES - A BALANCED TRUST
Details of Data on Page 36 - Exhibit A by Year

Starting Value of Trust	$625,000	Interest Paid on Bonds	6.00%
Percent in Bonds	50.00%	Dividends Paid on Stocks	1.30%
Percent in Stocks	50.00%	Trust Fees & Expenses	1.00%
Annual Growth in Stocks	11%	Charged to Income	0.50%

Year	Bond Amount	Bond Interest	Beg. Stock Amount	Stock Dividends	Stock Growth	End Stock Value	100%Trust Fees & Exp.	Net Income
1	$312,500	$ 18,750	$ 312,500	$ 4,063	$ 34,375	$ 346,875	$ 6,594	$19,516
2	312,500	18,750	343,578	4,467	37,794	381,372	6,939	19,920
3	312,500	18,750	377,902	4,913	41,569	419,472	7,320	20,003
4	312,500	18,750	415,812	5,406	45,739	461,551	7,741	20,285
5	312,500	18,750	457,681	5,950	50,345	508,026	8,205	20,597
6	312,500	18,750	503,923	6,551	55,432	559,355	8,719	20,942
7	312,500	18,750	554,995	7,215	61,049	616,045	9,285	21,322
8	312,500	18,750	611,402	7,948	67,254	678,656	9,912	21,742
9	312,500	18,750	673,701	8,758	74,107	747,808	10,603	22,207
10	312,500	18,750	742,506	9,653	81,676	824,182	11,367	22,719
11	312,500	18,750	818,498	10,640	90,035	908,533	12,210	23,285
12	312,500	18,750	902,428	11,732	99,267	1,001,695	13,142	23,911
13	312,500	18,750	995,124	12,937	109,464	1,104,588	14,171	24,601
14	312,500	18,750	1,097,502	14,268	120,725	1,218,228	15,307	25,364
15	312,500	18,750	1,210,574	15,737	133,163	1,343,737	16,562	26,206
16	312,500	18,750	1,335,456	17,361	146,900	1,482,356	17,949	27,137
17	312,500	18,750	1,473,382	19,154	162,072	1,635,454	19,480	28,164
18	312,500	18,750	1,625,714	21,134	178,829	1,804,542	21,170	29,299
19	312,500	18,750	1,793,957	23,321	197,335	1,991,293	23,038	30,552
20	312,500	18,750	1,979,774	25,737	217,775	2,197,549	25,100	31,937
21	312,500	18,750	2,184,998	28,405	240,350	2,425,348	27,378	33,466
22	312,500	18,750	2,411,659	31,352	265,282	2,676,941	29,894	35,154
23	312,500	18,750	2,661,994	34,606	292,819	2,954,814	32,673	37,019
24	312,500	18,750	2,938,477	38,200	323,232	3,261,710	35,742	39,079
25	312,500	18,750	3,243,838	42,170	356,822	3,600,661	39,132	41,354

STARTING VALUE OF TRUST	$625,000
VALUE OF TRUST AFTER:	
FIVE YEARS	816,423
TEN YEARS	1,130,998
FIFTEEN YEARS	1,647,956
TWENTY YEARS	2,497,498
TWENTY-FIVE YEARS	3,913,161

Note: Prepared using Estate Planning Program Two.

Chapter 7 - How to Test Your Financial Directives

On Page 61 of the text the data below was presented:

Listed below are the changes in the federal law that slowly increase your amount of estate-tax exemption to $1 million by the year 2006. Using the Default Rules, a surviving spouse's annual income is listed. The probable value of the Trust is shown in the last three columns.

Year	TRUST	SPOUSE'S ANNUAL INCOME			VALUE OF TRUST		
		1st Yr.	5th Yr.	10th Yr.	15th Yr.	20th Yr.	25th Yr.
1998	$625,000	$19,516	$20,597	$22,719	$1,648,000	$2,497,000	$3,913,000
1999	650,000	20,296	21,421	23,628	1,714,000	2,597,000	4,070,000
2000	675,000	21,077	22,245	24,537	1,780,000	2,697,000	4,226,000
2002	675,000	21,077	22,245	24,537	1,780,000	2,697,000	4,226,000
2002	700,000	21,858	23,069	25,445	1,846,000	2,797,000	4,383,000
2003	700,000	21,858	23,069	25,445	1,846,000	2,797,000	4,383,000
2004	850,000	26,541	28,012	30,898	2,241,000	3,397,000	5,322,000
2005	950,000	29,664	31,308	34,533	2,505,000	3,796,000	5,948,000
2006	1,000,000	31,225	32,956	36,351	2,637,000	3,996,000	6,261,000

This Table illustrates the low incomes from each of the different Trust amounts (about 3% of the value of the Trust). And the above low incomes are before annual state and federal income taxes. Yet the values of the Trusts, above, are high due to the restricted incomes.

Each of the above incomes in the first year could have been greatly increased if Directives were given by the Grantor. And the following years' incomes could have been increased at a much higher rate to offset inflation. As the columns under Value of Trust indicate, a greater income can be provided.

On the following pages the detail by year is given when the federal estate tax exemption is increased. Note the annual detail for 1998 is on Page 235.

All of the following Tables were prepared using Estate Planning Program Two explained in Appendix A.

In the Year 1999 the Federal Estate Tax Exemption is $650,000

Starting Value of Trust	$650,000	**Interest Paid on Bonds**	6.00%
Percent in Bonds	50.00%	**Dividends Paid on Stocks**	1.30%
Percent in Stocks	50.00%	**Trust Fees & Expenses**	1.00%
Annual Growth in Stocks	11%	**Charged to Income**	0.50%

Year	Bond Amount	Bond Interest	Beg. Stock Amount	Stock Dividends	Stock Growth	End Stock Value	100% Trust Fees & Exp.	Net Income
1	$325,000	$ 19,500	$ 325,000	$ 4,225	$ 35,750	$ 360,750	$ 6,858	**$20,296**
2	325,000	19,500	357,321	4,645	39,305	396,627	7,216	20,716
3	325,000	19,500	393,018	5,109	43,232	436,250	7,613	20,803
4	325,000	19,500	432,444	5,622	47,569	480,013	8,050	21,097
5	325,000	19,500	475,988	6,188	52,359	**528,347**	8,533	**21,421**
6	325,000	19,500	524,080	6,813	57,649	581,729	9,067	21,779
7	325,000	19,500	577,195	7,504	63,491	640,687	9,657	22,175
8	325,000	19,500	635,858	8,266	69,944	705,803	10,308	22,612
9	325,000	19,500	700,649	9,108	77,071	777,720	11,027	23,095
10	325,000	19,500	772,206	10,039	84,943	**857,149**	11,821	**23,628**
11	325,000	19,500	851,238	11,066	93,636	944,874	12,699	24,217
12	325,000	19,500	938,525	12,201	103,238	1,041,763	13,668	24,867
13	325,000	19,500	1,034,929	13,454	113,842	1,148,771	14,738	25,585
14	325,000	19,500	1,141,402	14,838	125,554	1,266,957	15,920	26,378
15	325,000	19,500	1,258,997	16,367	138,490	**1,397,486**	17,225	**27,255**
16	325,000	19,500	1,388,874	18,055	152,776	1,541,650	18,667	28,222
17	325,000	19,500	1,532,317	19,920	168,555	1,700,872	20,259	29,291
18	325,000	19,500	1,690,742	21,980	185,982	1,876,724	22,017	30,471
19	325,000	19,500	1,865,716	24,254	205,229	2,070,944	23,959	31,775
20	325,000	19,500	2,058,964	26,767	226,486	**2,285,451**	26,105	**33,214**
21	325,000	19,500	2,272,398	29,541	249,964	2,522,362	28,474	34,804
22	325,000	19,500	2,508,125	32,606	275,894	2,784,019	31,090	36,561
23	325,000	19,500	2,768,474	35,990	304,532	3,073,006	33,980	38,500
24	325,000	19,500	3,056,016	39,728	336,162	3,392,178	37,172	40,642
25	325,000	19,500	3,373,592	43,857	371,095	**3,744,687**	40,697	**43,008**

STARTING VALUE OF TRUST	**$650,000**
VALUE OF TRUST AFTER:	
FIVE YEARS	849,080
TEN YEARS	1,176,238
FIFTEEN YEARS	1,713,874
TWENTY YEARS	2,597,398
TWENTY-FIVE YEARS	4,069,687

Note: Prepared using Estate Planning Program Two.

In the Year 2000 the Federal Estate Tax Exemption is $675,000

Starting Value of Trust	$675,000		Interest Paid on Bonds			6.00%
Percent in Bonds	50.00%		Dividends Paid on Stocks			1.30%
Percent in Stocks	50.00%		Trust Fees & Expenses			1.00%
Annual Growth in Stocks	11%		Charged to Income			0.50%

Year	Bond Amount	Bond Interest	Beg. Stock Amount	Stock Dividends	Stock Growth	End Stock Value	100%Trust Fees & Exp.	Net Income
1	$337,500	$ 20,250	$ 337,500	$ 4,388	$ 37,125	$ 374,625	$ 7,121	**$21,077**
2	337,500	20,250	371,064	4,824	40,817	411,881	7,494	21,513
3	337,500	20,250	408,135	5,306	44,895	453,029	7,905	21,603
4	337,500	20,250	449,077	5,838	49,398	498,475	8,360	21,908
5	337,500	20,250	494,295	6,426	54,372	**548,668**	8,862	**22,245**
6	337,500	20,250	544,237	7,075	59,866	604,103	9,416	22,617
7	337,500	20,250	599,395	7,792	65,933	665,328	10,028	23,028
8	337,500	20,250	660,314	8,584	72,635	732,949	10,704	23,482
9	337,500	20,250	727,597	9,459	80,036	807,632	11,451	23,983
10	337,500	20,250	801,907	10,425	88,210	**890,116**	12,276	**24,537**
11	337,500	20,250	883,978	11,492	97,238	981,216	13,187	25,148
12	337,500	20,250	974,622	12,670	107,208	1,081,831	14,193	25,823
13	337,500	20,250	1,074,734	13,972	118,221	1,192,955	15,305	26,569
14	337,500	20,250	1,185,302	15,409	130,383	1,315,686	16,532	27,393
15	337,500	20,250	1,307,420	16,996	143,816	**1,451,236**	17,887	**28,303**
16	337,500	20,250	1,442,292	18,750	158,652	1,600,944	19,384	29,308
17	337,500	20,250	1,591,252	20,686	175,038	1,766,290	21,038	30,417
18	337,500	20,250	1,755,771	22,825	193,135	1,948,906	22,864	31,643
19	337,500	20,250	1,937,474	25,187	213,122	2,150,596	24,881	32,997
20	337,500	20,250	2,138,155	27,796	235,197	**2,373,353**	27,109	**34,492**
21	337,500	20,250	2,359,798	30,677	259,578	2,619,376	29,569	36,143
22	337,500	20,250	2,604,592	33,860	286,505	2,891,097	32,286	37,967
23	337,500	20,250	2,874,954	37,374	316,245	3,191,199	35,287	39,981
24	337,500	20,250	3,173,555	41,256	349,091	3,522,646	38,601	42,205
25	337,500	20,250	3,503,346	45,543	385,368	**3,888,714**	42,262	**44,662**

STARTING VALUE OF TRUST	$675,000
VALUE OF TRUST AFTER:	
FIVE YEARS	881,737
TEN YEARS	1,221,478
FIFTEEN YEARS	1,779,792
TWENTY YEARS	2,697,298
TWENTY-FIVE YEARS	4,226,214

Note: Prepared using Estate Planning Program Two.

In the Year 2002 the Federal Estate Tax Exemption is $ 700,000

Starting Value of Trust	$700,000		Interest Paid on Bonds		6.00%
Percent in Bonds	50.00%		Dividends Paid on Stocks		1.30%
Percent in Stocks	50.00%		Trust Fees & Expenses		1.00%
Annual Growth in Stocks	11%		Charged to Income		0.50%

Year	Bond Amount	Bond Interest	Beg. Stock Amount	Stock Dividends	Stock Growth	End Stock Value	100%Trust Fees & Exp.	Net Income
1	$350,000	$ 21,000	$ 350,000	$ 4,550	$ 38,500	$ 388,500	$ 7,385	**$21,858**
2	350,000	21,000	384,808	5,002	42,329	427,136	7,771	22,310
3	350,000	21,000	423,251	5,502	46,558	469,808	8,198	22,403
4	350,000	21,000	465,709	6,054	51,228	516,937	8,669	22,720
5	350,000	21,000	512,602	6,664	56,386	**568,989**	9,190	**23,069**
6	350,000	21,000	564,394	7,337	62,083	626,477	9,765	23,455
7	350,000	21,000	621,595	8,081	68,375	689,970	10,400	23,881
8	350,000	21,000	684,770	8,902	75,325	760,095	11,101	24,352
9	350,000	21,000	754,545	9,809	83,000	837,545	11,875	24,871
10	350,000	21,000	831,607	10,811	91,477	**923,084**	12,731	**25,445**
11	350,000	21,000	916,718	11,917	100,839	1,017,557	13,676	26,080
12	350,000	21,000	1,010,719	13,139	111,179	1,121,898	14,719	26,780
13	350,000	21,000	1,114,539	14,489	122,599	1,237,138	15,871	27,553
14	350,000	21,000	1,229,203	15,980	135,212	1,364,415	17,144	28,408
15	350,000	21,000	1,355,843	17,626	149,143	**1,504,985**	18,550	**29,351**
16	350,000	21,000	1,495,711	19,444	164,528	1,660,239	20,102	30,393
17	350,000	21,000	1,650,187	21,452	181,521	1,831,708	21,817	31,544
18	350,000	21,000	1,820,800	23,670	200,288	2,021,088	23,711	32,815
19	350,000	21,000	2,009,232	26,120	221,016	2,230,248	25,802	34,219
20	350,000	21,000	2,217,346	28,826	243,908	**2,461,254**	28,113	**35,769**
21	350,000	21,000	2,447,198	31,814	269,192	2,716,390	30,664	37,482
22	350,000	21,000	2,701,058	35,114	297,116	2,998,174	33,482	39,373
23	350,000	21,000	2,981,434	38,759	327,958	3,309,391	36,594	41,462
24	350,000	21,000	3,291,094	42,784	362,020	3,653,115	40,031	43,769
25	350,000	21,000	3,633,099	47,230	399,641	**4,032,740**	43,827	**46,317**

STARTING VALUE OF TRUST	$700,000
VALUE OF TRUST AFTER:	
FIVE YEARS	914,394
TEN YEARS	1,266,718
FIFTEEN YEARS	1,845,711
TWENTY YEARS	2,797,198
TWENTY-FIVE YEARS	4,382,740

Note: Prepared using Estate Planning Program Two.

In the Year 2004 the Federal Estate Tax Exemption is $ 850,000

Starting Value of Trust	$850,000	
Percent in Bonds	50.00%	
Percent in Stocks	50.00%	
Annual Growth in Stocks	11%	

Interest Paid on Bonds	6.00%
Dividends Paid on Stocks	1.30%
Trust Fees & Expenses	1.00%
Charged to Income	0.50%

Year	Bond Amount	Bond Interest	Beg. Stock Amount	Stock Dividends	Stock Growth	End Stock Value	100%Trust Fees & Exp.	Net Income
1	$425,000	$ 25,500	$ 425,000	$ 5,525	$ 46,750	$ 471,750	$ 8,968	$26,541
2	425,000	25,500	467,266	6,074	51,399	518,666	9,437	27,091
3	425,000	25,500	513,947	6,681	56,534	570,481	9,955	27,204
4	425,000	25,500	565,504	7,352	62,205	627,709	10,527	27,588
5	425,000	25,500	622,446	8,092	68,469	690,915	11,159	28,012
6	425,000	25,500	685,335	8,909	75,387	760,722	11,857	28,481
7	425,000	25,500	754,794	9,812	83,027	837,821	12,628	28,998
8	425,000	25,500	831,507	10,810	91,466	922,973	13,480	29,570
9	425,000	25,500	916,233	11,911	100,786	1,017,018	14,420	30,201
10	425,000	25,500	1,009,808	13,128	111,079	1,120,887	15,459	30,898
11	425,000	25,500	1,113,158	14,471	122,447	1,235,605	16,606	31,668
12	425,000	25,500	1,227,302	15,955	135,003	1,362,305	17,873	32,518
13	425,000	25,500	1,353,369	17,594	148,871	1,502,239	19,272	33,458
14	425,000	25,500	1,492,603	19,404	164,186	1,656,789	20,818	34,495
15	425,000	25,500	1,646,380	21,403	181,102	1,827,482	22,525	35,641
16	425,000	25,500	1,816,220	23,611	199,784	2,016,004	24,410	36,906
17	425,000	25,500	2,003,799	26,049	220,418	2,224,217	26,492	38,303
18	425,000	25,500	2,210,971	28,743	243,207	2,454,178	28,792	39,847
19	425,000	25,500	2,439,782	31,717	268,376	2,708,158	31,332	41,551
20	425,000	25,500	2,692,492	35,002	296,174	2,988,666	34,137	43,434
21	425,000	25,500	2,971,598	38,631	326,876	3,298,474	37,235	45,513
22	425,000	25,500	3,279,856	42,638	360,784	3,640,640	40,656	47,810
23	425,000	25,500	3,620,312	47,064	398,234	4,018,547	44,435	50,346
24	425,000	25,500	3,996,329	51,952	439,596	4,435,925	48,609	53,148
25	425,000	25,500	4,411,620	57,351	485,278	4,896,899	53,219	56,242

STARTING VALUE OF TRUST	$850,000
VALUE OF TRUST AFTER:	
FIVE YEARS	1,110,335
TEN YEARS	1,538,158
FIFTEEN YEARS	2,241,220
TWENTY YEARS	3,396,598
TWENTY-FIVE YEARS	5,321,899

Note: Prepared using Estate Planning Program Two.

In the Year 2005 the Federal Estate Tax Exemption is $ 950,000

Starting Value of Trust	$950,000			Interest Paid on Bonds			6.00%
Percent in Bonds	50.00%			Dividends Paid on Stocks			1.30%
Percent in Stocks	50.00%			Trust Fees & Expenses			1.00%
Annual Growth in Stocks	11%			Charged to Income			0.50%

Year	Bond Amount	Bond Interest	Beg. Stock Amount	Stock Dividends	Stock Growth	End Stock Value	100%Trust Fees & Exp.	Net Income
1	$475,000	$ 28,500	$ 475,000	$ 6,175	$ 52,250	$ 527,250	$ 10,023	$29,664
2	475,000	28,500	522,239	6,789	57,446	579,685	10,547	30,278
3	475,000	28,500	574,412	7,467	63,185	637,597	11,126	30,404
4	475,000	28,500	632,034	8,216	69,524	701,558	11,766	30,834
5	475,000	28,500	695,675	9,044	76,524	772,199	12,472	31,308
6	475,000	28,500	765,963	9,958	84,256	850,219	13,252	31,831
7	475,000	28,500	843,593	10,967	92,795	936,388	14,114	32,410
8	475,000	28,500	929,331	12,081	102,226	1,031,558	15,066	33,049
9	475,000	28,500	1,024,025	13,312	112,643	1,136,668	16,117	33,754
10	475,000	28,500	1,128,609	14,672	124,147	1,252,756	17,278	34,533
11	475,000	28,500	1,244,117	16,174	136,853	1,380,970	18,560	35,394
12	475,000	28,500	1,371,690	17,832	150,886	1,522,576	19,976	36,344
13	475,000	28,500	1,512,589	19,664	166,385	1,678,973	21,540	37,394
14	475,000	28,500	1,668,203	21,687	183,502	1,851,706	23,267	38,553
15	475,000	28,500	1,840,072	23,921	202,408	2,042,480	25,175	39,834
16	475,000	28,500	2,029,893	26,389	223,288	2,253,181	27,282	41,248
17	475,000	28,500	2,239,540	29,114	246,349	2,485,890	29,609	42,810
18	475,000	28,500	2,471,085	32,124	271,819	2,742,904	32,179	44,535
19	475,000	28,500	2,726,815	35,449	299,950	3,026,765	35,018	46,440
20	475,000	28,500	3,009,256	39,120	331,018	3,340,274	38,153	48,544
21	475,000	28,500	3,321,198	43,176	365,332	3,686,529	41,615	50,868
22	475,000	28,500	3,665,722	47,654	403,229	4,068,951	45,440	53,435
23	475,000	28,500	4,046,231	52,601	445,085	4,491,317	49,663	56,269
24	475,000	28,500	4,466,485	58,064	491,313	4,957,798	54,328	59,400
25	475,000	28,500	4,930,634	64,098	542,370	5,473,004	59,480	62,858

STARTING VALUE OF TRUST	$950,000
VALUE OF TRUST AFTER:	
FIVE YEARS	1,240,963
TEN YEARS	1,719,117
FIFTEEN YEARS	2,504,893
TWENTY YEARS	3,796,198
TWENTY-FIVE YEARS	5,948,004

Note: Prepared using Estate Planning Program Two.

In the Year 2006 the Federal Estate Tax Exemption is $ 1,000,000

Starting Value of Trust	$1,000,000	Interest Paid on Bonds	6.00%
Percent in Bonds	50.00%	Dividends Paid on Stocks	1.30%
Percent in Stocks	50.00%	Trust Fees & Expenses	1.00%
Annual Growth in Stocks	11%	Charged to Income	0.50%

Year	Bond Amount	Bond Interest	Beg. Stock Amount	Stock Dividends	Stock Growth	End Stock Value	100% Trust Fees & Exp.	Net Income
1	$500,000	$ 30,000	$ 500,000	$ 6,500	$ 55,000	$ 555,000	$ 10,550	$31,225
2	500,000	30,000	549,725	7,146	60,470	610,195	11,102	31,871
3	500,000	30,000	604,644	7,860	66,511	671,155	11,712	32,005
4	500,000	30,000	665,299	8,649	73,183	738,482	12,385	32,456
5	500,000	30,000	732,289	9,520	80,552	812,841	13,128	32,956
6	500,000	30,000	806,277	10,482	88,690	894,967	13,950	33,507
7	500,000	30,000	887,993	11,544	97,679	985,672	14,857	34,116
8	500,000	30,000	978,243	12,717	107,607	1,085,850	15,859	34,788
9	500,000	30,000	1,077,921	14,013	118,571	1,196,492	16,965	35,531
10	500,000	30,000	1,188,010	15,444	130,681	1,318,691	18,187	36,351
11	500,000	30,000	1,309,597	17,025	144,056	1,453,653	19,537	37,256
12	500,000	30,000	1,443,885	18,771	158,827	1,602,712	21,027	38,257
13	500,000	30,000	1,592,198	20,699	175,142	1,767,340	22,673	39,362
14	500,000	30,000	1,756,004	22,828	193,160	1,949,164	24,492	40,582
15	500,000	30,000	1,936,918	25,180	213,061	2,149,979	26,500	41,930
16	500,000	30,000	2,136,729	27,777	235,040	2,371,770	28,718	43,419
17	500,000	30,000	2,357,411	30,646	259,315	2,616,726	31,167	45,063
18	500,000	30,000	2,601,142	33,815	286,126	2,887,268	33,873	46,879
19	500,000	30,000	2,870,332	37,314	315,736	3,186,068	36,861	48,884
20	500,000	30,000	3,167,638	41,179	348,440	3,516,078	40,161	51,099
21	500,000	30,000	3,495,997	45,448	384,560	3,880,557	43,806	53,545
22	500,000	30,000	3,858,654	50,163	424,452	4,283,106	47,831	56,247
23	500,000	30,000	4,259,191	55,369	468,511	4,727,702	52,277	59,231
24	500,000	30,000	4,701,563	61,120	517,172	5,218,735	57,187	62,527
25	500,000	30,000	5,190,142	67,472	570,916	5,761,057	62,611	66,167

STARTING VALUE OF TRUST	$1,000,000
VALUE OF TRUST AFTER:	
FIVE YEARS	1,306,277
TEN YEARS	1,809,597
FIFTEEN YEARS	2,636,729
TWENTY YEARS	3,995,997
TWENTY-FIVE YEARS	6,261,057

Note: Prepared using Estate Planning Program Two.

Chapter 8   - Increasing The Value Of Your Trust For Your Children.

On pages 67, 68 and 69, Five-year summaries of the value of a Trust invested under the Default Rules and two Grantor options were presented. These Five-Year summaries are shown below.

Page 67 which stated:

Start	"DEFAULT RULES" - VALUE OF THE TRUST AFTER				
	5 yrs.	10 yrs.	15 yrs	20 yrs.	25 yrs.
$1,000,000	$1,306,000	$1,810,000	$2,637,000	$3,996,000	$6,261,000

The annual details for the above are given on the preceding page, Page 242.

Page 68 which stated:

Start	100% INVESTED IN STOCKS - VALUE OF THE TRUST AFTER				
	5 yrs.	10 yrs.	15 yrs	20 yrs.	25 yrs.
$1,000,000	$1,643,000	$2,701,000	$4,438,000	$7,293,000	$12,046,000
Increase Over Default Rule					
- Amount	337,000	891,000	1,801,000	3,297,000	5,785,000
- Percent	26%	49%	68%	83%	92%

The annual details for Exhibit B are on the following page, Page 244.

Page 69 which stated:

Start	100% INVESTED IN STOCKS & ALL FEES AND EXPENSES CHARGED TO INCOME - VALUE OF THE TRUST AFTER				
	5 yrs.	10 yrs.	15 yrs	20 yrs.	25 yrs.
$1,000,000	$1,685,000	$2,839,000	$4,785,000	$8,062,000	$13,585,000
Increase over Default Rules					
- Amount	379,000	1,029,000	2,148,000	4,066,000	7,324,000
- Percent	29%	57%	81%	102%	117%

The annual details for Exhibit C are on Page 245.

Exhibit B, Page 56, - Option 1: 100% Invested in Stocks

Starting Value of Trust	$1,000,000	
Percent in Bonds	0.00%	
Percent in Stocks	100.00%	
Annual Growth in Stocks	11%	

Interest Paid on Bonds	6.00%	
Dividends Paid on Stocks	1.30%	
Trust Fees & Expenses	1.00%	
Charged to Income	0.50%	

Year	Bond Amount	Bond Interest	Beg. Stock Amount	Stock Dividends	Stock Growth	End Stock Value	100%Trust Fees & Exp.	Net Income
1	$ -	$ -	$ 1,000,000	$ 13,000	$ 110,000	$ 1,110,000	$ 11,100	$ 7,450
2	-	-	1,104,450	14,358	121,490	1,225,940	12,259	8,808
3	-	-	1,219,810	15,858	134,179	1,353,989	13,540	9,088
4	-	-	1,347,219	17,514	148,194	1,495,413	14,954	10,037
5	-	-	1,487,936	19,343	163,673	1,651,609	16,516	11,085
6	-	-	1,643,351	21,364	180,769	1,824,119	18,241	12,243
7	-	-	1,814,999	23,595	199,650	2,014,649	20,146	13,522
8	-	-	2,004,575	26,059	220,503	2,225,079	22,251	14,934
9	-	-	2,213,953	28,781	243,535	2,457,488	24,575	16,494
10	-	-	2,445,201	31,788	268,972	2,714,173	27,142	18,217
11	-	-	2,700,602	35,108	297,066	2,997,668	29,977	20,119
12	-	-	2,982,680	38,775	328,095	3,310,775	33,108	22,221
13	-	-	3,294,221	42,825	362,364	3,656,585	36,566	24,542
14	-	-	3,638,302	47,298	400,213	4,038,515	40,385	27,105
15	-	-	4,018,323	52,238	442,016	4,460,338	44,603	29,937
16	-	-	4,438,037	57,694	488,184	4,926,221	49,262	33,063
17	-	-	4,901,590	63,721	539,175	5,440,765	54,408	36,517
18	-	-	5,413,561	70,376	595,492	6,009,052	60,091	40,331
19	-	-	5,979,007	77,727	657,691	6,636,698	66,367	44,544
20	-	-	6,603,514	85,846	726,387	7,329,901	73,299	49,196
21	-	-	7,293,252	94,812	802,258	8,095,509	80,955	54,335
22	-	-	8,055,032	104,715	886,053	8,941,085	89,411	60,010
23	-	-	8,896,380	115,653	978,602	9,874,981	98,750	66,278
24	-	-	9,825,607	127,733	1,080,817	10,906,423	109,064	73,201
25	-	-	10,851,891	141,075	1,193,708	12,045,599	120,456	80,847

STARTING VALUE OF TRUST	$1,000,000
VALUE OF TRUST AFTER:	
FIVE YEARS	1,643,351
TEN YEARS	2,700,602
FIFTEEN YEARS	4,438,037
TWENTY YEARS	7,293,252
TWENTY-FIVE YEARS	12,045,599

Note: Prepared using Estate Planning Program Two.

Exhibit C, Page 58, - Option 1 and Option 2:   100% Invested in Stocks & All Fees and Expenses Charged to Income

Starting Value of Trust	$1,000,000	Interest Paid on Bonds	6.00%
Percent in Bonds	0.00%	Dividends Paid on Stocks	1.30%
Percent in Stocks	100.00%	Trust Fees & Expenses	1.00%
Annual Growth in Stocks	11%	Charged to Income	1.00%

Year	Bond Amount	Bond Interest	Beg. Stock Amount	Stock Dividends	Stock Growth	End Stock Value	100%Trust Fees & Exp.	Net Income
1	$ -	$ -	$ 1,000,000	$ 13,000	$ 110,000	$ 1,110,000	$ 11,100	$ 1,900
2	-	-	1,110,000	14,430	122,100	1,232,100	12,321	3,330
3	-	-	1,232,100	16,017	135,531	1,367,631	13,676	2,341
4	-	-	1,367,631	17,779	150,439	1,518,070	15,181	2,598
5	-	-	1,518,070	19,735	166,988	1,685,058	16,851	2,884
6	-	-	1,685,058	21,906	185,356	1,870,415	18,704	3,202
7	-	-	1,870,415	24,315	205,746	2,076,160	20,762	3,554
8	-	-	2,076,160	26,990	228,378	2,304,538	23,045	3,945
9	-	-	2,304,538	29,959	253,499	2,558,037	25,580	4,379
10	-	-	2,558,037	33,254	281,384	2,839,421	28,394	4,860
11	-	-	2,839,421	36,912	312,336	3,151,757	31,518	5,395
12	-	-	3,151,757	40,973	346,693	3,498,451	34,985	5,988
13	-	-	3,498,451	45,480	384,830	3,883,280	38,833	6,647
14	-	-	3,883,280	50,483	427,161	4,310,441	43,104	7,378
15	-	-	4,310,441	56,036	474,149	4,784,589	47,846	8,190
16	-	-	4,784,589	62,200	526,305	5,310,894	53,109	9,091
17	-	-	5,310,894	69,042	584,198	5,895,093	58,951	10,091
18	-	-	5,895,093	76,636	648,460	6,543,553	65,436	11,201
19	-	-	6,543,553	85,066	719,791	7,263,344	72,633	12,433
20	-	-	7,263,344	94,423	798,968	8,062,312	80,623	13,800
21	-	-	8,062,312	104,810	886,854	8,949,166	89,492	15,318
22	-	-	8,949,166	116,339	984,408	9,933,574	99,336	17,003
23	-	-	9,933,574	129,136	1,092,693	11,026,267	110,263	18,874
24	-	-	11,026,267	143,341	1,212,889	12,239,157	122,392	20,950
25	-	-	12,239,157	159,109	1,346,307	13,585,464	135,855	23,254

STARTING VALUE OF TRUST	$1,000,000
VALUE OF TRUST AFTER:	
FIVE YEARS	1,685,058
TEN YEARS	2,839,421
FIFTEEN YEARS	4,784,589
TWENTY YEARS	8,062,312
TWENTY-FIVE YEARS	13,585,464

Note: Prepared using Estate Planning Program One.

Chapter 10 -The Safety Provision: Extra Money When You Need It.

Page 87. A problem arises when 5% is annually removed from a Trust where the Starting Income Requirement is high. In this example it was $54,529, increased 3% for inflation. Note: At the end of year 20, there is a negative "End Stock Value." The Bonds would then be sold.=

Starting Income From Trust	**$ 54,529**	**Year Starting Income Required**	**1998**
Annual Increase	**8.0%**	**Percent in Stocks**	**75%**
Starting Value of Trust	**$1,000,000**	**Stock Dividends**	**1.3%**
Percent in Bonds	**25.0%**	**Annual Stock Increase**	**8.0%**
Bond Interest	**6.0%**	**Trust Fees & Expenses**	**0.75%**

Year	Bond Amount	Bond Interest	Beg. Stock Amount	Stock Dividends	Stock Increase	End Stock Value	REMOVED from Principal	ANNUAL Income
1	250,000	15,000	750,000	9,750	60,000	810,000	$ 29,779	$ 54,529
2	250,000	15,000	772,271	10,040	61,782	834,053	33,852	58,891
3	250,000	15,000	792,070	10,297	63,366	855,436	38,306	63,603
4	250,000	15,000	808,840	10,515	64,707	873,547	43,176	68,691
5	250,000	15,000	821,944	10,685	65,756	887,700	48,501	74,186
6	250,000	15,000	830,666	10,799	66,453	897,120	54,322	80,121
7	250,000	15,000	834,194	10,845	66,736	900,929	60,686	86,531
8	250,000	15,000	831,611	10,811	66,529	898,140	67,642	93,453
9	250,000	15,000	821,887	10,685	65,751	887,638	75,245	100,929
10	250,000	15,000	803,861	10,450	64,309	868,170	83,554	109,004
11	250,000	15,000	776,230	10,091	62,098	838,328	92,633	117,724
12	250,000	15,000	737,533	9,588	59,003	796,535	102,554	127,142
13	250,000	15,000	686,132	8,920	54,891	741,023	113,394	137,313
14	250,000	15,000	620,197	8,063	49,616	669,812	125,236	148,298
15	250,000	15,000	537,678	6,990	43,014	580,692	138,172	160,162
16	250,000	15,000	436,290	5,672	34,903	471,193	152,303	172,975
17	250,000	15,000	313,480	4,075	25,078	338,559	167,738	186,813
18	250,000	15,000	166,407	2,163	13,313	179,719	184,595	201,758
19	250,000	15,000	(8,099)	(105)	(648)	(8,747)	203,004	217,899
20	250,000	15,000	(213,560)	(2,776)	(17,085)	(230,645)	223,107	235,331
21	250,000	15,000	(453,898)	(5,901)	(36,312)	(490,209)	245,058	254,157
22	250,000	15,000	(733,466)	(9,535)	(58,677)	(792,143)	269,025	274,490
23	250,000	15,000	(1,057,102)	(13,742)	(84,568)	(1,141,670)	295,191	296,449
24	250,000	15,000	(1,430,174)	(18,592)	(114,414)	(1,544,588)	323,757	320,165
25	250,000	15,000	(1,858,636)	(24,162)	(148,691)	(2,007,327)	354,941	345,778

STARTING VALUE OF TRUST	**$1,000,000**
VALUE OF THE TRUST AFTER:	
FIVE YEARS	**1,080,666**
TEN YEARS	**1,026,230**
FIFTEEN YEARS	**686,290**
TWENTY YEARS	**(203,898)**
TWENTY-FIVE YEARS	**(2,112,267)**

Note: Prepared using Estate Planning Program One

Chapter 12 -   Trusts for a Second Marriage

Numerous financial projections were made throughout this chapter to determine the amount of money required to fund a Trust for the second spouse. Estate Planning Program One was used for all of these calculations. Information on using this Program is in Appendix A.

Chapter 13 -   Marital Trust in Conjunction with a Credit Shelter Trust

On Page 115 of the text the following Exhibit was shown.

EXHIBIT 7

High Growth in Credit Shelter Trust for Benefit of the Children Coupled with a Marital Trust that Pays Any Shortage Based on the Stated Income Needs of the Surviving Spouse

Year	Income Needs From Trusts	Income Paid From Credit Shelter Trust[4]	Shortage Paid Paid From Marital Trust
1998	$ 28,000	$	$
2003	32,460		
2008	37,630	17,197	20,438
2013	42,353	23,386	18,967
2018	49,098	35,811	13,287
2023	56,918	56,746	172
2028	65,984	92,024	- 26,040

It was stated that the total to be paid over this 36-year period from the Marital Trust is $410,000. But as will be shown in this Appendix, only $280,000 is required to fund the Marital Trust if the amount was invested in bonds paying 5.5% interest.

This yearly detail is shown on the following page.

When Directives are given to Increase the Value of the Credit Shelter Trust (90% in stocks and all Trustees Fees and Expenses charged to income) an annual shortage occurs in the Income for the Spouse (Columns 2,3 and 4). To Supplement the Shortages, Funds can be placed in a Marital Trust (Columns 5, 6, and 7).

	Interest		5.50%			
	Amount in Marital Trust		280,000			

Year	ANNUAL Income Required	Credit Shelter Trust Net Income	Income Shortage	Marital Beginning Amount	Trust Ending Amount	Interest
1998	$28,000	$9,458	$18,542	280,000	261,458	14,380
1999	28,840	9,920	18,920	275,838	256,918	14,130
2000	29,705	10,434	19,271	271,049	252,129	14,130
2001	30,596	11,004	19,592	266,259	246,667	13,567
2002	31,514	11,637	19,877	260,234	240,357	13,220
2003	32,460	12,340	20,120	253,577	233,457	12,840
2004	33,433	13,120	20,313	246,297	225,984	12,429
2005	34,436	13,985	20,451	238,413	217,962	11,988
2006	35,470	14,946	20,524	229,950	209,426	11,518
2007	36,534	16,013	20,521	220,944	200,423	11,023
2008	37,630	17,197	20,433	211,446	191,013	10,506
2009	38,759	18,511	20,248	201,519	181,271	9,970
2010	39,921	19,970	19,951	171,301	151,350	8,324
2012	41,119	21,589	19,530	143,026	123,496	6,792
2013	42,353	23,386	18,967	130,288	111,321	6,123
2014	43,623	25,381	18,242	117,444	99,202	5,456
2015	44,932	27,596	17,336	104,658	87,322	4,803
2016	46,280	30,054	16,226	92,125	75,899	4,174
2017	47,668	32,782	14,886	59,673	44,787	2,463
2018	49,098	35,811	13,287	47,250	33,963	1,868
2019	50,571	39,172	11,399	35,831	24,432	1,344
2020	52,088	42,904	9,184	25,776	16,592	913
2021	53,651	47,046	6,605	17,504	10,899	599
2022	55,260	51,643	3,617	11,499	7,882	433
2023	56,918	56,746	<u>172</u>	8,315	8,143	
		TOTAL	$408,214			

Notes: The above Table was prepared by:

1. Calculating the annual income required by entering the starting amount of $28,000 (in 1998) into Estate Planning Program One. When the amounts were obtained, they were transferred to a new page of a spreadsheet program.

2.   Next, Estate Planning Program Two was used and the planning Directives of 90% in stocks and all Trustees fees and expenses charged to income were entered. And, as the starting value of Trust, $1 million was also entered since the Grantor's plan was based on his living past the year 2005. When the amounts of income were obtained, they were also transferred to a new page of the spreadsheet program.

3. A simple spreadsheet program was written to determine the shortage of income each year. This was followed by another program that would take an unknown starting value to be placed in a Marital Trust to pay the shortage each year. The program provided that after the shortages were paid, an unknown amount of interest would be paid on the remaining funds. After that was completed, actual amounts of initial funding of the Marital Trust and interest rates could be entered to test the amount of funds required.

Chapter 14 - Paying the Gross Income, Instead of the Net Income

On page 131, of the text the following was presented:

Key Measurements After	5 years	10 years	15 years	20 years
A. Value of each Trust:				
Gross Income provision	$800,470	$1,044,737	$1,436,170	$2,063,430
Net Income provision	771,068	980,205	1,323,889	1,888,684
Difference	$ 29,402	$ 64,532	$ 112,281	$ 174,746

Key Measurements After	5 years	10 years	15 years	20 years
B. Annual Income to Spouse:				
Gross Income provision	$ 26,793	$ 29,683	$ 34,314	$ 41,734
Net Income provision	25,754	27,164	29,483	33,292
Difference	$ 1,039	$ 2,519	$ 4,831	$ 8,442

The annual data on these key comparison follows.

Trust with Net Income Provision

Starting Value of Trust	$643,806	Interest Paid on Bonds	6.00%
Percent in Bonds	66.10%	Dividends Paid on Stocks	1.30%
Percent in Stocks	33.90%	Trust Fees & Expenses	1.00%
Annual Growth in Stocks	11%	Charged to Income	0.50%

Year	Bond Amount	Bond Interest	Beg. Stock Amount	Stock Dividends	Stock Growth	End Stock Value	100%Trust Fees & Exp.	Net Income
1	$425,556	$ 25,533	$ 218,250	$ 2,837	$ 24,008	$ 242,258	$ 6,678	$25,032
2	425,556	25,533	238,919	3,106	26,281	265,200	6,908	25,300
3	425,556	25,533	261,746	3,403	28,792	290,538	7,161	25,356
4	425,556	25,533	286,958	3,730	31,565	318,523	7,441	25,543
5	425,556	25,533	314,802	4,092	34,628	349,431	7,750	25,751
6	425,556	25,533	345,556	4,492	38,011	383,567	8,091	25,980
7	425,556	25,533	379,521	4,934	41,747	421,269	8,468	26,233
8	425,556	25,533	417,035	5,421	45,874	462,908	8,885	26,512
9	425,556	25,533	458,466	5,960	50,431	508,897	9,345	26,821
10	425,556	25,533	504,225	6,555	55,465	559,690	9,852	27,162
11	425,556	25,533	554,764	7,212	61,024	615,788	10,413	27,539
12	425,556	25,533	610,581	7,938	67,164	677,745	11,033	27,954
13	425,556	25,533	672,228	8,739	73,945	746,173	11,717	28,414
14	425,556	25,533	740,315	9,624	81,435	821,749	12,473	28,921
15	425,556	25,533	815,513	10,602	89,706	905,219	13,308	29,481
16	425,556	25,533	898,565	11,681	98,842	997,408	14,230	30,100
17	425,556	25,533	990,293	12,874	108,932	1,099,225	15,248	30,783
18	425,556	25,533	1,091,601	14,191	120,076	1,211,677	16,372	31,538
19	425,556	25,533	1,203,491	15,645	132,384	1,335,875	17,614	32,372
20	425,556	25,533	1,327,068	17,252	145,977	1,473,045	18,986	33,292
21	425,556	25,533	1,463,552	19,026	160,991	1,624,543	20,501	34,309
22	425,556	25,533	1,614,293	20,986	177,572	1,791,865	22,174	35,432
23	425,556	25,533	1,780,778	23,150	195,886	1,976,663	24,022	36,672
24	425,556	25,533	1,964,652	25,540	216,112	2,180,764	26,063	38,042
25	425,556	25,533	2,167,732	28,181	238,451	2,406,183	28,317	39,555

STARTING VALUE OF TRUST	$643,806
VALUE OF TRUST AFTER:	
FIVE YEARS	771,112
TEN YEARS	980,319
FIFTEEN YEARS	1,324,121
TWENTY YEARS	1,889,108
TWENTY-FIVE YEARS	2,831,739

Note: Prepared on Internet Calculator Number Two

Trust with Gross Income Provision

Starting Value of Trust	$648,038	
Percent in Bonds	55.36%	
Percent in Stocks	44.64%	
Annual Growth in Stocks	11%	

Interest Paid on Bonds	6.00%
Dividends Paid on Stocks	1.30%
Trust Fees & Expenses	1.00%
Charged to Income	0.00%

Year	Bond Amount	Bond Interest	Beg. Stock Amount	Stock Dividends	Stock Growth	End Stock Value	100% Trust Fees & Exp.	Net Income
1	$358,754	$ 21,525	$ 289,284	$ 3,761	$ 31,821	$ 321,105	$ 6,799	$25,286
2	358,754	21,525	314,307	4,086	34,574	348,881	7,076	25,611
3	358,754	21,525	341,804	4,443	37,598	379,403	7,382	25,969
4	358,754	21,525	372,021	4,836	40,922	412,943	7,717	26,362
5	358,754	21,525	405,226	5,268	44,575	449,801	8,086	26,793
6	358,754	21,525	441,716	5,742	48,589	490,305	8,491	27,268
7	358,754	21,525	481,814	6,264	53,000	534,814	8,936	27,789
8	358,754	21,525	525,878	6,836	57,847	583,724	9,425	28,362
9	358,754	21,525	574,300	7,466	63,173	637,473	9,962	28,991
10	358,754	21,525	627,510	8,158	69,026	696,536	10,553	29,683
11	358,754	21,525	685,984	8,918	75,458	761,442	11,202	30,443
12	358,754	21,525	750,240	9,753	82,526	832,766	11,915	31,278
13	358,754	21,525	820,851	10,671	90,294	911,145	12,699	32,196
14	358,754	21,525	898,446	11,680	98,829	997,275	13,560	33,205
15	358,754	21,525	983,714	12,788	108,209	1,091,923	14,507	34,314
16	358,754	21,525	1,077,416	14,006	118,516	1,195,932	15,547	35,532
17	358,754	21,525	1,180,385	15,345	129,842	1,310,227	16,690	36,870
18	358,754	21,525	1,293,538	16,816	142,289	1,435,827	17,946	38,341
19	358,754	21,525	1,417,881	18,432	155,967	1,573,848	19,326	39,958
20	358,754	21,525	1,554,522	20,209	170,997	1,725,519	20,843	41,734
21	358,754	21,525	1,704,677	22,161	187,514	1,892,191	22,509	43,686
22	358,754	21,525	1,869,682	24,306	205,665	2,075,347	24,341	45,831
23	358,754	21,525	2,051,006	26,663	225,611	2,276,616	26,354	48,188
24	358,754	21,525	2,250,262	29,253	247,529	2,497,791	28,565	50,779
25	358,754	21,525	2,469,226	32,100	271,615	2,740,841	30,996	53,625

STARTING VALUE OF TRUST	$648,038
VALUE OF TRUST AFTER:	
FIVE YEARS	800,470
TEN YEARS	1,044,737
FIFTEEN YEARS	1,436,170
TWENTY YEARS	2,063,430
TWENTY-FIVE YEARS	3,099,595

Note: Prepared on Internet Calculator Number Two

APPENDIX C

Additional Information for Completing Exhibit 1
INCOME NEEDS OF EACH SPOUSE

Introduction

Each person should complete a separate worksheet. Completing this worksheet is not meant to be an exhaustive time-consuming operation. Reasonable estimates can be made and placed in the various sections. Any errors should be made on the high-side. It is better that more income rather than less be available for the surviving spouse.

Section A

Insert the name of the person this form is being prepared for. A separate form should be prepared for the husband and for the wife.

A. - **Current annual income required** by (NAME) _____ as the surviving spouse excluding the cost of a new car, vacations and other items listed in "B" below. . . . . $ _____

Make an estimate of your current annual expenses. Many of the amounts especially for the annual costs of maintaining your home will remain the same for both the husband and the wife.(real estate taxes or rental payments, property insurance, cost of yard work and other normal annual maintenance items). Do not plan to immediately move after the first spouse dies to reduce your expenses. This can be a mistake.

Include auto insurance and your general liability policy (umbrella policy), medical gap insurance, drugs, etc.

If you entertain, belong to a club or other organizations include these expenses.

Generally the annual expenses of each person are about the same. In fact, the saying that two can live as cheaply as one has validity. If you know what your current annual expenses are, excluding the items in Section B, use this amount.

It is very important that you increase this amount by the annual state and federal income taxes you pay. If you want, you can adjust your standard deductions on your tax returns to increase your tax estimate by adding back the standard deductions taken as a husband and wife and then reduce this amount by the standard deduction for a single person.

Be sure to consider:

Your total annual income, less any expenses for items in Section B and any savings from your total income last year can be used. If you increased your credit card balances or used any of your savings or investments, these amounts should be added to obtain your total income needs.

A - 2 SOURCES OF INCOME excluding Trust:

In this section you will add items of income from sources other than the Trust. If you are currently working, do not include this current income. If your current position has retirement benefits and you will receive these, enter that amount.

For items such as Social Security, enter the current amount you are receiving as the husband. If the wife is receiving half of the husband's Social Security, enter the amount she will receive as a widow.

Do not increase current payments for Social Security or other items you list below. It is true that small upward adjustments are annually made for Social Security and the dividends you currently receive on stocks may increase. But these amounts of increases are small, especially in a short period of time.

a. Social Security $ _____
b. Pensions $ _____

Note: As indicated in Exhibit 2, The wife as the surviving spouse generally receives about half of the husband's pension at his death.

A - 2, c. Other: List by name & current value: (Examples below)

(CDs and Savings Accounts - Total Amount) $ (Annual Income)
(Interest Paying Bonds) $ (Annual Income)
(IRA Funds) $ (Estimated Withdrawals)
(Stocks & Mutual Funds) $ (Annual Income)
(Other Sources of Income) $ (Annual Income)
           TOTAL $ _____

The above section requires some careful thought on which assets are in the name of the other spouse in order to qualify for the Credit Shelter Trust. If your home, any stocks or other securities, mutual funds, etc. are in joint names with right of survivorship, they will pass directly to the surviving spouse. Enter all income producing assets that are either in your name alone or held jointly..

- **Subtract total of "Other Sources of Income" from "Estimated Annual Income Required"**   - $ _____

A - 3 TOTAL "A" INCOME REQUIRED FROM THE TRUST $ _____

This is the annual income you will need from the Trust your spouse established prior to adding the additional income you will need for items listed in Section "B," below.

Section B   Additional Special Needs for Annual Expenses not included in the above:

B - 1 New Car costing $_____ divided by ____ years = $ _____

As an example: A new car purchased every four years and costing $20,000 after trade-in of the old car, enter:
*New Car costing $ 20,000 divided by 4 years = $ 5,000 *

B - 2 Travel & Vacations $ _____

If you will be taking trips to visit your children and grandchildren, trips with friends, etc., enter the total costs of these trips including meals and lodging, airline tickets, etc.

B - 3 Family needs: assistance to children & grandchildren, gifts, etc. $ _____

This section requires thoughtful consideration.. In addition to gifts for birthdays and holidays, are there now or might there be in the future special needs for assistance for your children or grandchildren that you would like to provide for? If you will have high estates taxes, after the death of your spouse, do you plan to make use of annual gifts of $10,000 to any or all of your family, pay for the education of any of your grandchildren ,etc. If so, include these amounts here.

Other: List

_____ $ _____
_____ $ _____

In this section, list Other Special Needs. If you own a home, major appliances need to be replaced, roofs require repair, etc. You will need to set-up an annual reserve of at least a few thousand dollars a year for these types of items

B - 4 TOTAL FOR SPECIAL NEEDS $ _____

Note: In this section add an additional amount for the state and federal income taxes that must be paid for the total of the additional expense in Section B.

Example: If all of the additional expenses in Section B total $15,000 and your top tax bracket is 35% for both state and federal taxes, increase the $15,000 by 54% or $ 8,077 for a total of $ 23,077 required in additional income before a combined state and federal tax rate of 35%. Stated another way: A Taxable Income of $23,077 at a 35% tax rate pays $8,077 in taxes and nets $15,000.
INCREASE (For taxes) $ _____

TOTAL OF SPECIAL NEEDS (Including State
& Federal Income Taxes) $ _____

B - 5 PLUS TOTAL INCOME REQUIRED FROM "A" $ _____

Enter the "TOTAL "A" INCOME REQUIRED FROM THE TRUST" at the bottom of Section A above.

**C   TOTAL ANNUAL INCOME REQUIRED
FROM THE TRUST** $ _____

Add and enter the totals from Sections "A" and "B." If the above amount is over $19,000 you need to consider revising your estate planning documents if they are silent as to the income to be paid for the surviving spouse from the Credit Shelter Trust. This is discussed in Chapter 6. There are other important options that can be considered that are presented in this book.

NOTE:

THE SURVIVING SPOUSE SHOULD HAVE AMPLE FUNDS AVAILABLE. AND, IF POSSIBLE HAVE SUFFICIENT FUNDS FOR GIFTS AND OTHER NEEDS OF YOUR CHILDREN AND GRANDCHILDREN.   THE GOAL IS TO MAINTAIN A STRONG FAMILY RELATIONSHIP.

APPENDIX   D

Annually Evaluating the Investment Performance of the Trustee.

Introduction

Every investor should measure the performance of their investments. Professional investors and advisors continually do this but most individual investors do not devote full time to managing their investments. But they should measure the performance of their investments at least each quarter or semi-annually. This is especially important to do for common stock investments. The same concept of measuring performance applies to investments in a Trust that may be held by others as trustee.

If a bank Trust department is your trustee, information on the results of other banks can be obtained to compare their trustee performance compared to yours. This is especially important for that portion of the Trust invested in common stocks.

How to measure the performance of your stocks.

The key measurement of the performance of stocks is the S&P 500 index (Standard & Poor). It is composed of the S & P 400 Industrials, the S & P 20 Transportation, the S & P 40 Financial and the S & P 40 Utilities.

Most of the stocks in the S & P 500 are found on the New York Stock Exchange, though there are a few from the American Stock Exchange and the over-the-counter markets.

The S&P 500 index represents about 80 percent of the market value of all the issues traded on the NYSE. The S & P is commonly considered the benchmark against which the performance of individual stocks or stock groups is measured. It is a far broader measure of market activity than the DJIA (Dow Jones Industrial Average), even through the DJIA is quoted more widely.

Not matter who is controlling or advising you on the stocks that are purchased and sold, such as in a retirement account, a mutual fund, a Trust account or your personal account, the actual performance of your stocks should be measured against the performance of the S & P 500.

Consideration needs to be given in a Trust for both the income needs of the surviving spouse and other Income Beneficiaries and the growth of the assets to have the potential for a high end-value for the children and other heirs. A Grantor can state in the documentation that a high percentage of the investable assets of the Trust are to be invested in good quality growth stocks. The is a decision of the Grantor based on their knowledge and confidence in the market.

As a part of this consideration, the surviving spouse can be given an appropriate annual income, adjusted for inflation as determined by the use of Exhibit 1 -"Income Needs of the Surviving Spouse" or some other procedure to properly calculate the surviving spouse's needs. Recommendations to determine the proper income needs and how these needs might be stated in the Trust are in Chapter 6.

But even if this recommendation is not followed, or if the Trust is already in existence, the investment performance of a Trust should be measured. This appendix will show a simple method to continually make this measurement.

The two main investment vehicles for a trustee are stocks and bonds. Investments in stocks are made based on the belief that the total return (Dividends plus the growth in value), over time, will far exceed the return from bonds. Trustees do not invest in bonds for the growth of the investment. Speculation in bond futures, because of the high risks, is not an activity a trustee should engage in. Investments in bonds are made to obtain a higher interest income [1] than dividends provide.

Separate measurements are to be made of the investment results of the funds invested in stocks and the funds invested in bonds.

(1)   Investment in bonds carry an inflationary and interest rate risk. With inflation, the purchasing power of the funds invested in bonds are reduced. Even at a low inflationary rate of 2% a year, the purchasing power of bonds decreases in value 10% every five years. If the surviving spouse were to live for 20 years, the purchasing power of the funds invested in bonds would decrease 40% at 2% inflation. If inflation averaged 3% over these 20 years, the purchasing power of the funds invested in bonds would decrease 48%. To avoid interest rate risks, bond investments are normally made for short to medium term periods -five, eight or ten years.

To Measure the Investment Performance of U. S. Traded Stocks.

The S & P 500 index is widely used as a measurement of investment performance of stocks. Because of the large number of stocks in the index, 500, and their diversification, the S&P 500 index is considered the "market" and is the benchmark to which the performance of a stock portfolio is to be measured and compared.

The Dow Jones Industrial Average is perhaps more widely known and reported but it represents only 30 stocks.

To make this measurement only a few facts are required and they are illustrated below.

1. Value of the stock holdings, December 31, 1997	$ 765,000
Less: Stock Value when Trust funded, April 28, 1995	- 450,000
Unadjusted Gain in Account	$ 315,000
Percent Gain	70%
2. S&P 500 Index, Close December 31, 1997	970.43
Less: Index when Trust funded, Close April 28, 1995	514.71
Increase in the index	455.72
Percent Gain	88.5%

In the above example, the SP 500 index appears to have outperformed the trustee's investments in stocks. But the above example was not adjusted to make a true comparison. An adjustment is required for withdrawals. These withdrawals are for any trustee fees and expenses and payments of principal made to the surviving spouse that were charged to the stock portion of the Trust portfolio.

The above example has not been adjusted to take into account any withdrawals against the stock investments. This adjustment is made below.

1. Unadjusted Stock Gain in Trust		$ 315,000
Adjustments: withdrawals charged against stocks:		
a. 1995 withdrawals	$14,754	
b. 1996 withdrawals	31,379	
c. 1997 withdrawals	43,560	
Total Withdrawals		+ $ 89,693
Gross Gain in Stocks		$ 404,693

This adjusted gain is now the basis for comparison:

1. Value of the stock holdings, December 31, 1997	$ 765,000
Plus: Withdrawals charged against stocks	+ $ 89,693
Total	$ 854,693
Less: Stock Value when Trust funded, April 28, 1995	- 450,000
Adjusted Gain in Stocks	$404,693
Percent Gain	89.9%

On an adjusted basis, the trustee's investment performance was slightly better than the benchmark, the S&P 500 that gained 88.5%. No consideration should be given to replacing the trustee provided the gains were not made from very speculative stocks which would not normally be the case with a bank or other professional trustee.

The investment performance of a trustee should be made over several years. In a case of a change in trustees, the measurements should be made over the period that the particular trustee has handled the Trust. If a new trustee is appointed, you should start your measurement of the S&P 500 at the date the new trustee takes over the Trust and measure the new trustee's performance from that date forward.

Also note that the above measurement excludes any consideration of dividends paid on the stocks. In the past, trustees have justified a lower growth in their stock investments by stating that they invested in high dividend paying stocks that grow in value at a lower rate than the S&P 500 index, in order to produce a higher income for the surviving spouse.

This justification of sacrificing growth for a high income to be paid to the surviving spouse would have merit if the combined dividend and growth in value of the stocks are similar to the combined dividends paid on the S&P 500 stocks and the growth of the S&P 500. But this is not always possible. Growth stocks pay a low dividend because the profits generated are used to reinvest in the growing company.

Trustees who invest under the new Uniform Prudent Investors Act (UPIA in Appendix E) are required to achieve broad diversification in their stock holdings. To accomplish this, mutual funds or index funds are generally used. But there will still be cases in which individual stocks will be held.

A second level of measurement of the investment performance of stocks is to look at the investment return of each component in the stock portfolio measured to the S&P 500 index. These components might be several mutual funds and individual stocks. An example of this measurement follows:

John Doe Trust
Percentage Gain for the 12 months Ending June 30, 1997 [2]
of Mutual Funds & Stocks held for the past 12 months

Shares	STOCKS	Market Value June 30, 1996	Value June 30, 1997	Percent Gain
1500	Mutual Fund "A"	$136,121	$ 174,643	28.30%
1200	Mutual Fund "B"	124,743	155,854	25.55%
1440	Mutual Fund "C"	147,498	168,605	14.31%
480	Bristol Myers	21,600	39,420	82.50%
800	Coca Cola	39,200	56,800	44.90%
225	Eastman Kodak	17,494	17,663	0.96%
400	Exxon	17,375	24,175	39.14%
800	General Electric	34,700	52,250	50.58%
600	Hershey Foods	22,012	33,975	54.35%
400	Intel	29,375	56,900	93.70%
500	McDonalds	23,375	24,312	4.01%
500	Merck	32,312	51,250	58.61%
200	Mobil Corp	11,237	13,875	23.48%
500	Pfizer	35,687	61,000	70.93%
100	Procter & Gamble	9,062	13,931	53.73%
100	Schlumberger	8,425	12,500	48.37%
TOTALS		**$ 710,216**	**$ 957,153**	**34.77%**
S & P 500 Index		**671**	**848**	**26.45%**

(2)   The above Table has actual market prices for the individual stocks, the S & P 500 and their percent gains. The prices for the mutual funds and their gains are for illustration only.

The above analysis indicates that the growth of the Trust's total equity portfolio exceeded the S&P 500 index over the last 12 months. However, the purpose of the above example is to compare how individual mutual funds and stocks performed over this time period.

The stock market is very efficient. The market prices the stocks daily based on all available information. Therefore, it is best to assume that the market has priced each stock based on its value. There are exceptions, particularly for small companies, and occasionally with a medium and even a large company.

Therefore, the above illustration indicates that Mutual Fund "C," Eastman Kodak and McDonalds require special attention. What is the "market" telling us about Mutual Fund "C" and these two stocks? Why has Mutual Fund "C" only increased 14.31% compared to a 26.45% increase in the S&P 500 index.?

Was this a Mutual Fund that invested in a special sector such as small stocks, international stocks, etc.? Or, is it a case of poor fund management ? How well has this fund performed over the last three or five years? Should this fund be sold?

Why has the market priced Eastman Kodak and McDonalds to yield such a small gain over the last months? Two weeks after these market prices were available on June 30, 1997, Eastman Kodak announced that its earnings in the second quarter had dropped 16% compared to last year. The price of Eastman Kodak's stock dropped 10% with this news.

But if you were to look back a few months or longer, the market in its pricing of this stock knew that something was wrong. The same concept applies to McDonalds. Poor advice is to invest against the market.

To Measure the Investment Performance of International Stocks.

The U. S stock market now comprises 35% of the world's equity market valuation. An added risk in international investing is a change in currency valuations. Your gains from a foreign investment may be increased or decreased based on changes in the value of the foreign currency against the U.S. dollar. In recent years, the dollar has increased about 30% in value against most major foreign currencies.

There have been periods in the past, and therefore perhaps in the future, when the U. S. Dollar will drop in value compared to selected foreign currencies.

A well-diversified equity portfolio will hold a percentage of their investments in international stocks and foreign country or area mutual funds.

Again, indexes and index funds are available on international stocks by country and area of the world.

SUMMARY - On Measuring the Investment Performance of Stocks in a Trust.

1. Every Grantor of a Trust should give serious consideration to naming a trustee who has the knowledge, experience and time to properly invest and manage the assets in his Trust.

2. Each Trust should give the surviving spouse, or some other person, the power to replace the trustee.

3. In addition, a Grantor should consider leaving written instructions on how evaluations are to be made of the trustee's investment performance. Others in the family or friends can then assist the person, who has the authority to replace a trustee, with this evaluation.

4. Special and extra attention is generally given by the trustee who knows that their investment performance is being monitored.

There are measurements for other types of equity investments such as small cap stocks (Wilshire 4500), international stocks by country and areas of the world. But for most stock investors, the S&P 500 is the index to use.

Examples of Other Types of Equity measurements:

Wilshire 4500 Index - This index tracks that portion of the U. S. Stocks not included in the S&P 500 Stock Index.

Wilshire 5000 Index - This index tracks the entire U. S. Stock market. It includes the S&P 500 index and the Wilshire 4500 index.

Morgan Stanley Europe, Australia and Far East (EAFE) Index - This index tracks the world's major non-U.S. stock markets.

Morgan Stanley Europe Index -This is a sub-index of the Morgan Stanley EAFE Index (above) which tracks European Stocks.

Morgan Stanley Pacific Index - This is a sub-index of the Morgan Stanley EAFE Index (above) which tracks Pacific Rim Stocks.

The above concepts of measuring the performance of equity investments in a Trust can be applied to other investments as well.

To Measure the Investment Performance of Bonds

BOND INDEXES:

Lehman Brothers Government Bond Index - This index tracks U. S. Government agency and Treasury bonds.

Lehman Brothers Corporate Bond Index - This index tracks fixed-rate, non-convertible investment-grade corporate bonds.

Lehman Brothers Mortgage-Backed Securities Index - This index tracks fixed-rate securities of the Government National Mortgage Association (GNMA)(; the Federal National Mortgage Association (FNMA) and the Federal National Loan Mortgage Corporation (FHLMC).

Lehman Brothers Aggregate Bond Index - This index tracks some 4,000 investment-grade fixed income securities and is weighted by the market value of each security.

In addition to the above, there are short-term, intermediate-term and long-term Bond Index Funds.

APPENDIX E

Uniform Prudent Investors Act (UPIA)

Introduction

This Act is part of a group of "Uniform Acts" adopted by many states. The states that have adopted this new uniform act are listed on page 271. The Act is short and clearly written. It breaks new ground in Trust law. It allows your trustee to relieve themselves of the legal liability for investment decisions if they properly delegate the investment responsibilities to a professional trustee. This is stated in Section 9 of the Act.

An important reason the Act was created was to recognize modern investment techniques that can protect the investment assets in the Trust. Several individuals were awarded Nobel prizes for their work on these investment techniques now required in the Act.

A portfolio consisting of eight or ten stocks is not properly diversified for protection of the assets. Modern portfolio theory requires a wide range of securities such as those found in mutual funds and index funds. It also requires awareness of international securities.

The Act establishes investment requirements for your trustee that they must follow if they choose to manage the investable assets in the Trust. It would appear that failure to follow these investment requirements in the Act could be grounds for legal action against a trustee.

The Act clearly states that your son, daughter or friend that you select as your trustee "is not liable to the beneficiaries or to the trust for decisions or actions of the agent to whom the function was delegated."[1]

The Act, in the beginning Sections makes clear the investment responsibilities of your trustee. These are:

1.   ".. to comply with the prudent investor rule set forth in this [Act]"
     See: Section 1 (a).

2.   To follow the standards of care; portfolio strategy; risk and return objectives set forth in Section 2 of the Act.

(1)   See Section 9 (c) of the Act on the following pages.

This would appear to require your trustee to have a written plan for the investment and management of the assets and to include in that plan "an overall investment strategy having risk and return objectives reasonably suited to the trust." [2]

Also to be included in the trustee's plan are requirements for the recognition of several planning factors such as general economic conditions; expected tax consequences; expected total return from income and the appreciation of capital and five other requirements set forth in the Act. [3]

3.   Diversification of the assets as stated in Section 3.

4.   To do this work of establishing an investment plan to include the items required in the Act within a reasonable time after becoming your trustee. [4]

The Act also makes reference to the issue of Loyalty of your trustee. This is a very important legal requirement and is discussed in Appendix F.

"This [Act] applies to trusts existing on and created after its effective date *(the date adopted by your state)*. As applied to trusts existing on its effective date, this [Act] governs only decisions or actions occurring after that date." [5]

In Summary, What does this Act Require the Grantor to Consider?

1.   The Grantor can override this Act by Directives placed in the Trust. This is allowed since the Act is a Default Rule as clearly stated in Section 1 (b).

2.   However, the investment principals of diversification and other requirements in the Act such as having an investment plan containing the items required by the Act, are sound and should be considered.

(2)   From Section 2 (b) of the Act.

(3)   See Section (c) of the Act.

(4)   See Section 4 of the Act.

(5)   See Section 11 of the Act

3.   The Grantor after reviewing the Act may decide that they will name in their Trust the professional investment manager they want to handle their Trust instead of passing this decision to their trustee.

4.   In advance of the Grantor's state adopting this Uniform Act, the Grantor can select what sections of the Act they would want to include in their Trust.

Uniform Prudent Investors Act (UPIA)

SECTION 1. PRUDENT INVESTOR RULE.

(a)   Except as otherwise provided in subsection (b), a trustee who invests and manages assets owes a duty to the beneficiaries of the trust to comply with the prudent investor rule set forth in this [Act].

(b)   The prudent investor rule, a default rule, may be expanded, restricted, eliminated. or otherwise altered by the provisions of a trust. A trustee is not liable to a beneficiary to the extent that the trustee acted in reasonable reliance on the provisions of the trust.

SECTION 2. STANDARD OF CARE; PORTFOLIO STRATEGY; RISK AND RETURN OBJECTIVES

(a) A trustee shall invest and manage trust assets as a prudent investor would, by considering the purposes, terms, distribution requirements, and other circumstances of the trust. In satisfying this standard, the trustee shall exercise reasonable care, skill, and caution.

(b) A trustee's investment and management decisions must be evaluated not in isolation but in the context of the trust portfolio as a whole and as a part of an overall investment strategy having risk and return objectives reasonably suited to the trust.

(c) Among   circumstances that a trustee shall consider in investing and managing assets are such of the following as are relevant to the trust or its beneficiaries:

(1) general economic conditions;

(2) the possible effect of inflation or deflation;

(3) the expected tax consequences of investment decisions or
    strategies;

(4) the role that each investment or course of action plays within the overall trust portfolio, which may include financial assets, interests in closely held enterprises, tangible and intangible personal property, and real property;

(5) The expected total return from income and the appreciation of capital;

(6) other resources of the beneficiaries;

(7) needs for liquidity, regularity of income, and preservation or appreciation of capital; and

(8) an asset's special relationship or special value, if any, to the purpose of the trust or to one or more of the beneficiaries.

(d) A trustee shall make a reasonable effort to verify facts relevant to the investment and management of trust assets.

(e) A trustee may invest in any kind of property or type of investment consistent with the standards of this [Act].

(f) A trustee who has special skill or expertise, or is named trustee in reliance upon the trustee's representation that the trustee has special skill or expertise, has a duty to use those special skills or expertise.

SECTION 3. DIVERSIFICATION. A trustee shall diversify the investments of the trust unless the trustee reasonably determines that, because of special circumstances, the purposes of the trust are better served without diversifying.

SECTION 4. DUTIES AT INCEPTION OF TRUSTEESHIP Within a reasonable time after accepting a trusteeship or receiving trust assets, a trustee shall review the trust assets and make and implement decisions concerning the retention and disposition of assets, in order to bring the trust portfolio into compliance with the purposes, terms, distribution requirements, and other circumstances of the trusts, and within the requirements of this Act..

SECTION 5. LOYALTY. A trustee shall invest and manage the trust assets solely in the interests of the beneficiaries.

SECTION 6. IMPARTIALITY. If a trust has two or more beneficiaries, the trustee shall act impartially in investing and managing the trust assets, taking into account any differing interests of the beneficiaries.

SECTION 7. INVESTMENT COSTS. In investing and managing trust assets, a trustee may only incur costs that are appropriate and reasonable in relation to the assets, the purposes of the trust, and the skills of the trustee.

SECTION 8.   REVIEWING COMPLIANCE.   Compliance with the prudent investor rule is determined in light of the facts and circumstances existing at the time of a trustee's decision or action and not by hindsight.

SECTION 9. DELEGATION OF INVESTMENT AND MANAGEMENT FUNCTIONS.

(a)   A trustee may delegate investment and management functions that a prudent trustee of comparable skills could properly delegate under the circumstances. The trustees shall exercise reasonable care, skill and caution in:

(1) selecting an agent;

(2) establishing the scope and terms of the delegation, consistent with the purposes and terms of the trust; and

(3) periodically reviewing the agent's actions in order to monitor the agent's performance and compliance with the terms of the delegation.

(b) In performing a delegated function, an agent owes a duty to the trust to exercise reasonable care to comply with the terms of the delegation.

(c) who complies with the requirements of subsection (a) is not liable to the beneficiaries or to the trust for the decisions or actions of the agent to whom the function was delegated.

(d) By accepting the delegation of a trusts function from the trustee of a trust that is subject to the law of this state, an agent submits to the jurisdiction of the courts of this state.

SECTION 10. LANGUAGE INVOKING STANDARD OF [ACT].

The following terms or comparable language in the provisions of a trust, unless otherwise limited or modified, authorizes any investment or strategy permitted under this [Act]: "investment permissible by law for investment of trust funds," "legal investments," " authorized investments." "using the judgment and care under the circumstances then prevailing that persons of prudence, discretion, and intelligence exercise in the management of their own affairs, not in regard to speculation but in regard to the permanent disposition of their own funds, considering the probable income as well as the probable safety of their capital," "prudent man rule," prudent trustee rule," prudent person rule,' and "prudent investor rule."

SECTION 11. APPLICATION TO EXISTING TRUSTS. This [Act] applies to

trusts existing on and created after its effective date. As applied to trusts existing on its effective date, this [Act] governs only decisions or actions occurring after that date.

SECTION 12. UNIFORMITY OF APPLICATION AND CONSTRUCTION.

This [Act] shall be applied and construed to effectuate its general purpose to make uniform the law with respect to the subject of the [Act] among the States enacting it.

SECTION 13. SHORT TITLE   This [Act] may be cited as "[name of Enacting State] Uniform Prudent Investor Act."

SECTION 14. SEVERABILITY. If any provision of this [Act] or its application to any person or circumstances is held invalid, the invalidity does not affect other provisions or application of this [Act] which can be given effect without the invalid provision or application, and to this and the provisions of this [Act] are severable.

SECTION 15. EFFECTIVE DATE. This [Act] takes effect . . . .

States that have Adopted this new Uniform Act
As of August 1, 1998

Alaska	Nebraska
Arizona	New Hampshire
Arkansas	New Jersey
California	New Mexico
Colorado	North Dakota
Connecticut	Oklahoma
Hawaii	Oregon
Idaho	Rhode Island
Maine	Utah
Minnesota	Vermont
Missouri	Washington
	West Virginia

State Legislatures currently considering this Act.

District of Columbia	Mississippi
Indiana	Ohio
Massachusetts	Virginia
Michigan	Wisconsin

Note:

Some states have adopted this Act with changes. As an example, Florida adopted the Act with a change that makes the professional entity selected a "Trustee" instead of the position of an Agent" [6] as stated in the Act. Your Trust attorney can advise you of the status of this Act in your State.

Additional information on this Act and the "Uniform Principal and Income Act [1997][7] can be obtained from:

National Conference of Commissioners
On Uniform State Laws
211 e. Ontario Street, Suite 1300
Chicago, Illinois 60611
312/915-0195

(6)   See Section 9 of the ACT

(7)   Does not address the options contained in this book. But, does state that the Grantor can override the Act.

APPENDIX F

Duties of a Trustee

Introduction

The prime duty of a trustee is the investment management of the funds in the Trust and other types of assets that may be a part of the Trust such as real property. Some professional trustees will only manage the investment of funds. Others will also manage real estate such as homes, rental properties, vacant land, timber interests, oil and mineral rights.

Next, the trustee must know the laws regarding Trusts and properly administer the Trust according to these laws. And, annually your trustee must file state and federal fiduciary tax returns. These are the prime duties of a trustee.

Overshadowing the above and all other duties of the trustee is the duty of loyalty. Loyalty to serve the wishes of the decedent and loyalty to serve the beneficiaries of the Trust. This is an important duty. Acts that appear to be innocent of any personal gain by the use of the position of trustee may be declared by the courts to be a violation of this duty of loyalty.

The Duty of Loyalty

A trustee must not use the assets in a Trusts for their benefit - either directly or indirectly. Numerous court cases have ruled against trustees for violating this duty of loyalty.

Acts that may appear innocent have been ruled by the courts as a violation of a trustee duty of loyalty. For example:

A trustee purchasing from the trust any asset such as real estate, art or other personal property. The trustee may have paid the highest price (another duty of a trustee to obtain the highest price for the sale of any asset). But courts have ruled against the purchases by the trustee even if the asset purchased was sold at auction and the trustee was the highest bidder. [A-1]

And, if the property at some later, increases in value, the beneficiaries can recover the property. Or, if the property were sold, obtain the profit from the sale.

(A-1)   Numerous legal books on Trusts cite many court rulings and regulations regarding a trustee's duty of loyalty. A few of these books are mentioned at the end of this Appendix. And, reference to acts of trustees are by letter footnote for each book.

There are ways that the purchase of assets from The Trust by the trustee can be properly done. The laws and procedures for this vary by states. An Attorney should be consulted.[2]

"The fiduciary (trustee) always has the burden of proving full disclosure in dealing with beneficiaries and, in the situation where the fiduciary (trustee) is also a beneficiary, the further burden of showing that the transaction is fair to the other beneficiaries'" [A-2] [B-1]

So wide and far reaching is the duty of loyalty that a Co-Trustee who knows that another Co-Trustee has failed in a duty of loyalty is also guilty of that failure and is legally accountable.

Co-Trustees may divide minor trustee matters. "As to more important matters, however, one co-representative cannot act alone and unanimous action is required." [A-3] [B-2] This can happen when family members are co-trustees. Example:

Family Co-Trustees decide that one trustee will handle the investments and the other Co-Trustee will perform other duties - perhaps looking after the Income Beneficiary. But if the second Co-Trustee "was not exercising any control over the selection of investments . . (they) clearly breached (their) duties to act prudently and to perform (their) duties as a trustee. . . . A Fiduciary my not delegate to another the performance of a duty involving discretion and judgment." [A-4]

In most cases where a family member is the trustee, they are also the beneficiary of the trust.

The trustee may not favor one beneficiary at the expense of another. A son, as trustee, may not favor his mother, as the surviving spouse and Income Beneficiary, over his brothers and sisters and other heirs who will receive the funds in the Trust at the death of the surviving spouse. [B-3]

A trustee, especially a family member, has the added liability of documenting that each action taken was fair to all beneficiaries.

"It is important that he or she carefully preserve throughout the administration a record of activities. If the fiduciary is unable to explain or justify his or her acts, the fiduciary may be liable." [A-5]

(2)   This is just another of the many reasons why a family member or friend serving as trustee, must continually consult an attorney.

The above should clearly indicate that it is very important for the Grantor to clearly state in their Trust what they want to have happen. A Grantor should state the income their surviving spouse is to receive, how the funds are to be invested, and many other provisions recommended in this book.

Then the trustee will be following the Grantor's instructions stated in the Trust. A trustee must do this, follow the Grantor's instructions.

"Except where impossible, illegal, or where a change of circumstances occurs which would impair the purposes of the Trust, the nature and extent of the duties and powers of a trustee are determined by the Trust instrument." [A-6]

A Trustee's Greatest Problem - Managing the Investments.

Most legal action against a trustee, excluding fraud and other violations of loyalty, will be in the area of investments. And, a trustee may have the greatest problem in defending these types of suits.

In addition to carefully documented notes on all of their acts, especially those regarding investments, a family member or friend serving as trustee is encouraged to seek investment advice.

The new Uniform Prudent Investor Act (UPIA) strongly encourages a family member or friend to hire a professional trustee to manage the investments of the assets in the Trust.

So important did the drafters and the legislative bodies of the states consider the need for professional management of the investments in a Trust that they broke new legal ground and granted an exception in the new UPIA to the long standing rule of trustee responsibility. The new law relieves the trustee of any liability resulting from investing if the delegation was properly made. [3]

This is new law. The law in the past has always stated that responsibility cannot be delegated and the trustee who gives discretionary power to another is liable for the acts of another who has been given this delegated power.

[3] See Section 9 of the Uniform Prudent Investor Act in Appendix E and the commentary on this section

But now, an important responsibility of a trustee, in modern day Trusts, may be delegated and if properly done the trustee is relieved of any legal liability.

And, who will later say that the professional management of a trust by a major bank or a brokerage firm was not properly done.

Grantors should consider the reasons for this new law, and the relief it offers a family member or friend as trustee. It would be better if the Grantor selected the professional trustee rather than have a family, years later make the selection of the investment manager.

This would allow the Grantor to select a professional manager whose fees are reasonable and whose past investment performance would indicate proper handling of the assets.

Summary

The law regarding a trustee's duties is extensive. Most professional trustees understand these legal duties. Few family members or friends serving as trustees do.

That is why every individual serving as a trustee should quickly obtain the assistance of a competent Trust attorney before making any decisions as trustee. The special powers given to a trustee is in the document that created the Trust and the person named as trustee must follow these specific Directives in the Trust document. But there are numerous other legal and tax requirements that govern the work of a trustee not stated in the Trust document.

An experienced Trust attorney can interpret and guide an individual trustee in understanding the specific Directives in a Trust that must be followed. The assistance of this Trust attorney is particularly important in helping the individual understand the other problems that can result from the legal and tax requirements that govern the work of a trustee but that are not stated in the Trust document.

Proper documentation of the actions of a trustee is required.

Review the reasons for this new "Uniform Prudent Investors Act" and the relief it offers a family member or friend as trustee.

The Grantor should consider leaving a memo for their family member or friend selected to be their trustee. The memo would contain instructions and suggestions regarding their Trust. The first and most important instruction would be to:

First: Before taking any action as trustee:

    A.   Read the Trust document and make notes on any items you have questions about.

    B.   Then visit my attorney who prepared my Trust and review these items.

    C.   Ask what changes have been made in any of the regulations that you should be aware of. Are there recommendations concerning other items of your trusteeship that you should know about?

    D.   Obtain assistance in obtaining the tax I.D. number for the Trust and properly accepting the assets to be paced in the Trust.

    E.   Obtain advice on your record-keeping responsibilities as Trustee. Everything you do should be properly documented and saved during the life of the Trust.

Second: Determine what other professional assistance you will need as Trustee.

    A.   Proper state and federal tax forms must be filed. Obtain the assistance of a CPA who has experience in filing these forms.

    B.   Their may be other professionals recommended for your consideration whose services may be needed.

Third: After you have obtained the above guidance and understand what is to be done:

    A.   Review with my Income Beneficiary and the Remaindermen the Trust; how it will be managed, according to my Directives and Trust law.

    B.   While not stated in my Trust, I hope a strong family relationship will be maintained.

References:

(A)   "Decedents' Estates and Trusts" by John Ritchie, Neill H. Alford, Jr., Richard W. Effland and Joel C. Dobris, The Foundation Press, Inc. Westbury, New York Eighth Edition, 1993.

Used as a casebook for law students in wills, trusts, fiduciary administration and future interests. 1445 pages

(A-1)   Page 1247
(A-2)   Page 1248
(A-3)   Page 1252
(A-4)   Page 1254
(A-5)   Page 1260
(A-6)   Page 1265

(B)   "Loring A Trustee's Handbook" 1997 Edition Charles E. Rounds, Jr.,
Little Brown and Company, New York

Designed as a handbook for ready reference to be "user friendly." 352 pages

(B-1)   Page 20
(B-2)   Page 34
(B-3)   Page 21

APPENDIX G

Default Rules

Introduction

State Default Rules are not the cause of financial and management problems in Trusts. In fact, they are often the only thing that keeps a Trust instrument from failing. When a Trust fails because of a lack of specific instructions, those assets in it revert to the estate and pass by Will or intestacy.

When a Trust is silent on important issues that the Grantor neglected in their Trust, direction is provided by Default Rules. These Rules have been passed by each state's legislative branch in the United States and there are changes continually being proposed.[1]

An example of this work is the requirement in the new Uniform Prudent Investor Act for trustees to diversify the investments in a Trust. This is based on modern portfolio theory. A second act, The Uniform Principal and Income Act (1997)[2] was recently approved and is currently recommended for enactment in all the states. Both of these uniform acts are Default Rules designed to improve Trust investments and income paid when the Grantor fails to state what is required in the Trust. Neither of these acts provide the financial and management options a Grantor has that are presented in this book.

If the Grantor neglects to direct the trustee on how the funds are to be invested, then the Default Rules will govern this issue. In general the reasoning behind these Default Rules, while perhaps conservative in nature, has been well thought out.

(1)   In the United States the National Conference of Commissioners on Uniform State Laws, a confederation of state commissioners on uniform laws was founded in 1892. Its membership comprises more than 300 attorneys, judges and law professors who are appointed by each of the 50 states, the District of Columbia, Puerto Rico and the U. S. Virgin Island, to draft uniform and model state laws and work toward their enactment.

(2)   This new Act and comments on it are available on the Internet at site of the National Conference of Commissioners on Uniform State Laws at "www.law.upenn.edu/bll."

To assist in Trust situations where there is a lack of investment instructions, the Default Rules for investments were developed in response to the logical conclusion that since the Trust was silent, the investments should favor neither the Income Beneficiary nor the Remaindermen. Bonds produce a higher income, this favors the Income Beneficiary. Stocks while increasing in value over time (that would favor the Remaindermen), will produce a lower income. As a result, an equitable Default Rule for investments was written.

The Default Rules state - invest approximately 50% of the Trust in bonds and 50% of the Trust in stocks for a "Balanced Trust." As a result of this reasoning, it would appear that the investments of the Trust would favor neither the Income Beneficiary nor the Remaindermen.

The real point is that in our modern world, inflation is as great a danger as losing an investment outright. There is as great a risk of falling behind as there is of losing an investment. The Default Rules generally address the second of these two concerns because they are heavily influenced by conservative attitudes regarding investments.   This does not make them wrong. It makes them conservative, as far as investments are concerned. The reader should be aware of their own right to balance their own levels of risk and growth.

In this sense the Default Rules do not lower growth or income. The Grantor has simply lost the opportunity to decide in their Trust whether they prefer and are comfortable with their own investment options that allow more potential for growth.

The critical point however, is that the Grantor, as their own financial planner, has to be the one who chooses the level of risk they are willing to balance against growth. They already do this with the investments they make in their normal lives.

Another critical option the Grantor has is determining the annual payments to the Income Beneficiary (generally the surviving spouse) from the Trust.

As indicated in Chapter 6, if the Grantor does not plan and use their option of stating the annual payments to be made from their Trust, the actual amounts that will be paid are generally the Net Income[3] from the investments of the Trust.

---

(3)   The differences in the annual payments, as indicated in Chapter 14 is about 10% greater with the Gross Income provision than that received from the Net Income of a Trust.

This is generally a lower amount than may be required for the surviving spouse. The Grantor had the option of planning the income needs and increasing it for inflation and using their option of stating this in their Trust.

Also the Grantor has the option of giving Directives in the Trust that can increase the value of it for their children and other heirs. See Chapter 8.

Other options a Grantor has are summarized in Part Four of this book.

Default Rules Referenced in Trusts

Included in the draft or your executed Trust is an article, generally toward the end of the document. It makes reference to the state your Trust was constructed in along with a listing of the statutes of the state that become part of your Trust. You can read these state statutes that are part of your Trust in your attorney's office or they can be found in the reference section of most libraries.

You may not agree with some of the Default Rules you will read. But remember, they were written to be broad enough in scope to cover many situations Trustees may face.

As examples of trustee powers that are in Default Rules and that you may not want in your Trust are:[4]

1.   To invest in such assets as the trustee shall deem advisable, even though such investments shall not be of the character approved by applicable law but for this provision.

2.   To invest without diversification by making investments which cause a greater proportion of the property held by the trustee to be invested in instruments of one type or of one company.

For most people these powers would not be applicable. Even if stated by reference, a professional trustee would not use them. But they could be significant in the case of a closely held family business that the Grantor intended to have remain in the family.

(4)   General Statutes of North Carolina, Chapter 32-27, Items (3) and (4).

The shares would eventually pass to the Remaindermen after the death of the surviving spouse.

One could say that in such an instance, the Grantor should have used their option of stating in the Trust, wording that would accomplish this objective. But in the past, even when the Grantor had a family business, this Directive was left out. This is just one example of why such broad authority can be found in state statutes.

APPENDIX   H

Fees & Services of Professional Trustees

Introduction

Over 80% of Trusts do not use a professional trustee. A family member or friend is the trustee. Why? In most cases the Grantor:

1.   Believes the fees professional trustees charge are high.

2.   Does not understand the financial benefits to their surviving spouse and child of using a professional trustee to manage the investments.

3.   Believes that the care and concerns a family member can provide to their surviving spouse and other heirs are more important than the investment expertise of a professional trustee.

4.   Places the assets in the Trust without further safeguards for the protection of the assets and the family.

All of the above four points will be discussed. Hopefully after reviewing this material, a Grantor will give serious consideration to a professional trustee. Their annual fees can be as low as half a percent a year.

1. Believes the Fees Professional Trustees Charge Are High.

Professional trustees are able to manage the investments in securities for a low fee. The reason for these low fees is that actual costs today, to manage these investments is spread over a large number of Trusts.

The new requirements for investing Trust assets under the Uniform Prudent Investor Act (see Appendix E) is that the principles of modern portfolio theory are to be observed. No longer is an individual portfolio of eight of ten stocks considered to be properly diversified to protect the principal of the Trust.

Professional trustee management of investments has been moving away from individual securities placed in a Trust. Today, under modern portfolio theory, diversified groupings of similar types of securities are being selected.

If good quality bonds are required in the Trust, the selection is shifting from purchasing individual bonds to be placed in the Trust to allocating shares of a good quality bond fund centrally managed. The same is true of stocks.

These funds hold a large number of bonds or stocks to provide a greater diversification. Index funds are also used.

The result of this movement toward placing shares of mutual funds and index funds into Trusts has been a reduction in the cost of managing the investment function. The fees can be lower.

Now rather than review and perhaps change the individual securities held in each Trust, this function is centralized.

One example of reduced fees by using mutual funds and stock index funds is shown in the fee schedule below.

Trust Assets	Annual Fee[1]	Amount of Trust		
		$625,000	$ 1 million	$ 2 million
First $500,000	0.65%	$ 3,250	$ 3,250	$ 3,250
Next $500,000	0.35%	438	1,750	1,750
Over $1 million	0.20%			2,000
Total Annual Fee		$ 3,688	$ 5,000	$ 7,000
Percent of Total Assets		0.59%	0.50%	0.35%
Minimum Annual Fee		$ 3,250		

But if the Trust directs the holding of individual securities, which will increase the cost of investment management, an additional annual fee of 0.30% will be charged.

(1)   Source: Trust Fees of Vanguard Personal Trust Services as of 9/2/98

Another key point that needs to be considered is the management and other charges associated with the Trust owning fund shares. In many cases, not only are the annual fees of mutual funds not considered but the costs of buying and selling securities are not evaluated by the Grantor in determining who will manage the investments.

A family member or friend named as trustee will incur these transaction costs in managing the investments. But these costs are rarely considered.

Many professional trustees may not accept real estate as a Trust asset that they will manage. Therefore their fees may be lower since managing real estate requires different skills and generally a higher fee for the added expense.

Trustees may also charge an additional amount for fiduciary tax return preparation, court accounting (if required). All of these items need to be considered. Generally if this work is required of the professional trustee, a family member, serving as trustee, will also be required to have the same work done. And, the expense can be greater.

The fee schedule of a typical bank for personal Trust services is an annual fee as a percent of the market value of the account excluding illiquid assets.

Market Value of Assets	Annual Fee[1]	Amount of Trust		
		$625,000	$ 1 million	$ 2 million
$400,000 to 700,000	1.0%%	$ 6,250	$ 6,250	$ 6,250
$700,000 to 1.0 million	0.9%	---	2,700	2,700
$1 million to 2 million	0.7%	---	----	7,000
Total Annual Fee		$ 6,250	$ 8,750	$ 15,950
Percent of Total Assets		1.0%	0.88%	0.80%

Minimum Annual Fee varies generally at least $2,000.

Banks may charge additional fees for some special services:

1.   For management of illiquid assets, such as real estate, closely-held business interests, notes and liabilities. The annual fee may be 2% of the market value.

284

2.   If a Co-Trustee is used, along with the bank, some banks may charge an additional fee for the extra work required to obtain the co-trustees approval of any investment decisions. Generally this fee is very small and is waived for Trusts of $1 million or more.

3.   For the purchase or sale of illiquid assets an additional fee may also be charged.

All of the above items are in bank's fee schedules that a Grantor should review.

2. Does not Understand the Financial Benefits to Their Surviving Spouse and Child of Using a Professional Trustee to Manage the Investments.

Most professional trustees publish the performance of their Trust investments. And for most, the performance is compared to recognized benchmarks such the S & P 500 index (Standard and Poor) for Equity Funds and several Lehman Government/Corporate bond indexes for various bond funds.[2]

You can obtain copies free of charge. The investment results by these professional trustees may outperform what an individual trustee may obtain. And, the investments will be diversified.

The evaluation a Grantor needs to make is who can provide the highest reasonable investment returns for my Trust. The amounts involved are large. A 10% upward movement for a $1 million dollar Trust is $100,000. Who can best accomplish this - a professional trustee or my family member trustee?

A Trust should contain a provision for the removal of the professional trustee and appointing a new one (see Chapter 17). Perhaps the family member being considered as trustee could better serve as the watchdog of a professional trustee's performance.

3. That the Care and Concerns a Family Member can Provide to Their Surviving Spouse and other Heirs are More Important Than the Investment Expertise of a Professional Trustee.

(2)   These measurements of investment performance are similar to what is recommended in Appendix D.

This is true. A family member can, in most cases, do a much better job and will usually have greater concern for the surviving spouse and other heirs than a professional trustee.

As stated in Chapter 15, the care, advice and comfort given to your surviving spouse are best done by family members and friends. There is no requirement that only your trustee should do this for your surviving spouse. A professional trustee can provide some of this type of assistance, when nursing homes and other care is required for the survivor. But again, family members can best handle this need and look to the trustee to pay the bills, if needed.

Consider a "Special Trustee."

You can provide in your Trust for a "Special Trustee(s)" such as family members or friends whose responsibilities are clearly stated in the Trust and are different from the traditional role of a trustee. These "Special Trustee(s)" would have responsibilities such as, the care, advice and comfort given to your surviving spouse or other Income Beneficiaries.

If a nursing home or other medical care is required for the surviving spouse or Income Beneficiaries, this person would visit the nursing home to ensure that proper care was being given. This person would also have the Health Care Power of Attorney. Funds can be provided from the Trust for compensation for the "Special Trustee" and reasonable expenses could be automatically provided from the Trust for presents, travel expenses, etc. if needed.

4. Placing the Assets in the Trust without further safeguards for the protection of the Assets and the family.

In Chapter 18, it was recommended that all funds and securities in the Trust are to be held by an appropriate custodian or at least be held in a brokerage account.

When a professional trustee is used, this custodial function is performed. For additional information on this recommendation, review Chapter 18 .

APPENDIX I

Qualified Personal Residence Trusts
(Give it away, then keep it for awhile.)

Introduction

A major purpose of estate planning is to eliminate if possible, but at least reduce to a minimum, the taxes paid by your estate at your death. As you may know, each person can effectively transfer $625,000 estate tax free (this amount will go up every years under the new tax law until it reaches $1,000,000 in the 2006 tax year). One of the best ways to reduce your estate tax is to use this tax free amount as efficiently as possible. One of the best ways to maximize this tax free amount is to "leverage" or "spend" it by transferring, during your life, assets that will increase in value over your life. One of the ways you can accomplish this is to utilize a QPRT (Qualified Personal Residence Trust). As its name states, the QPRT is a Trust that consists of your residence, either your primary residence or a vacation home. Often, your residence represents a significant portion of your total estate value. A QPRT allows you to move your residence out of your estate for a gift value less than its present fair market value <u>and</u> before its value appreciates any further. The example attached illustrates that the gift tax value of a $300,000 home placed in a 10 year QPRT is only $105,366, or 35.12%of its value!

Mechanics

While the tax regulations that govern QPRTs are extremely complicated, the practical mechanics of a QPRT are fairly simple. First, you establish the QPRT by executing the Trust document. Second, you deed your residence to the QPRT. Third, the Trust document would state a set period of time during which the Trust holds title to your residence before it would transfer the title to beneficiaries of your choosing (i.e. your children). Fourth, during the Trust term, you would treat your home no different than you do now, For example, you would pay for repairs and if you rented the home, you would receive the rent. Fifth, as explained later, after the Trust term you could remain in the home by renting it from the beneficiaries.

Advantages

As stated in the introduction, the tax benefits of a QPRT are two-fold:

A.   Your residence is transferred out of your estate at a reduced tax value. In other words, the amount of your tax free transfer amount you would have to "spend" to move your residence out of your estate would be less than the actual value of the residence (in the attached example, only $105,366 rather than $300,000!). This is possible because the tax regulations states that the value of the residence deeded to the Trust is reduced by the value of your use of the residence during the set time the Trust holds the residence.

B.   Your residence is transferred out of your estate as of the day it is deeded to the Trust. This saves the estate tax that would have been paid at your death on the increased value (appreciation) of the residence during your lifetime. In the example, at an inflation rate of only 5%, the house value grew from $300,000 to $488,668 in ten years.

C.   In addition to these tax advantages, there are non-tax advantages. A QPRT also accomplishes the transfer of your residence during your lifetime. This reduces the administrative work and expense that will be required of your family at your passing. Also, since you will be around to oversee the transfer, your intentions are clear and your presence could reduce any potential tension among beneficiaries. Finally, since you no longer "own" your home, it should receive some "asset protection" in the event you later experience financial or legal hardship.

Disadvantages

As with most estate planning tools, there are advantages as well as disadvantages. A QPRT is no exception. In addition to the advantages explained above, there are two potential disadvantages:

A.   After the set period of time in the QPRT expires, the titles to the residence is transferred to the beneficiaries and your residence no longer belongs to you. While this is the legal result of a QPRT, the actual effect on you can be minimized. If you want to continue living in your residence after the QPRT expires, then you and the beneficiaries can sign a lease contract <u>at the same time</u> you execute the QPRT documents. The lease would give you the right to rent your residence from the beneficiaries at a fair rental after the QPRT time period has expired. This would have the additional beneficial effect of transferring the rental money out of your estate with no transfer tax and no reduction in your $10,000 annual exclusion per donee.

B. Since your residence is passed to your heirs without being exposed to estate tax, the income basis (used in calculating gain or loss on a sale, and used to compute any depreciation deduction if it is rented) "carries over" to your Trust beneficiaries and is <u>not</u> "stepped-up" to fair market value at death. If the home is later sold, then a 20% capital gains tax will probably be owed, <u>unless</u> one of the beneficiaries first acquires titles from the other beneficiaries and converts the home into their own personal residence. If this is done, then the personal residence exclusion of either $250,000 (or $500,000) would probably offset most, if not all, of any gain. Keep in mind if the 20% capital gains tax must be paid, this is still probably less than ½ of the estate tax, therefore, the tax savings are substantial.

Death During the QPRT Term

There is another effect of a QPRT that is neither an advantage nor a disadvantage. According to terms of the QPRT that are required by the tax law, if the grantor of the Trust (you) passes away before the end of the set QPRT time period, the full value of your residence is included in your estate. In this event, your tax free transfer amount would be replenished in the amount "spent" to transfer the residence to the Trust. The reason this is neither an advantage nor a disadvantage is because if you die before the QPRT expires, the tax position of your estate will be no better nor any worse than it is right now.

<u>CAVEAT</u>

This discussion paper is for educational purposes only and should not be relied upon as legal advice. Legal advice can only be rendered after all the relevant facts are known to the attorney and only after many complex alternatives are considered. Seek out competent help <u>before</u> proceeding!

Webb & Craven P.L.L.C.

Principal Office Located at:
910 N. Sandhills Blvd., (U.S. Highway No. 1)
P. O. Box 1437
Aberdeen, North Carolina 28315

(910) 944-9555
Fax: (910) 944-7641

Second Office Located at:
Landfall Executive Offices
1213 Culbreth Drive
Wilmington, North Carolina 28405
(910) 256-1120
Fax: (910) 256-1240

© Webb & Craven, P.L.L.C. August, 1998

Example of a 10 Year QPRT

Age of Grantor (nearest birthday) if applicable	68
Age of other person (nearest birthday) if applicable	0
Term of Trust in years	10
Projected marginal estate tax bracket of grantor	40%
Projected growth -inflation rate of Trust property	5%
Value of property transferred to Trust	$300,000
120% Applicable Federal Midterm Rate (AFMR)	6.84%
Discount Rate (AFMR rounded to nearest.2)	6.80%
Present value to grantor(s) factor	
(Term, life or shorter of term life)	0.41808
Reversion factor	0.23070
Present value of property use to grantor(s)	$125,424
Present value of reversion	$ 69,210
Present value of use and reversion to grantor(s)	$194,634
Gift taxable portion of value placed in Trust	$105,336
Gift taxable percent of value transferred to Trust	35.12%
Value of property in the Trust at the end of term	$488,668
Estate tax on property if retained by grantor	$195,487
Estate tax on gift taxable portion of Trust property	$ 42,146
Potential estate tax savings at grantor's FET rate	**$153,321**
Total value to grantor plus tax savings	$347,955

"A" AND "B" TRUST or "A/B" TRUST: See Credit Shelter Trust.

ACCOUNTING PERIOD: A calendar year unless a different 12-month period is selected.

ADVANCEMENT: An amount of funds or other type of assets given to an heir during the lifetime of that person, intended as an advance against the future heir's share of the estate.

ANNUAL EXCLUSION: Up to $10,000. per year that a person is allowed to give to another person without having to pay a gift tax.

ATTORNEY in FACT: Your agent given authorization by you to represent you and to take certain actions on your behalf. This should be in writing and for some acts, may require notarization.

BENEFICIARY: A person named in your Will or Trust to receive gifts. An organization can also be named as a beneficiary. In the case of a Trust, an Income Beneficiary and a Remainder Beneficiary (generally called the Remaindermen).

BEQUEST: Property transferred under your Will.

BYPASS TRUST: See Credit Shelter Trust.

CAPITAL: The value of an asset. Referred to as principal in Trusts.

CASE LAW: Laws established by court decisions.

CHARITABLE REMAINDER UNITRUST: The donation of assets to a Trust in which you receive a lifetime income. You may name a second recipient, such as a child to also receive this lifetime income after your death. Has great tax advantages. See Chapter 18.

CODICIL: An amendment to a Will. It must be properly executed as the Will was.

COMMUNITY PROPERTY: Property acquired by a husband and wife during their marriage and subject to special laws in several states.

CORPORATE TRUSTEE: An organization such as a bank that acts as trustee.

CO-TENANCY: When two or more parties own the same property and it remains undivided.

CO-TRUSTEE: Two or more individuals serving as trustee, a family member serving with a corporate trustee.

GLOSSARY

CREDIT SHELTER TRUST: A Trust established to retain your federal-estate tax exemption for your heirs, $625,000 in 1998 and increasing to $1 million in 2006, while providing your Income Beneficiary with income and other benefits during their lifetime. A Credit Shelter Trust is referred to by several other names.

DECEDENT: A term used for the person who died.

DEFAULT RULES: When your Trust is silent on any of the financial and management options, the state will determine each of these options such as how the funds will be invested. You may not want your Trust controlled by many of the Default Rules. See Appendix G; page 4 of Chapter 1 and other references to Default Rules, Chapters 6 to 8.

DEVISE: Real Estate that is transferred under a Will.

DIRECTIVE: An instruction given by the Grantor as to what is to be done, such as "I direct my trustee to pay my surviving spouse $35,000 a year starting on the date this Trust was executed and increased 3% a year from that date."

DISCLAIMER: If an heir does not wish to accept all or part of a bequest, they may disclaim it. If the disclaimer is made within the required time, it can be made without tax consequences.

DOMICILE: The place a person permanently resides.

DURABLE POWER OF ATTORNEY : A legal document in which you give a person(s) the authority to handle your financial matters. If you become disabled, a Durable Power of Attorney will continue to be valid. See page 170 of Chapter 21.

ESTATE TAX: A tax that the states and federal government place on your assets at the time of your death. Currently the federal estate tax applies to estates with a market value of over $625,000 and this increases to $1 million in 2006. State taxes on estates and exemptions vary by state. See federal tax table on page 146 in Chapter 18 and in Appendix B, Chapter 2.

EXECUTOR (the male form) : **EXECUTRIX** (the female form): A person named by you in your Last Will and Testament" to account for all your assets, paying your expenses, just debts and taxes and to make the distribution of your assets to your beneficiaries and/or trustee according to the terms of your Will and any other documents.

EXEMPTION TRUST: See Credit Shelter Trust.

FIDUCIARY: A person in a position of responsibility. The person may be the executor of your Will or the Trustee of your Trust. See duties in Appendix F.

GENERATION-SKIPPING TRANSFER TAX: A special tax assessed on transfers in excess of $1 million to anyone two generations below the Grantor such as grandchildren and great grandchildren.

GIFT: Transfer of an asset without requiring payment of any type.

GRANTOR: (Also called a **Trustor, Donor, Settlor, Testator, Creator).** An individual who forms the Trust and transfers assets into the Trust. The transfer of assets into the Trust can be done at any time - while the Grantor is living or at their death. Proper legal documentation is required.

GROSS INCOME PROVISION: All of the fees to manage the Trust and expenses of the Trust are paid out of the principal of the Trust. The Income Beneficiary receives all of the income from the Trust. A Gross Income provision provides for a greater income paid to the surviving spouse or other Income Beneficiaries. See Chapter 13.

GUARDIAN: The person you appoint to be responsible for your minor children or other persons who require special care and attention by a court appointed person

GUARDIANSHIP: The responsibility for a minor or a person requiring special care.

HEALTH CARE POWER OF ATTORNEY A legal document in which you give another person the power to make medical decisions if you are unable to do so. See page 170 of Chapter 21

HEIRS: The persons who are to receive the assets after your death..

INCOME: Interest paid on Bonds, CDs and other securities generally called "Fixed Income Investments" and dividends paid on equities. Can include property a Trustee receives from a principal asset.

INCOME BENEFICIARY: Generally your spouse. This is the person who will receive income from the Trust and if properly stated in your Trust be able to receive additional funds from the principal of the Trust. NOTE: This person has no authority to change how the assets will be distributed upon their death unless provided for in a Directive that the Grantor can give. See Chapters on Grantor Options.

INCOMPETENT: An individual who ha been declared by a court to be unable to handle and manage their own affairs.

INSURANCE TRUST: See Irrevocable Life Insurance Trust in Chapter 19.

GLOSSARY

INTER VIVOS TRUST: See "Living Trust"

INTESTATE: A person who dies without a Will or any other device to transfer their property.

INVASION OF PRINCIPAL: This is an act of taking funds from the principal of the Trust for the benefit of one or more of the beneficiaries of the Trust. Special instructions are in the Trust that indicate the conditions upon which the trustee will take funds from the principal of your trust for the benefit of your spouse or others. See Chapter 9.

INVESTMENT CLASSIFICATIONS OF TRUSTS: The right a Grantor of a Trust has to state how the assets of a Trust will be invested. If the Grantor of a Trust states that 100% of the assets of a Trust will be invested in good quality medium term bonds or 100% invested in stocks and these instructions may include the type of stocks, or any other percentage combination, the trustee must follow these instructions. But if the Trust is silent on this or any other key rights a Grantor has, then state's "Default Rules" will be followed. See Chapter 6.

IRREVOCABLE: A Trust a Grantor establishes that cannot be changed once it has been executed.

JOINT TENANCY WITH RIGHT OF SURVIVORSHIP: A legal form of ownership used by many husbands and wives for assets they own together and the title is in both of their names with this right of the survivor to fully own the property such as real estate (their homes) and their securities. The tax consequences of this type of ownership is not properly understood by many people

NOTE: Assets held in "Joint Tenancy with Right of Survivorship" cannot be placed into a Credit Shelter Trust. As an example: If your home is held in your name and your spouse's name as "Joint tenancy with right of survivorship" you have already, by a legally recorded document, willed your ownership interest directly to your surviving spouse or to anyone else you jointly held the property with. Therefore, you cannot remove this prior ownership agreement by now placing your ownership of the real estate or brokerage account into your Credit Shelter Trust. There is an exception for assets owned with your spouse if your Will or "Living Trust" has a disclaimer provision in it. But this is not generally recommended.

LIVING TRUSTS: A type of Trust established to avoid probate, See Chapter 20.

LIVING WILL: A legal document in which you generally state that you choose a natural death; you do not want your life maintained by artificial means and in it you also have the option of stating several other key items of medical care that you want or do not want. See Chapter 22.

MARITAL LIFE ESTATE TRUST: See Marital Trust and Chapter 13.

MARITAL DEDUCTION: Any amount of assets given to a spouse are exempt from estate taxes.

MARITAL TRUST: To control other assets you pass tax-free to your surviving spouse. See Chapter 13.

MINOR: A person who under state law is not old enough to be considered an adult.

NET INCOME PROVISION: 50% of the annual trustee fees and expenses are charged against the Gross income of the Trust, The other 50% is charged against the principal. This reduces the income that the Income Beneficiary will receive by about 10%. See Chapter 13.

PER CAPITA: A distribution from an estate made equally to a class of people such as grandchildren

PERPETUITIES, RULES AGAINST: Federal Tax law which restricts the numbers of years assets may be held in a Trust. Generally a Trust can last during the entire lifetime of someone who is alive when the Trust was established and for an additional 21 years. This restriction does not apply to Charitable Trusts. For more detailed information, consult your attorney.

PER STIRPES: A distribution from an estate made equally among family lines. As an example, if the Grantor had three children the funds would follow the family line. Therefore, grandchildren could receive more or less than if the distribution had been made per capita.

POUR-OVER WILL: See Chapter 22.

PRINCIPAL: Assets held by the trustee for distribution to the remainder beneficiaries when the Trust is terminated.

PROBATE: A court procedure that all of your assets not excluded by other documents will pass through. Among the several key things that probate does is to change title of your assets from your name to those you have named in your Will, if you had one. In probate your executor is appointed, generally the person you have named in your Will. Your debts are to be paid and states require that advertisements are to be placed many times in newspapers announcing your death and asking that any debts you owe be submitted by a certain date. Other issues are concluded prior to the distribution of your estate to your heirs. Many people use a "Living Trust" and other means to avoid the delays of probate and to keep their assets and other information from becoming part of the public record. See Chapter 20.

GLOSSARY

REMAINDERMEN: Generally your children. These are the individuals named in your Trust who are to receive the assets in your Trust after the death of the Income Beneficiary or the person(s) who is receiving the income no longer does so because their right to receive income from the Trust was terminated by other conditions in your Trust.

REVOCABLE TRUST: See Living Trusts.

RULE AGAINST PERPETUITIES: The law that voids a future interest in property if the transfer will take effect within a stated period of time. Generally the period is the lifetime of a person living when the Trust became effective plus an additional 21 years.

SETTLOR: A person who establishes a Trust. See Grantor.

SILENT: A legal term meaning that the document neglected to state what was to be done. In these cases the issues may be decided by what are called Default Rules. Each State has their own set of Default Rules.

SPOUSAL BYPASS TRUST: See Credit Shelter Trust.

SPRINKLE POWER: A Trust that gives sole authority in its documentation to the trustee the authority to determine how the income from the Trust and the principal may be given to different Trust beneficiaries or retained in the Trust. See Option 3 in Chapter 8.

STEPPED-UP BASIS This is a tax term and very important to understand what it means and how it is used. When a person dies, the assets a person owns is "Marked-to Market."

In the case of listed securities, such as stock, the newspapers report the current value at the date of death. Appraisals are also made on other types of property such as the value of the real estate owned, objects of art, etc.

These "Stepped-up" values are the values that will be used for tax purposes. It is the value of the items you can place into your $625,000 Bypass Trust in 1998 . And, missed by many in estate planning, it is the tax base of all assets given to your wife who receives these tax free. Therefore, as an example, if you left your wife stocks with a low cost value to you these stocks will now have a "Stepped-up" value (the market) and your wife could sell these with no capital gain taxes. This could be a good time to sell these stocks and instruct your spouse to invest in a better diversified holding such as mutual funds and index funds.

SUCCESSOR TRUSTEE: The person designated in a Trust to replace the original trustee or another successor trustee when the prior trustee is unable to serve.

TENANCY IN COMMON: Two or more people own the same property and there is no right of survivorship. Therefore a deceased person's share passes to their estate.

TESTAMENTARY TRUST: A Trust that is established at your death generally under your Last Will and Testament. The most common example is the Credit Shelter Trust that uses the $ 625,000 federal estate tax exemption(in 1998) for each individual.

TRUST: A document that provides for assets to be held and managed by a person or entity, such as a bank, called the trustee. The trustee manages these assets according to the terms of the Trust.

TRUST ASSETS: Can be in any form, cash, securities, property, etc. This is what is transferred to your trust to be managed by your trustee for the benefits and objectives stated in your Trust documentation. Trust assets Remember, if your trust is silent on any of the options and objectives of your Trust, state "Default Rules" will than determine how these assets are invested and other important issues that you had an option to determine.

TRUSTEE: The person or organization that will manage your Trust. Be sure to name successor trustees in case the person named initially as your trustee is not able to serve. Otherwise a court will name your trustee and this could be someone you may not want as your trustee. Your Trust can have a Directive in it that allows your Income Beneficiary or others to replace the trustee and successor trustee and name a new trustee. See Appendix F and Chapters 14 to 17.

UNIFIED CREDIT: A federal exemption from federal estate taxes that every person is entitled to obtain. Currently the value of the Unified Credit is $625,000 in 1998 and increases to $1 million in 2006. A Credit Shelter Trust was designed to make maximum use of this unified credit to shelter up to $2 million in 2006 of assets of a husband and wife from federal estate taxes and by doing so, save $235,000 or more in estate taxes. The tax credit can be applied toward gifts and that part of the remaining unified credit not used during a person's lifetime can be used for estate taxes.

UNIFIED CREDIT SHELTER TRUST: See Credit Shelter Trust.

WILL: A document that should be properly prepared with the assistance of an attorney in your state of your residence in order to conform to the laws of that state. This document appoints an executor of your estate and successor executors if the initial person so named is unable to serve.. It states how your assets are to be distributed and if there are beneficiaries who are minors, it names trustee or guardians of the funds you gave to minors. It may name the trustee and successor trustees for special Trusts you established such as a Credit Shelter Trust and the terms and conditions for investing, managing and payments from the Trust.

INDEX

INDEX

Exhibit 1
INCOME NEEDS OF EACH SPOUSE

A. **CURRENT ANNUAL INCOME NEEDED**
before Income Taxes Excluding the cost of
a new car and other items listed in "B" below. . . . . $ _____

A -2 **SOURCES OF INCOME excluding Trust:**
a. Social Security $ _____

b. Pensions $ _____

A -2, c. Other: List by type, current value and Income:

_____ $ _____
_____ $ _____
_____ $ _____
              TOTAL $ _____
- Subtract total of "Sources of Income" from
  Annual Income Required   - $ _____

A -3 **TOTAL "A" INCOME REQUIRED FROM TRUST** $ _____

B. **Additional Special Needs for Annual Expenses not included in the above:**

B - 1 New Car costing $_____ divided by _____ years = $ _____

B - 2 Travel & Vacations $ _____

B - 3 Family needs: assistance to children & grandchildren,
Gifts, etc. $ _____

Other: List

_____ $ _____
_____ $ _____
_____ $ _____

B - 4 **TOTAL OF SPECIAL NEEDS** $ _____
Convert Total needed for special needs to an amount prior
to federal and state income taxes: If your top tax bracket
is 20% in income taxes, increase by 25%; if you top tax
bracket is 25%, increase by 33%; if you top tax bracket
is 30%, increase by 43%; if you pay 37% increase by 59%.
              INCREASE $ _____

B - 5 **PLUS TOTAL INCOME REQUIRED FROM "A" ABOVE** $ _____

C **TOTAL ANNUAL INCOME REQUIRED FROM TRUST**
IN   YEAR   IT   WAS   EXECUTED $ _____

*NOTE: The surviving spouse should have ample funds available. If possible have
sufficient funds to buy gifts and other needs of your children and grandchildren. The
goal is to maintain a strong family relationship unaffected by financial strain.*

301

Exhibit 1
INCOME NEEDS OF EACH SPOUSE

A.   **CURRENT ANNUAL INCOME NEEDED**
before Income Taxes Excluding the cost of
a new car and other items listed in "B" below. . . . . $ _____

A -2   **SOURCES OF INCOME excluding Trust:**
    a. Social Security $ _____

    b. Pensions $ _____

A -2, c. Other: List by type, current value and Income:
    _____ $ _____
    _____ $ _____
    _____ $ _____
             TOTAL $ _____
   - **Subtract total of "Sources of Income" from**
    Annual Income Required   - $ _____

A -3   **TOTAL "A" INCOME REQUIRED FROM TRUST** $ _____

B.   **Additional Special Needs for Annual Expenses not included in the above:**

B - 1   New Car costing $_____ divided by _____ years = $ _____

B - 2   Travel & Vacations $ _____

B - 3   Family needs: assistance to children & grandchildren,
    Gifts, etc. $ _____

    Other: List

    _____ $ _____
    _____ $ _____
    _____ $ _____

B - 4   **TOTAL OF SPECIAL NEEDS** $ _____
    Convert Total needed for special needs to an amount prior
    to federal and state income taxes: If your top tax bracket
    is 20% in income taxes, increase by 25%; if you top tax
    bracket is 25%, increase by 33%; if you top tax bracket
    is 30%, increase by 43%; if you pay 37% increase by 59%.
                 INCREASE $ _____

B - 5   **PLUS TOTAL INCOME REQUIRED FROM "A" ABOVE** $ _____

C   **TOTAL ANNUAL INCOME REQUIRED FROM TRUST**
    IN YEAR IT WAS EXECUTED $ _____

NOTE: The surviving spouse should have ample funds available. If possible have sufficient funds to buy gifts and other needs of your children and grandchildren. The goal is to maintain a strong family relationship unaffected by financial strain.

Exhibit 1
INCOME NEEDS OF EACH SPOUSE

A. **CURRENT ANNUAL INCOME NEEDED**
before Income Taxes Excluding the cost of
a new car and other items listed in "B" below. . . . . $ _____

A -2 **SOURCES OF INCOME excluding Trust**:
a. Social Security $ _____

b. Pensions $ _____

A -2, c. Other: List by type, current value and Income:

_____ $ _____
_____ $ _____
_____ $ _____
TOTAL $ _____

- Subtract total of "Sources of Income" from
Annual Income Required   - $ _____

A -3 **TOTAL "A" INCOME REQUIRED FROM TRUST** $ _____

B. **Additional Special Needs for Annual Expenses not included in the above:**

B - 1 New Car costing $_____ divided by _____ years = $ _____

B - 2 Travel & Vacations $ _____

B - 3 Family needs: assistance to children & grandchildren,
Gifts, etc. $ _____

Other: List

_____ $ _____
_____ $ _____
_____ $ _____

B - 4 **TOTAL OF SPECIAL NEEDS** $ _____
Convert Total needed for special needs to an amount prior
to federal and state income taxes: If your top tax bracket
is 20% in income taxes, increase by 25%; if you top tax
bracket is 25%, increase by 33%; if you top tax bracket
is 30%, increase by 43%; if you pay 37% increase by 59%.
INCREASE $ _____

B - 5 **PLUS TOTAL INCOME REQUIRED FROM "A" ABOVE** $ _____

C **TOTAL ANNUAL INCOME REQUIRED FROM TRUST**
IN   YEAR   IT WAS EXECUTED $ _____

*NOTE: The surviving spouse should have ample funds available. If possible have
sufficient funds to buy gifts and other needs of your children and grandchildren. The
goal is to maintain a strong family relationship unaffected by financial strain.*

Exhibit 1
INCOME NEEDS OF EACH SPOUSE

A.   **CURRENT ANNUAL INCOME NEEDED**
before Income Taxes Excluding the cost of
a new car and other items listed in "B" below. . . . . $ _____

A -2   **SOURCES OF INCOME excluding Trust:**
    a. Social Security $ _____

    b. Pensions $ _____

A -2, c. Other: List by type, current value and Income:

    _____ $ _____
    _____ $ _____
    _____ $ _____
    TOTAL $ _____
    - **Subtract total of "Sources of Income" from**
      Annual Income Required   - $ _____

A -3   **TOTAL "A" INCOME REQUIRED FROM TRUST** $ _____

B.   **Additional Special Needs for Annual Expenses not included in the above:**

B - 1 New Car costing $ _____ divided by _____ years = $ _____

B - 2 Travel & Vacations $ _____

B - 3 Family needs: assistance to children & grandchildren,
    Gifts, etc. $ _____

    Other: List

    _____ $ _____
    _____ $ _____
    _____ $ _____

B - 4 **TOTAL OF SPECIAL NEEDS** $ _____
    Convert Total needed for special needs to an amount prior
    to federal and state income taxes: If your top tax bracket
    is 20% in income taxes, increase by 25%; if you top tax
    bracket is 25%, increase by 33%; if you top tax bracket
    is 30%, increase by 43%; if you pay 37% increase by 59%.
              INCREASE $ _____

B - 5 **PLUS TOTAL INCOME REQUIRED FROM "A" ABOVE** $ _____

C   **TOTAL ANNUAL INCOME REQUIRED FROM TRUST**
    IN   YEAR IT WAS EXECUTED $ _____

*NOTE: The surviving spouse should have ample funds available. If possible have
sufficient funds to buy gifts and other needs of your children and grandchildren. The
goal is to maintain a strong family relationship unaffected by financial strain.*